How to
Change Your Career

How to
Change Your Career

Debbie Andalo

gb
guardianbooks

First published by Guardian Books, an imprint of Guardian News and Media

Copyright © Debbie Andalo 2007

A CIP record for this book is available from the British Library

ISBN:
978-0-85265-066-0

Cover Design: Two Associates
Text Design: Jane Daniel

Printed and bound in Great Britain by William Clowes Ltd, Beccles, Suffolk

CONTENTS

PREFACE

Are you spending eight hours of every day doing work that doesn't satisfy you? Are you bored at work? Or stressed out? Or do you simply feel that you could achieve much more in another field?

There are times in most people's careers when they feel like walking out of their job and stalking off into the sunset. While this is not an option for many of us - mortgage payments still need to be made and we have to eat - there are opportunities for planning a complete change in your working life.

The main thing to remember is that job satisfaction is within your control, but it is going to take a lot of effort on your part.

Job satisfaction is based on a number of factors:
- Recognition by your managers and peer group
- Rewards through pay, perks or praise
- Intellectual challenge
- Absorbing but not overly stressful work
- Career development that fits in with your long-term goals
- Good work/life balance

Given that you have picked up this book, you are probably looking for a more satisfying career, whether you want to earn more money, work in a more stimulating environment, or reduce the amount of stress you suffer at work.

And what if your new career is forced upon you? While a complete change in your working life can be invigorating, and the transition can be an exciting and enjoyable process, for many people, especially those who have been made redundant or who are returning to work after a career break, the thought of doing something new can be terrifying. How do you know what you want to do? And once you've decided the direction in which you want to go, what are the first steps in making the switch?

The most successful career changes are those that have been carefully thought out and systematically planned. Taking time to analyse your skills, strengths and interests is the first step. As someone who has considerable insight into the working world, you will have a better idea about what you want than the average 21-year-old graduate. However, before you leap into (or out of) anything, it is essential that you ensure your qualities and motivations are well matched with the career you are considering. For example, it's no use training as a nurse if you're squeamish, no matter how caring you are.

This book is your starting point. From which career to select, to the hurdle of securing a job, this guide is designed to steer you through the process of your career move.

The first step is to find out what you really want: use the personal audit in this book (page 14) to help you to identify your skills, find out how to build on your strengths, and how to choose your next career. You may be surprised to discover how many transferable skills you have and how easy the transition might be. You will almost certainly have more to offer in terms of experience than the average recent graduate.

While many of your skills will be transferable, it's likely that some retraining will be necessary. It might seem off-putting at first when you discover the time and financial investment you need to make the switch. Try and think of the move as something you can achieve in a number of steps. This guide will help you on your way and tell you all you need to know about retraining and funding your studies, and where to get the help and support you need.

The **first section** of this book will help you to decide if you want to change your career, what you want to change to and how to set about it.
● Chapter 1 encourages you to think about your reasons for changing your career, and spells out some of the realities of such a change.
● Chapter 2 will help you to focus on finding work that will use your talents to the full.
● Chapter 3 gives help in getting the qualifications you need.
● Chapter 4 explains the pros and cons of freelance work – a big step to take for people more used to working within a corporate structure in a big organisation.
● Chapter 5 helps you to find the funding you will need to pursue your new goal.
● Chapter 6 gives you essential practical tips on getting your dream job.

The **second section** of the book gives detailed analysis of a selection of careers, from Accountant to Yoga teacher. You will find helpful job descriptions, details of the qualifications required and how to get them, plus contact addresses for the professional organisations involved in each field.

Appendix One is a series of examples of the funding available to those wishing to study as a mature student. **Appendix Two** gives helpful contacts and information about funding for setting up your own small business. And finally, at the end of the book there is a list of **useful contacts.**

It's great if you can do something that you feel passionate about and even better if you can get paid for doing it. Bear in mind that a career change will probably be a strain on your time, money and emotions. Perhaps you will have to take a pay cut, start at the bottom again, or go without a social life while you combine work with study. But do your research carefully, plan ahead, be prepared for the sacrifices you will have to make, and you could find yourself embarking on the best adventure you have ever had.

CHAPTER ONE

WHY SWITCH?

C areer changes are on the increase in today's workplace. There is plenty of evidence to suggest that employers value the benefits that people with previous work experience can bring to a new job. What's more, today's workplace culture welcomes older people and is keen to attract career changers.

For example, in the fields of accountancy and law, people with previous work experience in an unrelated field are often welcomed. Two of the UK's top accountancy firms say they look favourably on the increasing number of older graduates and career changers applying for their training schemes because they are often 'strong performers'. Large city law firms report greater interest in trainee solicitors' posts from 'second jobbers' and the Law Society has a recognised route of entry to legal training for non-graduate career changers who have management experience.

The average age of new medical students is rising too. From 2000 to 2003, the number of students aged between 25 and 39 applying to medical school doubled, and in 2002, 43 per cent of first-year medical students fell into this age group. This followed an increase in alternative options to study medicine offered by some medical schools to mature applicants and graduates. According to research published in *Nursing Standard* magazine[1], the typical profile of a student nurse is likely to be somebody aged over 30 who is also a parent.

Horticulture is another favourite venture for the career changer. A survey initiated in 2005 by English Heritage[2] revealed that 55 per cent of people working in the horticulture industry are in their thirties or forties. Significant numbers of these are career changers coming from such diverse backgrounds as banking or the mining industry.

The same applies to the teaching profession. These days, student teachers are often older men and women entering the profession after several years in a totally different field. A third of newly qualified teachers, according to the Teacher Development Agency for Schools, are aged over 30 and a third of all career changers who come into the profession come from a senior management background.

Age should be no bar to changing your career. Employers' organisations such as the Employers Forum on Age and those working in human resources believe the UK's ageing population is inevitably influencing employers' attitudes. The business arguments for creating an age-diverse workforce make common sense. Because the

UK workforce is growing older, the labour pool is shrinking, and employers cannot afford to dismiss prospective employees on the basis of their age. Sam Mercer, director of the Employers Forum on Age, explains: 'It isn't just that there are older people in the workforce, it's also that there are fewer young people entering the workplace. Employers facing skills shortages have to recruit and the obvious place to look is in the older workforce.' (See page 7 for more on new legislation on age discrimination.)

Stuck in a rut

If you feel as if your career is going nowhere, or if you think you are in a dead-end job, the danger is that you may begin to assume that you yourself are not interesting. This catch-22 problem can throw you into a downward spiral, making it increasingly difficult – and frightening – to take control of your career.

Career consultant Mary Maybin speaks from personal experience when she says it can be quite difficult to haul yourself out of your comfort zone to pursue a new career path. Eighteen years ago she turned to career coaching after giving up her former career as a secondary schoolteacher. She says: 'A lot of people find a career change hard or are resistant to it. It's asking people to give up their sense of security. It's scary for them and it takes a lot of energy.'

A combination of fear and low self-esteem can make taking that first step seem insurmountable. Many people remain in jobs which they aren't happy with because they don't quite have the courage to make the move. While security and knowing the nature of your work are perfectly valid reasons for staying in a job, if you are dissatisfied with where you are heading then you need to change.

Running the risk of going stale can be as damaging as being stuck in a job you really hate. According to occupational psychologist Sheila Panchal, dissatisfaction at work manifests in a number of negative ways. She says, 'The whole idea of being somewhere where you don't want to be can cause anxiety, feeling low or even physical symptoms.'

But if chronic Monday Blues and debilitating migraines are not enough to push you into action, consider this: occupational psychologist Dr Charles Johnson has this warning. 'Being stale in your work is a way of ageing quickly. If you are thinking "this work doesn't interest me any more, I'm bored, I want to do something different", then you should do something about it. Because the chances are that by doing nothing you will be shortening your life.'

This is Mary Marsh, a former head teacher, who is now chief executive of the National Society for the Prevention of Cruelty to Children. She says, 'I'm expecting to get my OAP bus pass soon, and the people I originally graduated with are thinking of retiring. I don't have the first thought about that.' If, like Mary, you have been in the same job for many years, it might be that you have reached a plateau. A change of direction could be the kick-start you need to keep your mind active, allowing you to grow and develop. Mary says, 'The move has been hugely revitalising. If I had stayed in teaching I suspect I would have gone flat and stale. I have found it very refreshing.'

Unfulfilled ambitions

'I have to acknowledge that I might fail and that I've taken a big risk. But I never regret what I have done,' says Stephanie Allen, who gave up her job as a high-flying City accountant with a £60,000 salary to become a student nurse.

Stephanie had always wanted to be a nurse, but at 16 she was the main carer for her grandmother and was unable to pursue her ambition. Instead, she got a job as a filing clerk. Four years later, her employer offered to pay for her training to become an accountant. 'It offered me the chance of good money and security so I agreed,' she says. Although she moved to the top of her career ladder, Allen admits she was miserable. 'Money wasn't the be-all and end-all. I wasn't happy. There wasn't enough job satisfaction. So about six years ago I started to think about what I wanted to do with the rest of my life, and accountancy wasn't it.'

Stories like this are not hard to find. Stephanie is one of a growing number of people who decide, after 20-odd years in the same career, that it is time for a change. And like Stephanie, many people take a lower salary for the sake of job satisfaction. These people have found the confidence to say that they have decided to take their career in a new direction, rather than justifying a move in terms of money. Stephanie says, 'I looked at what makes me happy and I realised it was people interaction and sorting out problems. I began to realise that I had in fact come full circle and that nursing was what I had always wanted to do so maybe I should take a look at that.'

Work/life balance

More than two million people who took part in a survey by the Trades Union Congress[3] said they wanted to work fewer hours even if it meant taking home less money every month. The Department of Trade and Industry revealed at the same time that 40 per cent of all employees, or 9.7 million people, are now working flexible hours.

There is increasing evidence that employees can make themselves ill if they fail to get the right work/life balance. A study of 2,000 men commissioned by the makers of vitamin supplements Wellman[4] and published in June 2006 revealed that 40 per cent of them had difficulty switching off from work, 20 per cent admitted they suffered from depression because of job-related stress while more than 25 per cent said their work exhausted them.

These statistics speak for themselves and show just how important getting the right work/life balance has become.

The issue is also at the forefront of our political leaders' minds. Work/life balance has always been on the agenda of New Labour, and in spring 2006, it was the focus of a speech by Conservative Party leader David Cameron when he talked about the need for employers to support family-friendly workplace practices to boost employees' sense of 'wellbeing'.

As the work/life balance debate gains political momentum and the culture of a long working day becomes increasingly unacceptable, a new climate is being created in the workplace, which is good news for career changers.

It means you will be able to use the argument for creating a better work/life balance convincingly as one of the reasons why you want to work in a different way or in a totally different environment. Dr Charles Johnson, an expert in career change, predicts it will no longer be unusual for people to make three or four career changes in their working life as their work/life priorities alter. He says: 'A career change will no longer be seen as an indication that there is something wrong with you but rather that it is a positive thing to do.'

Never too old to change

Your age should no longer be an obstacle to a change of career. In October 2006 the law changed so that it is now illegal for employees to be discriminated against in the workplace on the basis of their age. The new regulation gives you legal protection if you believe your new career path has been thwarted because an employer thinks you are too old. The new legal protection also potentially gives financial redress in the courts.

'As far as I'm concerned it's a no-brainer on age – look at the figures, look at the demographics and look at your customers – why wouldn't you want to recruit a highly talented, highly skilled older individual?' says Sam Mercer, director of the Employers Forum on Age, a network of leading UK businesses promoting age diversity in the workplace. 'This legislation is hopefully putting a stake in the ground. It may make people think twice about what they are doing as individuals, and employers will be able to educate their managers and their employees about their recruitment decisions.'

The Chartered Institute of Personnel and Development (CIPD) represents professionals working in human resources and people development. The CIPD is confident that outlawing ageism in the workplace will create greater career opportunities for older people and career changers. In addition, a survey of Employers Forum on Age members revealed that 80 per cent of them believed that the new anti-age discrimination legislation would increase the career opportunities for older workers. Half of the companies quizzed also predicted that the law would have a greater impact than existing race and gender anti-discrimination legislation.

The views of the Employers Forum on Age are significant because it has more than 230 members, who between them employ 14 per cent of the UK workforce – more than four million people. It includes high-street names such as Marks and Spencer,

Shell, BT and Sainsbury's as well as City firms GFK and the big banks, including HSBC and the Royal Bank of Scotland Group. British Airways, Procter and Gamble and the pharmaceutical giant GlaxoSmithKline are also members, as are public sector employers such as the Department of Work and Pensions, some local authorities and the Cabinet Office. It is a diverse and influential group of employers who should, if they practise what they preach, welcome you if you are after a new career.

Importantly, age equality in access to training and education is also covered by the regulations. It will be illegal for employers to discriminate against you in terms of decisions governing promotion and career development. This, according to the Open University, will have significant implications for career changers. The head of the careers advisory service at the OU, Clare Riding, says: 'We are still getting feedback from students that they have a sense of age discrimination going on in the workplace, although sometimes this is just a feeling that they get and they can't prove anything. The anti-age discrimination legislation is something we welcome.'

The regulations are especially useful if you are looking for a career change with your present employer. Dianah Worman from the CIPD says: 'If you are looking for a career change it's not always about looking outside of the organisation you are working for. Even if you are with one particular organisation it may be that you can move on within that organisation by increasing your skills portfolio.'

If you want to work beyond the statutory age of retirement, which is currently 65, the potential number of years you have in the workplace is now higher than it was before the directive came in. For example, an employer interviewing a 50-year-old career changer will no longer be able to assume that they only have a maximum 15 working years left. Worman says: 'I think it will encourage people not to be put off by thinking that they haven't got much longer left in the workplace to achieve their goals.'

Another proposal to change the law governing the state pension is also likely to increase the age at which workers choose to retire in the future. The white paper[5] proposes increasing the state pension age for men and women from 65 to 68 by 2046. Changes are already in the pipeline for the women's state pension age to rise to 65 – equalling that of men – by 2020. The new law proposes that the state pension age for both sexes will increase to 66 between 2024 and 2025; to 67 between 2034 and 2036 and finally to 68 between 2044 and 2046.

These legislative changes will help to create a workplace culture which is more sympathetic to people who choose to change career in later life. Sam Mercer says: 'If we are looking at extending the working life, the thought of doing the same kind of job all the time doesn't appeal to most people. I think it will mean that people will have two or three different careers in a working lifetime, and that people will become less averse to the risk of taking time out of the workplace to retrain. But at the same time I think it also means that the government has to look very carefully at how it lets people re-skill or retrain mid life, because this is definitely the direction which people are moving in.'

Before you leap

You will have realised by now that it's not a matter of handing in your notice and starting from scratch the next day. Any careers adviser will tell you that a change in career should be taken in a series of steps, rather than one giant leap. Planning and thorough research before you do anything is crucial. Think very carefully about what you are giving up. Don't underestimate the time that you are going to have to give to training, and your finances must be sorted out to the penny.

A career change is a major life event and it is not something to be done alone. It is crucial, right from the start, to have the support of your family and friends. You need them to understand why you are making the move, not only because you may want their practical and emotional support, but also because you may need them to motivate you when you feel overwhelmed or disillusioned about what you are doing.

So, how will you explain your new career path to your family and friends, and ensure that you have their essential support?

Here are some pointers to help you to work through the process.

Information: the more information you can give them as to why you reached your decision, the less scared they will feel about the change.

Explanation: sit down and explain your plan. The plan should include your immediate short-term goals, where you expect to be in a couple of years and where you intend to be in the long term.

Stress the positive: don't just tell them 'I'm really fed up at work and want to change careers.' You have to show them that you are not acting on a whim.

Evidence: make sure you support your plan with detailed evidence, so that you can tell them what your transferable skills are and how they can be used in your new career.

Motivation: explain what motivates you at work and how you can combine that with your transferable skills in a new career.

The alternative – staying put: point out how you would feel if you don't make the move. Be frank – explain how miserable, trapped or unfulfilled you will continue to be if you stay where you are.

It's also very important that at this stage, before you make any major decision, you are honest with yourself about your own ability to cope with the psychological pressure of giving up one successful career, only to start another at the bottom of the ladder. Ask yourself whether it's important to you that you move through the ranks quickly. If the answer is yes, are you prepared to take the initiative, and do you have the energy to develop your new career and move up the ladder?

Look at your current job

Being clear about why you want to change your career includes making sure you have explored why you are unhappy in your current role. It could be that making your current situation work more effectively for you will give you the confidence it takes to switch, or that you will improve things at work to the extent that you decide to stay put after all.

Some of the most common reasons people give for wanting to get out of their current role are:

Wanting more responsibility. If this is you, try these options first:

- Discuss taking on additional roles or responsibilities.
- Take up the issue with your line manager in the first instance, or with a higher authority if you don't get anywhere.
- Explain you are feeling stale and need more responsibility.
- Make the discussion positive – try not to moan.
- Suggest a placement or secondment to another part of the organisation.
- Negotiate a move where you can develop new skills within the company structure.

No promotional opportunities. If you feel you have progressed as far as you can in your current role:

- Discuss the possibility of secondments outside the company which will benefit your professional development.
- Make it clear that a secondment means you would be bringing back fresh ideas to the organisation, and new ways of thinking which could benefit the company.
- Ask about the possibility of placements in a different department within the organisation.
- If you have an idea for a new project, spend your own free time working on a business plan to present to your manager. Maybe suggest a financial reward if the project improves the efficiency of the company. This could prove lucrative. A welder working in the docks for the car manufacturer Toyota in America was given a 2 per cent share of the £250 million the company saved after he came up with a more efficient way of loading freight onto cargo ships.

Feeling bad at your job. This can be soul-destroying. Instead of putting up with the stress and anxiety, why not:

- Discuss possible courses designed to develop your areas of weakness.
- Ask yourself whether you are in the right organisation but in the wrong role. If the answer is yes, speak to your personnel department or your manager to discuss a possible move elsewhere within the organisation.
- Remember it's in your employer's interest to keep you – they know your strengths and have already invested time and money in your development – and it's also in their interest to maintain a happy and motivated workforce.

Feeling bored with your job. If you think your talents and skills are under-used at work:

- Discuss potential avenues for development with your manager.
- If repetitive tasks are getting you down, discuss the possibility of delegating some of your work in return for undertaking new tasks.

● Consider asking your employer for further training in new skills.

● Volunteer for additional responsibility at work or suggest your boss allows you to spend more time developing the tasks you enjoy.

● Remember that boredom at work can damage your health.

Simply not liking your job. Take time to analyse the problem:

● Examine the way you work. Something like your organisation habits could considerably affect how much you enjoy your job. It's possible that if you leave these habits unaddressed, you will take them with you to your next job.

● Talk to your manager, be honest about how you feel and explain your desire for change to rekindle your motivation.

● Start thinking seriously about changing your career.

Is it possible to change careers within your existing company?

Of course you will still need to recognise and take action to address any skills gaps that you may have. Be prepared to do lots of development work to catch up. But remember that career development does not always require spending money on a formal course. It could include secondment within the organisation or work shadowing a colleague. Another option is being given an assignment within another department so that you can practise new skills.

Taking the initiative in your career development is likely to reap rewards, according to research published by the National Institute for Careers Education and Counselling (NICEC). Academics concluded that employees who had experienced positive discussions about their career at work had initiated the discussion themselves. Surprisingly, most of those positive talks took place outside any formal career development meetings – only 7 per cent of employees questioned in the study said they had occurred during their regular appraisal.

Practical tips for boosting career development[6]

● Put yourself in the driving seat. Think about who can help you address career issues.

● Make sure you get the help you need by asking for it.

● Try to develop a relationship with your boss such that they will actively support your career. If this is impossible try to keep your boss informed.

● If you want to raise a career issue in appraisal, tell your appraiser beforehand. Ask for a follow-up to the appraisal meeting if there are career issues you could not discuss fully. Take advantage of other types of career support offered by your organisation.

● Prepare for a career discussion meeting by thinking about your situation and skills and their fit with the business. Think about what you want to discuss and what you want from the discussion.

● Share your agenda with the career support person.

- Show you realise how your career plans relate to the business. Try to link your skill development to the organisation's needs.
- Think about what you want in your work and how it fits into your life. Be prepared to discuss broader personal issues if you wish. But if the discussion gets too personal for your comfort, say so.
- Make sure you come away with a clear view of what to do next. Ask if you can come back if you need to.
- Agree what information should remain confidential. If information needs to be shared with others, clarify who will do this, how and when.
- Try to leave with concrete things to do.

Stockbroker to plumber: Jeremy Dunnill (41)

'I've got an HND in marine civil engineering and originally thought I would go into the army but I didn't get into Sandhurst. Then I thought I'd always wanted to work with money, because money was never going to go out of fashion, so I became a stockbroker at Gerrard in the City. It was just after the time of the Big Bang and it was great fun, the financial environment wasn't as stringent as it is now, because of 9/11. But after 9/11 there was so much regulation brought in which I just found a bit anal. I just didn't enjoy coming into work any more. Then I was made redundant and worked for another City firm for four months before I was diagnosed with cancer. After my treatment was completed I resigned from that job and decided to get work as a plumber. It appealed to me as a career change because I liked working with my hands and I wanted to do a job which brought satisfaction. Also, having done mechanical engineering before, I was mechanically minded which I think helped me make my mind up.

A friend told me about the NVQ qualifications I would need, then I went on the internet and did some research and found out about colleges near me that ran the courses. I know that some people work as plumbers who aren't qualified but I thought it was important to get decent qualifications. I started working towards my career change while I was still at Gerrard and did two days a week at college in the evenings studying for the NVQ. But what gets you the jobs in plumbing is the practical experience. So as I had a friend who was a good plumber I worked for him for two days a week so that I could get the practical experience I needed to complete my NVQ in plumbing, which I've now done. I'm now a qualified self-employed plumber.

It was interesting because all my friends at Gerrard didn't think I was mad – they said good on you. They told me they wished that they could do it too but they couldn't because they were stuck in a rut in the City.

When I first told my father I think he thought I was mucking around – I'd gone from a major public school into the City – it was the right sort of line. But when I explained to him why I wanted to do it he said I should do whatever made me happy. I was earning in the mid £30,000s in the City and then there was the possibility of an annual bonus which went into four figures. Maybe if I'd have stayed there and got my qualifications I could have gone on to earn £70,000 plus. But I wasn't after money – it was all about job satisfaction.

I was only out of work without an income for about three months between resigning from my job in the City and starting working in plumbing. I had my redundancy money to fall back on and my wife was still working in the City, so we had money coming in.

I love what I'm doing now. There are no regrets – every day is different, I'm working with my hands. There is also great job satisfaction – when you go to somebody's house and they have a problem and you sort it out, it's a great feeling.'

CHAPTER TWO

WHICH CAREER?

Now that you know you want to leave your old career behind and you've got family and friends on your side, the next challenge is to find out what new career suits you best.

But before you can make that decision, you must decide what it is you can offer a new employer. The best way is to carry out what is known as a **personal audit**, a detailed process of self-examination which will help you to identify what your skills and values are, what sort of issues are important to you at work and what motivates you.

A personal audit won't on its own reveal what kind of career you should move into, but it will give you the answers you need about yourself before you can make that decision. It's then up to you to research different jobs and careers to discover whether they match the results of your personal audit profile.

Personal audit

Here is a list of the kinds of issues you should be considering in your personal audit. You may well think of other questions for yourself, and some of the questions below may not seem relevant in your situation, but carrying out such an audit will help you to focus on your strengths and weaknesses as well as your aims for the future.

What are your work achievements to date?

What have you achieved at work that made you proud? Think back to the early days when your motivation levels were high. Was there a project you managed which was especially successful? Or was there a time when your negotiating skills were invaluable to colleagues or managers? It's easy, when you are fed up with your present job or have been stuck in the same organisation for years, to forget about earlier achievements. Look back through your employment history and think of other proud moments with other employers. The list will help boost your self-esteem and you will also have a good supply of workplace examples which you can use when you come to complete your CV.

What are your skills, abilities and personal qualities?
It is essential to identify your core skills, abilities and personal qualities, because these are the transferable skills which you will be able to take with you to your new career. List your intellectual and cognitive abilities. Are you numerate and literate? What about computer skills? Do you have good spatial reasoning? Maybe you see yourself as a good listener and communicator – somebody who can empathise with people easily? Are you assertive and persuasive? Can you negotiate well?

Don't restrict your analysis to the workplace – think about the skills, abilities and qualities you have outside your job. What parenting or caring skills have you developed at home? What personal qualities do you bring to other non-work organisations like clubs or voluntary organisations you might be involved in?

What do you like about your current job, and what do you want to change?
Being able to identify what it is you like about your job, or remembering what it was that attracted you to it in the first place, is a good way of finding out what motivates you at work. Once you have a list of personal motivators you can use it when you start to consider an alternative career. You will be able to scan job adverts or check person specifications to discover whether the job offers you the kinds of things that you enjoy about working.

To find out what motivates you, consider whether you like working in a competitive environment. Are you somebody who likes to work alone or do you prefer teamwork? Do you prefer to work inside or outside? Are you somebody who enjoys working with your hands or would you rather use your head?

It's equally important, however, to be frank about what you *don't* like – to be able to identify the kinds of things that get you down at work, which can also help inform your next choice of career. Do you hate working shifts? Does commuting drive you mad? Have you realised over time that you are not a natural leader?

Feedback on your skills and performance – what do you need to develop and improve?
Personal appraisal at work can be useful in helping you to discover what your strengths and weaknesses are. It's a good way of identifying any further training you might require to boost your professional development and your self-esteem, and you may wish to undertake this before making your career move. But it's worth bearing in mind that the quality of the appraisal is only as good as the quality of the appraiser. Also consider speaking to friends at work to get a different perspective on your skills and performance.

What are your career aspirations?
Think about the kind of career you would like to follow next and consider both your

short and long-term hopes. Try to be realistic. Some new careers, such as law or medicine, will require years of studying – are you really prepared to make that kind of commitment? If you think you know what you want to do, find out if you have any skills gaps – if it means further training or qualifications, can you achieve these while still in your current role? It may require huge time and financial commitments, but the desire for change should be enough to keep you going. Also if you can show a new employer that you spent your own time and money on filling these skills gaps it shows a high level of commitment to your career change.

Set yourself short and long-term career goals. Include this in a written career plan which you keep up to date.
Career changes never happen overnight and it can sometimes take years to fulfil ambitions. A good idea is to create a career plan that details the targets you aim to meet in the long and short term. Keep referring to the plan to make sure you are still on track. Adapt it if you have to, but if you hit the point where you feel disillusioned about your long-term ambitions, read it again: you may be surprised to discover just how far you have come.

Next steps
Now that you have decided to change your career and have carried out your personal audit, what are the next steps to take before you decide what kind of work will suit you best?

Take advice to avoid pitfalls
People traditionally fall into two categories – those who are change averse and those who seek out change.

If you are change averse but feel it's time to switch careers, the idea of a move can be traumatic. The way around the potential trauma is to plan carefully and to seek advice from as many people as possible. Don't just talk to your friends and family, use the trained experts in the field of career change and life choices. There are many sources of guidance available, such as professional career counsellors who will be able to help you to assess your strengths and decide which way to turn. Although there is no national register of career counsellors, the British Psychological Society has a directory of qualified occupational psychologists and life coaches who are trained in this role. If you live in southern Ireland you might find the Institute of Guidance Counsellors useful.

Another potential source of advice is the career guidance office at your former university or college. The government-run career advice agency Learndirect also offers callers three supported telephone calls from specialist advisers.

Make a list of your career goals

As advised in the personal audit section above, create a list of long and short-term career goals. This list will be a vital tool in the years to come and can be adapted as your aspirations change – it's not set in stone, but will help you to focus on your achievements as you progress through any new training and to clarify the next steps you need to take.

Staying put

Make another list of how you would feel if you *do not* make the move.
● Would staying put make you more stressed?
● Is it going to damage your health – physically and mentally?
● Is your misery at work affecting your personal relationships as well as those in the workplace?
Just being able to identify what could happen to you, and those around you, if you accept the status quo, can be a huge motivator.

Be honest with yourself

Knowing yourself and understanding what you want from work are the very first stages of successful career planning. But if this personal audit or self-scrutiny is to be of value you have to be honest with yourself, and realistic. Being realistic doesn't mean doing yourself down – it has to be a **really can do** exercise. If you find it difficult to identify your own skills and personal qualities, consider asking a friend to assess you – provided they promise to be honest, the results could be illuminating.

Mary Marsh says she had to be very honest about her strengths when she moved from head teaching to become chief executive of the NSPCC charity. She says: 'There must have been huge anxiety when I was taken on, although I didn't feel any hostility. I have however had to be very robust about my self-reflection and my own competencies.'

Identify your transferable skills

Once you've completed the personal audit you will know what your different skills are. You then have to be able to identify which of them you can take with you to a new career. Try to look for generic transferable skills, such as:
● experience of project management
● being good at settling arguments
● being a good listener
● being the person in the office that new recruits turn to for advice and help, even if you are not officially employed in that role
But if you are still unclear about which of your skills are transferable it may be worth considering expert advice from a career coach or a recruitment consultant.

Matching skills to a new career

Now you know what your transferable skills are and you know what it is about a job that motivates you, the next challenge is to find a career that matches these results.

Do your homework

When you are researching a new career, it's important to look past the job you will be doing, and think about the context in which you will be working. You aren't just researching how to get a toehold in the labour market. You should consider the long term and work out where you want to be in five, even ten years' time. That means thinking in terms of choosing sectors to move to, not just occupations. Thoroughly researching the sector you plan to move into will help you to think about your possible career development.

If, for example, you are thinking of going into social care, you should understand any changes taking place within the health and social care sector. Try to determine the skills the sector will need in five years' time, as this will have an impact on the potential you have to develop your career.

Furthermore, you should find out about the ethos of the sector you plan to move to. There are some sectors where you have to be very collaborative, and others where the only way to get noticed is to show that you are better than anybody else. Are you coming from a sector where people are very pushy and moving to a sector where this is inappropriate? You will have to be able to adapt yourself to new environments.

Find out as much as you possibly can about your future industry and its work culture. Making an informed decision about your career move will not only help to ensure you are doing the right thing, but could also become part of your job hunt.

Use your personal and professional networks to track down somebody who is already doing the kind of job you are interested in. Finding out about the nature of the job will help you to make useful contacts and also help you to pitch any future job application at the right level. You may also be able to arrange some work shadowing or work experience in your chosen field. This is not the occasion to be reticent or shy – it takes an awful lot of energy and time to find a new career. Don't give up after just a couple of phone calls.

The time and effort you put in now, at the planning stage, will bring benefits later when you face the realities of making a big change in your life, and will certainly help you not to make mistakes you will later regret.

Dancer to doctor: Kirsty Lloyd (33)

'I went to the Arts Educational School in Hertfordshire, which is a specialist performing arts school. I spent half the day training in dance, drama and music, and the other half doing school work. I took seven GCSEs and three A levels including human biology. I wanted to go to university to do a history of art degree but at the same time I applied to dance college – I got places to do both and went with dance at the London Contemporary Dance School. After I graduated I worked as a freelance professional dancer, but I also carried on with a variety of part-time jobs because, as a performer, you need that flexibility of income. Looking back, I realise that I was always looking at what new skills I could develop, like gaining management experience or being a front-of-house manager, and it's something I still do today.

While I was still dancing professionally and doing part-time jobs I became involved in arts administration. I put a tour together for a dance director who was having huge problems communicating with his dancers. I then volunteered to help at a conference organised by the International Association of Dance Medicine and Science. During my days at college I'd injured my back so had always been interested in dance injury. I was put in charge of managing the volunteers and took on that responsibility at future conferences. But that first conference was a turning point for me – I attended some of the sessions and heard this new language, this exciting scientific language which completely captured my imagination. It opened my eyes to dance medicine. At later conferences I spoke to osteopaths, physios, pilates and yoga specialists and realised, eventually, that I didn't want to do what they did – I wanted to be a doctor. So I began to find out what qualifications I would need. I studied GCSE chemistry at night school and then found out I would also have to study for another science A level.

At the time I remember thinking that I'd aim to be a doctor and then see where I ended up. I knew I could give up at any time and I thought my ambition was pretty unrealistic. I didn't see it as a career change. I just saw the move as a series of steps – this is what I need to do next if I was going to get there. I wrote to all the medical schools in the country. I also spoke to further education colleges, but most of them were so negative; they told me medicine was very competitive, but they were talking to a professional dancer and you can't get more competitive than that. Then purely by chance I found out about an 'access to medicine' course – it's aimed at students who have no experience of higher education and who want to get into medical school. It was at a further education college and there were other mature students there from a variety of backgrounds including an opera singer, an English teacher and a journalist. I was offered a place on the access course but deferred it for three years so that I could clear as much debt as possible.

Although being on the course didn't guarantee me a place at medical school, I was given good advice. I was advised to write to the medical schools telling them

I used to be a professional dancer and asking if they would accept an application from me. So I did that and I eventually got three offers of a place and chose Leicester because it matched my learning style. I'm now in my fourth year of medical training with two more years to go before I become a junior doctor and can have a salary.

I'm going to end up with the most enormous amount of debt. It's going to be between £40,000 and £50,000 – even though I have worked part time and have had a student loan and a professional study loan which I have to pay back within 10 years. It's an enormous amount of money. It's like a mortgage. I'm going to be 36 when I finish my training – that's normally at the point in people's lives when they start a family, buy a car and a house.

It's taken me a long time to understand that I am clever enough to be a doctor. That's only happened in the last four months – I got a first in the research degree I completed in year four. It was at that point I felt for the first time that I'm one of them. I'm going to be a doctor.'

CHAPTER THREE

RETRAINING

S ome careers will be easier to switch into than others. Some require a large amount of knowledge or skills and many years of retraining: if you're moving from tree surgeon to brain surgeon, it's not going to happen overnight. On the other hand, other professions allow career changers to rocket through the system. Teaching, for example, is full of people who have got on successfully because the skills they are being asked to use are those that they have brought with them from their previous career.

As a career changer you will inevitably need to gain some extra knowledge, but often you will be bringing valuable skills with you. The amount of retraining you will need will of course depend on where you're going, and where you came from, but also on your life experience and natural abilities.

How do I find out what qualifications I need?

The **Learning and Skills Council**, the government agency devoted to promoting vocational training and education, should be at the top of your list when seeking advice about qualifications for a career change. It runs a variety of different services with people like you in mind, from over-the-phone advice or more in-depth face-to-face help and support (more details on page 22).

Also think about approaching the **human resources departments** of businesses established in the career you are interested in following. Make it clear you are not searching for a job but want to find out the minimum qualifications and training you need in order to make your new career move. At the same time try to discover if they would offer on-the-job training for somebody like you or if the acceptable route is to get qualified elsewhere.

For those with few formal qualifications, **access courses** may be the answer. If you have ambitious plans for a new career, maybe a burning desire to be a lawyer or a doctor, but have few qualifications, don't despair – there is still a good chance that you can follow your dream. There are around 1,000 access courses run by further education colleges and adult education centres which are designed as a route into higher education for students with few academic qualifications.

Access courses can be followed full time or part time for between one and two years. They cover many subjects, including

- medicine
- law
- teaching
- nursing
- art and design
- humanities

Completing an access course does not guarantee you a place on a higher education training programme or a degree course, but it will increase your chances of being accepted if you have few academic qualifications. Contact the University and Colleges Admissions Service (UCAS) for details of all accredited and recognised access courses.

It may be useful to contact the training and development department of the **professional organisation or trade union** that represents those working in the new career which interests you, in order to find out more about any essential qualifications or training you may need. They will be able to explain the minimum qualifications needed and also point you in the direction of relevant courses and course providers.

Learning and Skills Council (LSC)

The Learning and Skills Council is the government agency devoted to improving the skills of the workforce in England through a range of information, advice and guidance services. At the heart of this organisation is the website **Learndirect** (see useful contacts at the back of this book). Learndirect should be your first port of call if you know what you want to do but do not know what qualifications you require. The site offers more than 700 job profiles with details of the necessary qualifications and a national database so you can search for a local course provider. If you do not have access to a computer and the internet, then you can still contact a Learndirect adviser by phone.

Nextstep is a face-to-face career advice service run by the LSC aimed specifically at career changers, the over-50s and young parents. Nextstep advisers provide free core career advice services including up-to-date information about funding for education and training courses, information about the local jobs market and help with interview skills and completing a CV. They can also provide, for a nominal fee, more in-depth career coaching and psychometric testing to help you reach a decision about your new career. Learndirect telephone advisers have an automatic telephone link to the service and may put you through to your local provider if they think it would help you in your career change.

Nextstep is available at different venues across England. It can be found in further education colleges, Citizens' Advice Bureaus or other centres run by voluntary and community groups. To find where your local nextstep provider is you should log on to the website and tap into its directory. (See also useful contacts at the back of this book.)

Other sources of advice in the workplace

The Union Learning Fund is managed by the LSC and run by the Trades Union Congress. Trade unions have learning representatives who can advise members how to improve their skills in the workplace. To access this support you will have to be working in a unionised workplace and you will have to be a union member. For more information see useful contacts at the back of this book.

Train to Gain, the national employers training programme, was due to be launched in August 2006. The initiative is aimed at boosting the skills of employers' existing workforces. It may prove a valuable resource if you are hopeful that your employer will fund and support your career change, although you would have to make the change within the company. For further details see useful contacts at the back of this book.

Distance learning

Learning at home may be an attractive option if it means you can fit your study in around your work and domestic commitments. Distance learning qualifications are increasingly available and can be studied in a number of different ways – through correspondence; online via the internet; using CDs, DVDs or videos; or via a mixture of all these options.

Learndirect has a database of different distance learning study programmes available across a range of disciplines, including IT, business management skills, foreign languages, and basic numeracy and literacy skills.

The **Open and Distance Learning Quality Council**, originally established by the government to set the standards for correspondence distance learning courses, is also worth checking out. It's now an independent organisation and has offices in London.

It's also worth checking with **professional organisations** that represent people in the career you are interested in working in, to see if they offer distance learning opportunities.

Distance learning with the Open University

What can the Open University offer?

The Open University (OU), the biggest university in Europe, offers you the option to study for a degree, diploma, professional certificate or postgraduate qualification through distance learning. This means you can study and stay in full-time employment at the same time. It can be an attractive option for some career changers who need a full-time income while they prepare for their new career.

How does it work?

It offers realistic flexible learning – OU students choose when, where and how they complete their study so it really can be tailored to meet your work or domestic commitments. OU students can also choose to dip in and out of study, as their personal circumstances change. The courses are modular so you can complete one module and accrue the credits for that in one year and, if you need to, put studying on hold until a later date. The credits you have already achieved remain on your credit account and can be added to when you return to OU study and go on to complete more modules.

What qualifications would I need?

The OU is unique because it has no minimum entry qualifications, so it may be an appealing option if you need to study for a degree but have not got the statutory qualifications – usually a minimum five GCSEs A–C grades or equivalent O Levels, and good A Level passes – which would secure entry to a university through the more traditional route. According to OU statistics, about a third of its undergraduates have lower entry qualifications than those at other universities. About 70 per cent of OU undergraduates are also in full-time employment.

What does it cost?

According to OU statistics, completing one of its degrees costs around £4,860, which is considerably cheaper than the costs faced by undergraduates at other universities.

What support structures do OU students have?

The OU stresses the support infrastructure it has built for its students and says the fact that 70 per cent of its students are juggling study alongside full-time work speaks for itself. The issue you will have to confront about whether to go down the OU route is whether you have the self-discipline and motivation to study by distance learning. Clare Rider, head of the career advisory service at the OU, says: 'It is very common for career changers or people seeking career development to study with the OU. But OU study doesn't suit everybody. Not everybody wants to study at a distance. To study with the OU you do need to be self-motivated. But we do give our students a lot of help with study and time management skills. The biggest advantage studying with the OU offers is the ability to earn and learn. It is also very flexible – it means if you move around the country with your work you can take your studying with you.'

The courses

The OU offers more than 600 different courses, including degrees, diplomas and certificates as well as postgraduate qualifications.

The OU subject areas are:

- Business and management
- Education and teacher training
- Environment
- Health and social care
- Arts
- Languages
- History
- Information technology and computing
- Law and criminology

- Mathematics and statistics
- Psychology
- Philosophy
- Politics
- Economics
- Science
- Social science

Courses start each year in February and October and last for a maximum of nine months. Exams, if the course requires them, take place in June and October. Academic results are based on a combination of student assessment, course assignments and exam results.

You only have to commit to the module or the course you have registered for. You do not have to commit to completing a degree or other qualification at the outset – even if that is your intention. The OU also offers the flexibility to study for its OU Open BA or BSc, which can be made up of different modules from different subject areas.

If you are thinking about becoming a **nurse**, the OU is a good alternative route to qualification as it offers the higher education diploma qualifications in adult or mental health branches of nursing. The OU is also an alternative option if you want to stay in full-time employment and train to become a **social worker** by completing the social work degree, which entitles you to register and practise as a professional social worker. If you want to become a **teacher**, you can use the OU route to study for the qualification you need to become a probationary teacher, the postgraduate certificate in education (PGCE) qualification. Aspiring **lawyers** can gain an LLB degree, the first step to becoming a solicitor or a barrister before the vocational training stage.

Regional centres

The regional centres are the local hub of the OU. They have student support teams which can help students decide which courses to study, how to plan their career, how to cope with the financial issues and any other problems that affect your study or course. OU students also have access to the OU online library, which includes a database of OU subject and course-related internet sites. The OU also provides learning skills support online and has an online conferencing facility for students and tutors.

The 13 OU regions (with their regional centre headquarters in brackets) are:

- London (Camden)
- South (Oxford)
- South East (East Grinstead)
- South West (Bristol)
- West Midlands (Birmingham)
- East Midlands (Nottingham)

- East of England (Cambridge)
- Yorkshire (Leeds)
- North West (Manchester)
- North (Newcastle upon Tyne)
- Wales (Cardiff)
- Scotland (Edinburgh)
- Ireland (Belfast)

Modules and credit points

The OU relies on a system of points and gives each qualification a total number of points which have to be achieved before that qualification is complete. Each module in the course is in turn awarded a specific number of points, so you can pick and choose the modules you want to study.

An OU honours degree is made up of a total of 360 points, while a non-honours degree requires 300 points and a foundation degree is 240 points. OU students on a degree course would usually aim to gain 60 points a year, which means on average it takes six years to complete a degree. It is up to each student to decide how many points they want to achieve in a single year. It is possible to achieve 120 points in a year so that your OU degree would be completed in three years rather than six, but the commitment to study means you would be expected to study full time.

The OU calculates one credit point is equal to 10 hours of study, so if you plan to have a target of 60 points a year it will require you to put in 600 hours of study, or around 16 hours a week.

Financial support

There is financial support available for OU students on undergraduate courses from both the government and the OU. This can consist of:
- help with course fees
- study expenses for books and equipment
- help for students with a disability, medical condition or learning difficulty
- help for students who get into financial difficulty during the course

Eligibility is linked to welfare benefit entitlement; income; marital status and family dependants; household income and employment status.

For students facing financial difficulty, the OU can provide emergency financial support from its charitable funds. Students can also apply for money from the government's **Access to Learning Fund**. Although this funding is restricted, mature students with existing financial commitments are identified as a priority group. Further details about the OU's Student Assistance Fund are available from the OU. Details about the Access to Learning Fund are available from **Aimhigher**, the Department for Education and Skills initiative promoting access to higher education.

Textile conservator to science teacher:
Rosalind Tuckwell (45)

'I resigned from my job as a textile conservator after more than 17 years in the summer of 2006 to study full time for the postgraduate teacher certificate, the PGCE, to become a science teacher. I suppose the catalyst for considering a career change happened a few years earlier with the break-up of my marriage and the fact that I needed new challenges. I realised that I was going to have to support myself, probably for the rest of my life, and decided then to study for a science degree with the Open University with the eventual intention of training to be a teacher.

Teaching appealed because I believe that people can turn things around through education. I knew it would give me job security and also that I would be able to work anywhere I wanted. As a textile conservator I really had been tied to working in London, and not only in London, but to the same workplace as well for nearly 18 years. Teaching also offers me a pension, which was important to me. I was also looking for a career which would give me continuing challenges, which I knew teaching 12 to 18-year-olds would give me.

If you look back through my CV, though, you can see that there is a thread which has led me to teaching. One of my first jobs, which I did on a casual basis when I was still at high school in Sydney, Australia, and which I continued when I was studying for a science degree after leaving school, was working with children in an after-school club. I was working with children again when I got a job as a children's hostess on a cruise liner which toured all around the Pacific and the Far East. I also remember when I was still in high school walking around the building thinking "I'm going to be a teacher one day". So you could say that was like a premonition.

After I had completed the science degree with the OU I had planned to study for the PGCE full time at Cambridge University, and I had a place offered twice, but I had to turn both of them down because it wasn't practical. So I changed my mind and decided instead to complete the PGCE with the OU which again meant I would be studying and working at the same time. My boss was really relieved because he wanted me to stay. But although I'm a great promoter for the OU, it wasn't that easy to do a PGCE at the same time as working full time. There is an awful lot of theory with teaching and there is teaching practice to do as well. Also with the OU, although you have support from a tutor, you don't have that contact with other students, or at least not to the same extent as you do studying full time where you can discuss the course or talk about teaching amongst yourselves when you want. Now that I'm studying for the PGCE full time at university I can *totally concentrate on it.*

I was able to afford to do the full-time course because I had some savings I could use, and also, because I'm studying to be a science teacher, I qualified for a £9,000 government bursary. I also qualified for a £2,700 maintenance grant and I was given another £1,500 from the university. I have had to pay my own tuition fees but I don't have to pay council tax. I've estimated that I've got about £14,000 to live on for the year, and although that doesn't sound a lot, it's tax free. Also I wasn't expecting the money and had anticipated that I would be living on my savings instead. Once I qualify I'll earn around £20,000 and I'll also get a £5,000 'golden hello' from the government. It's substantially less than I was earning as a conservator, which was around £40,000 – but it isn't always about money.'

CHAPTER FOUR

GOING IT ALONE

Making a career change and setting up your own business at the same time may seem an impossible task. In some cases, such as becoming a journalist, a cab driver or a plumber, starting off as a freelance and being self-employed can be the perfect way to test the water and build up a business before making the switch permanent and full time.

But for other career moves, such as running your own pub or bed and breakfast, there are no half measures. You will have to dive in head first and it's going to require minute planning and possibly huge personal financial risk if you want to increase your chances of success.

Whichever self-employed route appeals to you, it's crucial to do your homework first and get as much specialist advice and support as you can before making your decision.

How do I decide to be self-employed?

This is not the easy option, even though you may like the idea of being your own boss. It's essential that you are honest with yourself and assess whether you have the right personal qualities to make it work.

- Are you self-motivated?
- Do you have strong personal discipline?
- Are you confident about your own abilities?
- Are you able to make your own decisions?
- Can you sell yourself?
- Do you have good networking skills?
- Are you happy working alone?
- Can you work to a budget?

What are the pros and cons of being self-employed?

It's a good idea to make a list of the advantages and disadvantages of being your own boss to help you reach your decision.

The advantages may be:
- Working for yourself means you don't get embroiled in company politics.

- You can choose the hours you want to work.
- You can structure your own job to suit you.
- You can work for a variety of different clients, so the risks of getting bored or stale are minimal.

But there may be disadvantages:

- It is hard work and you may find you work more hours than you planned, sometimes for little or no financial return.
- Your cash flow may be unpredictable, especially at the beginning.
- It can be difficult to live with the stress of an uncertain income, especially if you are the main breadwinner in the family.
- You are going to be responsible for the cost of your own professional development and training.
- No more paid holidays!

How do I know how much to borrow?

Your start-up costs are going to vary depending on the kind of business you intend to run and whether you expect to meet the cost of business premises as well.

Setting yourself up as a self-employed taxi driver, for example, can cost as much as £35,000 if you want to own your own brand-new cab, but there are cheaper alternatives – renting a vehicle instead can be as little as £160 a week, or buying a second-hand cab would set you back just £2,000.

Alternatively if you want to become a self-employed tour guide, your start-up costs are going to be the price of a mobile phone and a good pair of walking shoes.

As a leasehold publican you should expect to invest at least £20,000, while a tenanted landlord could have start-up costs of £10,000. But if you want to own your own pub outright, be prepared to invest possibly hundreds of thousands of pounds.

It's a good idea to talk to professional associations involved in the business you are thinking of setting up to get realistic advice about costs and then seek further help from specialist advisers at **Business Link** (see below); they will help you to develop a fully costed business plan. (See also Appendix Two for funding options for setting up your own business.)

Where can I get advice on setting up a business?

There is plenty of help out there for people who want to start their own business. The Guardian's Guide to Careers is a good starting point. Professional associations which represent the business sector you want to move into will be able to help by pointing out the pitfalls, and should be able to put you in touch with others who have set up their own business as well.

Business Link, which has branches all over the country, can also provide invaluable support and give you step-by-step help in how to go about setting up your own business. There's also support available from your local enterprise agency (for more details see below).

Sources of general business support

Business Link

Business Link is a national government service which offers advice and support to new and small businesses. It should be top of your list if you are planning to become self-employed and run your own business. Each branch of Business Link has a team of specialist business advisers who can point you in the right direction if you are looking for financial backing – including sources of government funding to help launch a new business.

There is currently a Business Link office in every county but from April 2007 the service is being reorganised on a regional basis. To find your local Business Link office you should log on to its national website and access its national directory. By typing in your postcode you will find details of your local office.

Each Business Link branch has a team of specialist advisers to guide you. They will help you with your business plan and can provide a model template for you to work from. High-street banks may also have business plan templates which could be useful.

The plan should tackle issues like marketing, the structure of the business and funding. Your funding plan should include what assets you can release and what your 'survival budget' is, that is the money you have to live on while you wait for your business to start making a profit.

Business Link will help you to be realistic and make sure that you have completed proper market research to assess whether your business is likely to be successful. As one Business Link adviser says: 'Most businesses fail because people haven't thoroughly researched their market. You have to know what your market is, what your product or service is and whether it's relevant to the market place. That is key.'

Business Link will also help you with the legal demands of establishing a business, whether you want to be a sole trader or set yourself up as a limited company, for example. It has a range of fact sheets looking at issues such as VAT and tax and national insurance for a self-employed person.

Business Link will be able to give advice on turning your business plan into an action plan, and can direct you towards any statutory grants or sponsorship available, which may help to meet some of your start-up costs for things like necessary equipment.

Once your business is established, Business Link will still offer support and advice through your early years as a self-employed person. It runs a series of short training courses or workshops, most of which are free, to help you to develop any new business skills you need such as accounting, basic selling skills, marketing your business and legislation that applies to small businesses. There are other courses that target IT and E-commerce, such as how to create a website and how to market on the internet and create an online store.

Enterprise agencies

An enterprise agency is a not-for-profit organisation that can offer advice to anybody thinking of setting up a business. The National Federation of Enterprise Agencies (NFEA) has 130 agency members in England, but not all enterprise agencies are members of the NFEA. NFEA members give help to around 45,000 existing businesses each year and help another 20,000 businesses to start up.

An enterprise agency will tell you what you need to know before setting up a business, will talk through the idea and help you to develop a business plan. Advisers can point you towards sources of business funding, although some agencies will have access to their own budget for business support and development, so they can provide financial backing themselves. Enterprise agencies can also help you to find funding for training if you need to learn new skills to run your business.

The NFEA provides an online business advice line which you can find on its website (see useful contacts at the end of the book).

Through its members and other business support organisations, the NFEA manages the Business Volunteer Mentor programme. Under this scheme businessmen and women, either still working or retired, give mentoring support to people new to business.

The NFEA is also running the national New Entrepreneur Scholarship programme (NES) on behalf of the government, which encourages enterprise in disadvantaged areas of the country (see website for more details or contact them direct).

Regional Development Agencies

It is also a good idea to contact your local regional development agency – the government agency with responsibility for economic and sustainable development and employment skills and training across its region. There are nine regional development agencies in England.

PRIME

The charity PRIME is the only national organisation devoted to helping people aged over 50 to set up their own business.

The support is targeted at people who, through redundancy or other circumstances, are forced to look at setting up their own business because it is their only employment option. But it also helps others in this age group who have made a deliberate decision to give up a career to start working for themselves. A survey it carried out in 2006 on the people who used its services revealed that 23 per cent of them claimed that difficulty in finding financial backing was the reason that they gave up starting a business, while another 40 per cent admitted they had to delay their plans because of lack of funding.

Shell LiveWire

This scheme is limited to people between 16 and 30 years old who are planning to set up a business. There are a number of free services that you can make use of, including a Start a Business toolkit which can be tailor-made to match your business idea. You also have the chance to enter your business in the Shell LiveWire Young Entrepreneur of the Year Awards, which has a top prize of £10,000.

PR executive to acupuncturist: Marian Casey (43)

'I left university with a language degree and worked for a few years as a bilingual personal assistant, and then became interested in public relations. I was in the press office for Revlon for more than six years and went on to become a PR executive for BAAMcCarther Glenn, which runs designer outlets. Then I just decided I wanted a change of career. It wasn't that I hated the job but I was working long days with long hours. I was stressed. It was the constant deadlines and I knew that it wasn't going to change. I was 37 then and just felt that unless I did something drastic my life wasn't going to improve, so I decided to give up my job and train to become an acupuncturist.

I'd always been interested in Chinese medicine and I'd read a book about acupressure which got me thinking about acupuncture. My husband didn't seem to mind at all and my family were a bit bemused although they knew I'd always been interested in this kind of thing. They were all very encouraging. But I suppose it took me about a year to make the switch, from leaving my job in PR to starting the acupuncture degree course, which was part time over four years. I found out about the course from the British Acupuncture Council, having seen their name on a leaflet I'd picked up somewhere. It was important to me that I trained properly and got onto a good course. I used my savings to pay for the course, which cost around £15,000.

I'd been earning around £30,000 in PR but didn't really think about the money I wasn't earning at the time. When I did think about money it was in terms of the money I needed to buy books or stationery. My priorities changed. Also my husband was still earning so we still had an income. I carried on working part time, doing a variety of different jobs so that I had a couple of days a week to do the course work. I also had to study every other weekend for four years to complete the degree. I think when you get older it's a lot harder to study – you need a lot of stamina, and also I wasn't working part time when I did my first degree, which made a difference.

But with acupuncture it's not just the academic side – there is also the clinical work you have to complete. The amount of work was phenomenal but I just had to keep going. It was very tough, but I have no regrets. I qualified in May 2006 and am now self-employed as an acupuncturist. I rent out a room in the clinic of a colleague one day a week but I eventually want to build up and work full time. Although my costs are low I think at the moment I'm just about breaking even from my practice. I'm also working as an administrator three days a week at the British Acupuncture Council, which gives me enough money to live on.

When I look back I remember even after A levels I'd thought about being a physiotherapist, so I suppose in some ways this kind of career has always been in me.'

CHAPTER FIVE

FUNDING

'I didn't save before I started my training but I did make sure I was completely debt-free.' Stephanie Allen, career changer from accountant to nurse. The biggest hurdle to a successful career change, once you have decided which new path you want to follow, is going to be money. As we have seen, a new career will be likely to mean undertaking some training or study in order to fulfil your ambition. Whether you have to study for a first degree, a postgraduate qualification or an NVQ, the reality is that you are going to have to fund your own study.

Stephanie Allen's preparation for her move to nursing – where she had to survive on a £6,000-a-year bursary instead of her £60,000 accountancy salary – was to clear all her debts. Although finding enough time to study, train and work to supplement her income has been difficult, the most important issue for her before making the career change was the financial one. Every week she spends four days on the ward training, one day at university and one day a week working as a healthcare assistant. She hasn't had a holiday for four years. Of the 450 students who began her nursing course, only 100 were still with her as her training drew to an end. She says: 'Some people dropped out because nursing wasn't what they had expected, but for others it was for financial reasons – it was just too tough for them.' Combining training with maintaining an income can be difficult for career changers, but there is sometimes no alternative if you still have financial commitments.

There is some statutory funding available from the government if your new career is in one of the caring professions like nursing or social work – there are bursaries to be had as well as help with tuition fees and other financial support (see the entry on government bursaries below and Appendix One for further details). The amount of money available will depend on whether you are following a degree or diploma course, and in some cases the funding will be means-tested, so your household income will influence the amount you will be entitled to.

There is also some financial help for those career changers who want to study medicine, but the amount of money available depends again on the kind of medical degree you are studying. (See the entry on NHS student grants unit and medical students, below, and Appendix One for further details.)

Career changers who are entitled to the most generous statutory help are those who decide to become teachers – especially those who want to teach one of the subjects where there are definite skills shortages, such as maths (see entry on government bursaries below and Appendix One for further details).

Where to get funding

Your **local education authority** will be able to give you details of what funding you are statutorily entitled to and tell you if there are any other pockets of funding which you can dip into. But if you have studied in higher education before, you are not automatically entitled to financial support for more higher education study. If you have not studied for a degree before, your entitlement to funding will be linked to your household income, so do not automatically assume you will be eligible for student loans.

Learndirect and **nextstep** advisers will also give you advice about any statutory funding available to you as an older student and career changer.

The **Educational Grants Advisory Service** has an up-to-date online database of educational trust funds. It also has a telephone advice line which is open three afternoons a week. But because it has only a small team of staff it prefers enquiries about available funds to be made online (see useful contacts at the back of this book).

The **Student Grants Unit** provides up-to-date information on NHS bursaries and other financial aid available if you plan to retrain as a health professional. The bursaries can be either non-means-tested or means-tested and are available for specific NHS training courses. There is other financial help available from the NHS, such as contributions towards childcare costs and an older person's allowance (for students aged over 26).

The **General Social Care Council** administers the non-means-tested bursaries that are available to students in England who are studying for the professional social work degree.

The **Training and Development Agency for Schools** has details of the bursaries and other financial support that is available to students on postgraduate teacher training courses, or those who have taken the employment route to professional training.

High-street banks have a range of different financial packages aimed at career changers who are returning to education or training. The help available depends on the type of course being studied and its duration. They also have funding packages if you are thinking of setting up your own business. These packages are detailed below. Case studies of examples of funding available for mature students from high-street banks can be found in Appendix One.

Most high-street banks have a variety of different financial packages available, from student bank accounts, which offer interest-free overdrafts, to career development loans, which are targeted at helping to fund mature students through two years of study. There are also professional trainee loans available for would-be doctors and lawyers and other specific professions. There is also the option of having a short-term holiday from your mortgage repayments, but this is not practical if you are looking for long-term funding. The longest repayment holiday you are likely to be able to negotiate is around six months.

If you are planning to study for a degree

There are two different funding options for people studying for a degree.

If you have not studied in higher education before you are entitled to apply for two government student loans. There is a loan available to help meet your tuition fees, and another maintenance loan to help meet your living costs while studying. But both loans are means-tested so there is no guarantee you will be entitled to anything. The loans, like those to younger undergraduate students, also have to be repaid once you are earning. To find out more details, see The Guardian Student Finance Guide or contact your local education authority.

If you are already a graduate but need to study for another first degree, you are not entitled to a student loan to help towards your tuition fees. You are, however, entitled to a student maintenance loan towards meeting your living costs at university. To find out more details, see The Guardian Student Finance Guide or contact your local education authority.

If you are planning to study for a postgraduate qualification (including a Master's degree)

There is no student loan available if you want to complete any postgraduate education. However if the course qualifies you to be a teacher (see entry on teacher training bursaries below) or a social worker (see entry on social work bursaries below) or you are continuing your medical qualifications (see medical students entry below) there is funding available.

It is more than likely, then, that you are going to have to pay your tuition fees from your own pocket. The cost of tuition fees will also vary according to the course you are studying and can be between £3,000 and £6,000 a year, and up to £18,000 a year for some medical degrees or an MBA.

The financial advice from experts at Learndirect is to approach your own university in the first instance to see if they have any bursaries or other sources of money which they can draw on to help meet your costs. If your university cannot help, the next port of call should be the Educational Grants Advisory Service, which has a database of charities and other trusts to fund education.

If you are planning to study for an NVQ qualification

Adult learning grants are available to help towards the cost of studying for an NVQ, although in the majority of cases it is likely that your employer will meet all your costs.

If that is not the case, the amount of grant available depends on the level of NVQ being studied. The grant, which is non-repayable, is not expected to meet the course fees, but rather to be a contribution towards the expenses you incur in order to study, such as travel costs. The current grants available are £250 for a level 2 NVQ, £750 for a level 3 and £2,000 for a level 4.

The grants are not available to all students across the UK. They are only available in pilot areas, which are: **Bedfordshire** (Luton); **Berkshire; Black Country** (Dudley, Sandwell, Walsall, Wolverhampton); **Buckinghamshire; County Durham; Devon & Cornwall** (includes Isles of Scilly); **East Sussex; Hampshire and the Isle of Wight; Humberside** (East Riding, Hull, North Lincolnshire, North East Lincolnshire); **Kent and Medway; Lancashire** (Accrington and Rossendale, Blackburn, Blackpool and Fylde, Burnley, Chorley, Hyndburn, Lancaster, Morecambe, Nelson and Colne, Pendle, Preston, Ribble Valley, Rossendale, Runshaw, Skelmersdale, South Ribble, West Lancs, Wyre); **Leicestershire; London West** (Brent, Ealing, Hammersmith and Fulham, Harrow, Hillingdon, Hounslow); **Milton Keynes; Northumberland; Oxfordshire; Shropshire; South Yorkshire; Surrey; Tees Valley; Tyne and Wear; West Sussex.**

The City and Guilds, which awards NVQs, also has some bursaries available.

Other ways to fund study

Student bank account

Banks offer free overdrafts on student bank accounts, which in some cases can cover five years of full-time study, but there are conditions attached and each bank is different.

Career development loan

A bank career development loan is the most common funding choice for career changers. In order to be eligible for the loan you must be over the age of 18 and have been resident in the UK for at least three years. Under the scheme you are able to borrow between £300 and £8,000. However not all banks offer career development loans, and if you apply for the loan it is not automatically guaranteed. Whether you are successful or not will depend on your credit history, and you will also have to show that the course is one which improves your prospects of employment. The course has to be registered with the Learning and Skills Council.

The loan is available to cover up to two years of study so it is a useful financial source for a variety of different degree courses and other professional training qualifications.

You will be expected to start repaying the loan a month after you finish your course. Banks will expect the loan to be repaid between 12 and 60 months of finishing your course. It may be possible however to defer the start of your repayments if you have problems finding employment. It is important to discuss and agree repayment options with the bank before taking out the loan.

Professional trainee or studies loan

These are offered by some banks and are available for specific training courses or degrees in medicine and law. They offer up to a maximum £25,000. Details vary, but generally the first repayment is not expected until six months after the course is completed, and you can have up to 10 years to repay the money.

Production manager to trainee accountant: Charlie Wale (34)

'I've been out of university, where I did a degree in biochemistry, for 12 years. When I graduated I joined the graduate management training scheme at Procter and Gamble because I wanted a job working with people, and my university career adviser suggested production management. I worked at a cosmetics factory in a number of different roles for five years, starting in process engineering where I had to manage a line in the factory and improve its reliability. I then became a production manager in charge of a whole department with responsibility for around 70 employees.

The catalyst for change for me was when the factory moved to southern Ireland. I'd felt for a while that the job wasn't really me and I didn't want to move to Ireland so I took voluntary redundancy. The money bought me time to reflect on what I wanted to do next. I decided to do a taught Masters degree in applied theology as I had been thinking about a move into the Christian ministry. But after a couple of years I realised it wasn't what I wanted to do.

I was like a blank sheet – I really didn't know what I wanted. I bought myself a self-assessment book and worked through all the questions, which is how I settled on accountancy. It did surprise me. I hadn't tried to manipulate the answers. I was confident enough about the conclusions to follow it up in depth – I went back to my university careers department and used their resources to find out more about accountancy. They also put me in touch with alumni who worked in the profession, so I rang three or four of them and discussed their experiences.

I applied to KPMG for their graduate programme, and they took me on with the idea that I would complete an MBA rather than go through the traditional accountancy exams. It was something the company was trying out and it was very tempting – I knew the pattern of study would be less intensive than the professional accountancy exams and that the MBA had more self-study and ongoing assignments. At the interview I showed them that I already had five years of experience in industry and I explained that in some ways my first career had been a false start in the sense that it didn't lead on to further things. I did a book-keeping course at evening class to see if I liked it and could do it, and I *realised it was what I wanted to do.*

I've been trained on the job and have done the same accountancy courses as others on the graduate scheme except I haven't had to do the exams. I'm completing the MBA part time over four years and am now halfway through. It's proved to be what I expected it to be. I was prepared for the fact that I would be coming in at the bottom of the tree in terms of progression and I knew I had to take a fairly hefty pay cut to come here. But the fact is this feels like my natural path and it makes it much more worthwhile.

My potential future income may eventually exceed what I was earning before, but that isn't really an issue for me. In my other career I felt like a square peg in a round hole. I think it was about my personality and the kind of skills that you needed for the job. It was a very masculine environment with aggressive targets.

I was engaged at the time I decided to change career and am now married. My wife, who is a teacher, has always been extremely supportive. I think she's seen that I have found a job which I enjoy doing and she notices the difference in me at the end of the day.'

CHAPTER SIX

FINDING A JOB

Finding the right job can become a full-time occupation, whether you are a career changer or looking for a new position within your existing profession or sector. You have to know where to look for job opportunities and find out how to create those opportunities for yourself. This can be difficult enough if you already know the market you are working in, but if you are trying to break in as a career changer the challenges can be even greater.

This is the time when all that hard work on identifying your transferable skills is going to pay off. It's vital that you understand what it is you can bring from your old career to your new one.

Another hurdle you are going to have to confront is how you can make your CV work for you. Why should an employer take you on ahead of another applicant who has masses of experience in the profession or sector you are trying to break into? The answer is to customise your CV to reflect the needs of the job and the organisation. That's where your research into the necessary skills for the job and the role of the company is going to reap rewards.

As a career changer, your principal strategy should be to try and minimise the number of opportunities an employer has to turn you down. The good news is that there are sources of information and specialist advisers available to help make that task more manageable.

Job hunting

Newspapers
Broadsheet national newspapers are useful for job hunting. Each has days of the week when it focuses on particular industries or professions. Newspaper websites, especially the Guardian's, are also worth looking at as they can provide wider careers advice and are a source of useful contacts.

The Guardian
- Monday – creative, media, marketing and general
- Tuesday – education, academic and research
- Wednesday – health, public services, housing, environmental and voluntary sectors

- Thursday – computing, science and technology, engineering and finance
- Saturday – second jobber and graduate vacancies in the Rise supplement

The Independent

- Monday – computing, science, engineering and technology
- Tuesday – accountancy, finance and public sector
- Wednesday – arts, creative media, marketing and sales
- Thursday – education and secretarial
- Friday – legal, arts and media

The Times

- Tuesday – computing, engineering, technology, legal and general
- Wednesday – computing, arts, creative and media, sales and marketing and secretarial
- Thursday – accountancy, engineering, technology, science, public sector, sales and marketing
- Friday – arts, creative and media

The Financial Times

- Wednesday – accountancy, finance, insurance, sales and marketing

The Daily Telegraph

- Monday – general vacancies
- Thursday – general vacancies

Trade magazines

National trade magazines and newspapers are a good starting point if you want to find out more about the industry or profession you want to move into. They will bring you up to date with current issues and give you an insight into market leaders and their movers and shakers. They are also a good source for job vacancies when you start looking for that first step on the new career ladder.

Many of the trade magazines also have online versions that carry job vacancies so you may be able to start your job hunt without having to buy the magazine.

If you do not know the titles of the trade magazines in your new industry or profession, it is worth getting hold of a copy of the Guardian's Media Guide, which is updated annually. It contains an authoritative A to Z of the names of trade magazines with their contact numbers.

Another option is to track down a copy of brad – a comprehensive directory of UK media information which includes 13,500 different entries. Brad has details of trade magazines listed according to different categories. Each listing will also include an editorial profile, which will give you an idea about the magazine and its target audience. Like the Guardian's Media Directory it also includes contact numbers so you can contact them if you need to clarify anything.

Although brad is available by subscription – it offers both an online and hard copy directory – many public libraries will hold a copy or have access to its online directory. Alternatively your local university business faculty or local Business Link office – the government's national network of small business support – may have access.

If you cannot find access to brad you can buy individual magazine entries for £10 an entry by going online and logging on to its company website (www.intellagencia.com). This is useful if you know the title of the magazine you are seeking, but could be expensive if you need to trawl through various titles before finding the one you need.

Networking and cold calling

The Chartered Institute of Personnel and Development, the professional organisation for human resources and people development, suggests networking as a key part of your strategy to find the job you want. This could include writing letters to prospective employers outlining what you are looking for. Even if they do not have something available at that time they may know somebody who does or may even be willing to offer work experience.

Cold calling is another option. Even if you find this difficult, it is worth a try to help get your foot in the door. But be prepared – know the name of the person you want to talk to, make sure you know what you want to say, and most of all, be polite.

Internet job boards

An internet job board is an online job vacancies listing. Some of the sites will also offer a careers advice service and help with compiling CVs. A job board offers a similar service to the job advertisement pages in a newspaper, with the significant difference that, unlike a newspaper, it has no limit on space so the number and variety of job vacancies it can offer is potentially endless. Most sites will have a search facility enabling the user to look for a job according to criteria such as job title, geographical area or salary. Most sites will have a web link to the home page of the company advertising the job and another link that enables job applicants to forward their CV to the company online.

According to the British Market Research Bureau, from information based every year on 4,000 phone calls, 13.1 million people who were looking for a job in 2005 used the internet. The BMRB's TGI.net research survey revealed that during 2005, an average 27 per cent of all adults of working age in Great Britain, or 41 per cent of all internet users, relied on the internet to look for job opportunities.

Although internet job boards may appear to make the whole process of finding a job easier, they are unregulated, so they must be used with some caution. There is anecdotal evidence that some unscrupulous recruitment agencies have used job boards to advertise non-existent dream jobs in an attempt to entice job seekers to register their details with them and hand over their CV, thereby gaining the agencies more custom. However it is also worth remembering that a similar criticism has in the past been levelled at recruitment agencies who have been accused of using the advertisement pages of newspapers and magazines in the same way. One way to avoid falling into this potential trap is only to reply to job vacancies that are advertised directly by clients or only those advertised by agencies that have professional credentials such as REC membership. The Recruitment and Employment Confederation (REC) is the organisation that represents recruitment professionals and companies in the industry.

Recruitment consultants and recruitment agencies

The recruitment industry in the UK has an annual turnover in the region of £24.5 billion, so it is a hugely successful operation. Although it is a regulated industry, governed by national standards, recruitment agencies and consultants do not need a licence to practise. With this in mind, it is important to check whether they are reputable. One issue to consider, which may influence your decision about using a recruitment agency or consultant, is that the consultant is paid a fee or commission by the client if they fill the vacancy – their priority is the employer, not the candidate. It is worth remembering that it is illegal in the UK to charge individuals for a job-seeking service.

Where can I find details of recruitment consultants or agencies?

The internet and Yellow Pages are obvious places to look as well as local and national newspapers. The REC has a database of its members on its website (see useful contacts at the back of the book).

How can I make sure they are reputable?

The REC represents more than 7,000 corporate members, and around 5,000 individual members. It aims to improve professional standards in the industry. If an agency or consultant is an REC member, that suggests they observe its code of good recruitment practice. The organisation also has a complaints procedure, so if you are unhappy with the service you have been given, you have a means of redress. It is also worth checking whether your consultant has the REC's certificate or diploma in recruitment practice. The Chartered Institute of Personnel and Development (CIPD) also offers specialist coaching and mentoring qualifications so it is worth asking recruiters if they are either members of the CIPD or have a CIPD qualification.

What else should I look for?

A consultant is the link between you and your next job. The company will have a list of clients' vacancies which they will be working to fill. So it's important to select the right kind of specialist recruitment consultancy you need. One option you have is to phone the companies you are interested in working for to find out which recruitment agencies they use and then register with them.

The REC has launched its diversity charter, in conjunction with the Department for Work and Pensions. Companies which have made the REC diversity pledge will be making a public declaration of their commitment to equal opportunities regardless of age, disability, gender or race.

What can I expect from a recruitment consultant?

It is the consultant's job to match suitable candidates to suitable vacancies. John Lees, a career coach and former chief executive of the Institute of Employment Consultants, which later became the REC, has this advice for anybody on a job search using a recruitment consultant:

● Ask the recruitment consultancy to explain its policy on submitting your CV or details to a prospective employer.

● Will they always contact you before putting you forward? If this is what you want, tell the consultancy.

● Employers often put consultancies under a great deal of time pressure, so to avoid missing opportunities, stay in close contact with the consultancy.

● Make sure you inform the consultant in writing of any companies that you do not wish to work for.

● Always ask the recruitment consultancy for a copy of the CV they are intending to send to clients.

● Only allow the consultancy that first contacts you about a specific vacancy to act on your behalf.

● Be wary of signing up with a number of different consultancies – multiple submissions by different consultancies can confuse potential employers and do not increase your chances of success.

Career Fairs

Career Fairs represent an opportunity to meet a number of potential employers under one roof at the same time. It is a chance to talk to people who may already being doing your dream job and can give you an additional insight into what the job is about and whether it is for you. They may also be able to give some advice about how you may be able to change careers. It is also possible to find out more about a particular company – you have the ability to make a fuller assessment from talking to them face to face, without any obligation.

Career coach

A career coach is a specialist who gives careers advice and support. There is no national register of qualified career coaches but the British Psychological Society has a directory of qualified occupational psychologists and life coaches, which could be useful. If you live in southern Ireland it's also worth checking out the Institute of Guidance Counsellors.

You can expect to have regular sessions with a career coach, and the contact can range from six months to a number of years. Career coaches are frequently used by top executives who want to work through work-related issues with an adviser from outside their workplace, but they can also be used to help to guide you through the process of deciding on a career change and then fulfilling that aspiration.

It's important that you feel at ease with your coach and that you trust them. It is also important to check their training credentials. The International Coaching Federation, a global organisation offering training and professional accreditation to life and professional coaches, has its own qualifications. But it's also worth looking to see if coaches are CIPD qualified or are members of the REC.

Follow up references and testimonials from former clients. You will have to make up your own mind about whether you like the models or methods they use and feel confident that they can adapt their skills to meet your own needs. It is also important to make sure that they are prepared to be flexible and fit in with the times you are available to see them.

The fees for hiring a career coach vary but a consultant working independently is likely to charge between £25 and £75 an hour outside London or from £50 to £200 if they work in the capital. Expect to pay from £400 and up to £1,000 for packages designed by career consultancy firms.

A good recruitment consultant, say REC and the CIPD, should be able to provide you with similar support to a career coach, so this is worth bearing in mind as it's likely to be free advice.

Some employers will also offer employees the option of support from a career consultant if the person is facing redundancy or losing their position within the organisation. If you are offered this option do not turn it down – it would be a free service and the intervention could be useful in helping you to reach decisions about your next career move.

Learndirect

This organisation provides a regularly updated database of job profiles, with information about training and qualifications. Although it cannot find you that career-changing job, it can help you to address some of the key issues you need to confront before making the change. Apart from dealing with one-off queries, its trained advisers are also able to offer three supported telephone calls that can cover a period of months. There is no time limit. The adviser can help you to draw up an action plan and support you through achieving your goal. This could include advice about how to market yourself, identifying transferable skills, how to deal with a CV and interview strategies.

Specialist agencies
Forties People Ltd
This agency was set up in 1992 after its founder, a professional recruiter, was made redundant at the age of 50 and found it impossible to find another job.

The agency focuses on older people and job opportunities and careers in the office sector across the board, from office administrator to finance director. Its client group is generally people aged over 35. Like other agencies it will help career changers to identify their transferable skills. It estimates it places around 75 per cent of job candidates, most of whom have come to the agency on personal recommendation. It covers London, Essex and Watford and is expanding. It is an REC member and has won Age Positive awards. The awards are given annually by the Department for Work and Pensions to companies or individuals who are positive about age and who challenge ageist attitudes in the workplace.

Aged2Excel Ltd
This is a specialist search-and-select company aimed at placing older people in employment. Although 60 per cent of clients are aged over 50, it also has people in their 30s and 40s. It is a supporter of the government's Age Positive campaign. Its services include job search and selection; online CV development; online job application; management of job applications and management of covering letters. It offers email job alerts, and careers advice including training advice and options.

Other useful organisations
Age Positive
This is a government-led campaign to promote age diversity in the workplace. Its website includes a list of employers and other organisations which support its aims and promote themselves as age-diverse employers.

PRIME
See details in chapter 4, page 32.

The Employers Forum on Age
This is an employer-led organisation which supports and promotes age diversity in the workplace. It has more than 230 members who between them employ 14 per cent of the UK workforce – more than four million people. See details in chapter 1 page 7.

The mechanics of the job hunt
Of course, it's not just a question of spotting an ideal position in a newspaper ad and moving straight to a new company. Plenty of homework needs to be done first, and there may be many disappointments along the way. But if you follow these tips on how to apply and how to cope with an interview, you will stand a good chance of landing your perfect job.

What should go in my covering letter?

- Be positive. Never draw attention to any gaps in your experience, knowledge or skills which could give the reader an excuse to bin the letter.
- Explain *briefly* why you want to move into the sector or new career.
- Highlight what the move will bring to the organisation – they aren't really interested in what you think the move will do for you.
- Illustrate that you are up to date with the industry and its trends.
- Avoid using 'I' – it shouldn't be all about you – remember it's what you can bring to them.

Example of a good covering letter:[7]

Heading (e.g. Mr X Andrews)
Address
—————
—————
—————
(Leave 2 lines between Address and Date)

Date——
(Leave 2 lines between Date and Salutation)

Dear Mr Andrews,

1st paragraph: talk about the company – not you!

2nd paragraph: purpose of your application and very brief background.

3rd paragraph: what precisely can you do for them?

4th paragraph: closing sentences.

Closing (e.g. Yours sincerely)

(Signature)

Name

How do I make my CV work for me?

A well-written CV that highlights your transferable skills, rather than your skills gaps, will get you a step nearer to your dream job.

As a career changer it's especially vital that you customise your CV to reflect the needs of the job and the organisation. That may sound obvious, but a surprising number of candidates will just send out their standard CV. If you want to take a new career path then you are going to have to use the CV to market yourself differently.

So what needs to go in? At this point, you will have identified your transferable skills. Pick out any strengths that are meaningful to the organisation you wish to work for. Find out as much as you can about the company. While you are researching the company, research the sector you are hoping to move into. Be well informed.

Your CV and covering letter are not limited to selling your potential. They should also manage the risk. If you don't have the relevant experience or qualifications, then you have to pitch it right to persuade potential employers why somebody with your background has something to offer them. It's about minimising the opportunities they have to turn you down.

Top tips from the experts on presenting the perfect CV:

Go back and look at your list of transferable skills and illustrate them with action you took in your current or previous employment.

The idea is to show your prospective employer that although the organisation you worked for before may be totally different, the skills you used there benefited the organisation in ways that you can bring with you.

● Think of an anecdote that shows for example that you have good leadership skills. Is there another story from your career history that illustrates how you work well under pressure?

● Don't get carried away – limit the number of action points to around half a dozen.

● Remember your aim is to highlight the skills you already have, which are needed for the job you are applying for.

Careers coach John Lees, former chief executive of the Institute of Employment Consultants, which later became the REC, has these tips for older job seekers:

● Put your date of birth, rather than your age, and put it on the back page of your CV.

● If you are a parent and decide to reveal you have children, do not include their ages if they are grown up.

● Do not include the dates of qualifications.

● Only include an email address that reflects a professional image. An email address like *hotchick@yahoo.com* will not cast you in a good light. The same goes for your voicemail message.

Example of the perfect CV:[8]

ANGELA MIDDLETON

Address: 5 Poppy Grove London
Telephone: 07968 785425

Nationality: British
E-mail: angela.middleton@hotmail.com

PERSONAL ATTRIBUTES

I am a hardworking and motivated individual who constantly strives to achieve high standards. I am industrious and creative with a keen eye for detail and enjoy working as part of a team, with the ability to work autonomously if required.

EDUCATION

1998–2001 **Sheffield University**
Bachelor of Arts in English

1996–1998 **Morshead Sixth Form College**
4 A levels: Geography B, General Studies B, Economics C, English Language D

1991–1996 **Morshead Comprehensive School**
9 GCSEs graded A-C, including English and Mathematics

PROFESSIONAL DEVELOPMENT

Aug 2005 **St John's Ambulance**
First Aid in the Workplace

1993–1998 **Duke of Edinburgh**
Bronze and Silver Awards

CAREER HISTORY

Aug 2003–present **LB Hounslow**
Project Co-ordinator
- Ensured standards of service delivery are consistent and of the highest quality
- Produced a service development plan for each centre
- Ensured plans were implemented
- Monitored health and safety for staff and premises in compliance with the Health and Safety at Work Act, Environmental Health Regulations
- Provided consultancy on the development of activities that promote and support healthy living and active ageing
- Monitored centres to ensure appropriate activity programmes were being used
- Ensured all materials and equipment in centres were used correctly and kept in good repair
- Line managed Centre Managers through regular support, supervision, appraisals and training
- Was involved in the recruitment and selection of Centre Managers, staff and volunteers
- Provided appropriate induction and training
- Organised regular rotation of managers throughout the centres
- Ensured liaison with statutory authorities such as Social Services, Health Authority, PCTs, fire services and outside agencies such as transport services, leisure centres, colleges, other voluntary/community organisations

Mar 2003–Aug 2003 **Suttons Haulage**
Administrator
- Performed filing and data entry duties
- Had responsibility to ensure records were up to date
- Scanned invoices ready for processing
- Took incoming calls from customers and colleagues
- Ensured deliveries were timely

Dec 2002–Feb 2003 *Independent travel*

Oct 2002–Nov 2002 **Lincraft, Australia**
Data Entry / Administration Assistant
- Responsible for data entry of product codes and new order information
- Reorganised product descriptions

Aug 2002–Sep 2002 *Independent travel*

May 2002–Jul 2002 **Nutworth Partnership Recruitment, Australia**
Recruitment Assistant
- Carried out data entry of résumés into the database
- Formatted résumés to send to clients
- Interviewed potential candidates and assessed their ability for specific positions

Dec 2001–Apr 2002 **Skiworld plc, France**
Chalet Host
- Looked after a chalet of ten guests in the French Alps
- Responsibilities included cleaning the chalet and cooking breakfast and lunch
- Ordered shopping and managed spending within an allocated budget
- Received 'Chalet host of the month' award

Oct 1997–Nov 2001 **Judges Hotel**
Waitress (during holiday periods)
- Waited tables in an à la carte restaurant and at silver service functions
- Worked within bar areas

IT SKILLS
Proficient in Microsoft Word, Excel, WordPerfect, email and the internet

OTHER SKILLS AND RELEVANT EXPERIENCE
A full and clean driving licence

INTERESTS
Travelling – travelled around Europe after university, worked in France for 6 months and then took a year to travel around Australia, New Zealand and Thailand
Photography – currently attending a Intermediate Photography course

REFEREES
Available on request

How do I make the most of an interview?

'I think what you have to do as a career changer is really think through where you might be exposed in the interview because you don't have the career experience. You should use examples from other parts of your life, such as your family life or voluntary work you may have done, to help fill those gaps.' Mary Maybin, career consultant and former teacher.

Before going for the interview make sure you have done your homework and do not undersell yourself. Research the company and its culture. It's easy to find out the facts about a company, but the facts alone do not tell you why people stay with the firm and what they enjoy about the company.

The easiest way to find out the answers to these questions is to spend some time in the company ahead of the interview and chat to people in the department where you are applying to work. Visiting the department ahead of the interview will give you a much better understanding about the job you are applying for. You could try speaking to the company's personnel department. Explain that you have been asked to come for an interview, that you are really interested and that you want to do some research first. Rely on your networking skills to help you to reach the people you want to talk to ahead of the interview. You can't afford to be reticent. It takes a lot of commitment and energy to find a new career. Don't give up if you don't get anywhere at first.

If you can get a foot in the door before the interview it is often enough to put you ahead of your competitors. It raises your profile above those who just turn up for the interview on the day. It shows that you are an interested professional who has been prepared to find out as much as you can about the company and the job. You may be put to the front of the queue just by showing you are serious. It also helps you with the interview in other ways, as you will be more informed and can ask relevant questions about the organisation and the job.

Finally, here are some tips from career coaches in getting through an interview:

- This is your chance to market yourself face to face. Be confident. Remember your CV has worked and they are interested in you.
- Do not undersell your skills and knowledge.
- Show them that you know about the company and the sector. It's the chance for all that research to pay off.
- Talk about your transferable skills.
- Suggest that your new blood means you may bring creativity.
- Be clear about why you are career changing.
- Make the case that it was a deliberate choice. Make sure they realise you are somebody who has thought through the move. Be clear that you are not acting on a whim.
- Explain what your ambition is and where this new career and new job fits in with your long-term plans.

- Interviewers are looking beyond your skills and competences. They are judging your commitment, dedication and enthusiasm.
- If you have completed an evening class or course to increase your skills in your new career, tell them. What about unpaid work experience or work shadowing?

Charity worker to plumber: Natalie Gowers (30)

'When I finished university and graduated with a degree in sociology I took a gap year before working. I've done a number of different jobs – I've worked in retail and even tried teaching. For the last four years I was working as a researcher in a fund-raising department of a charity. What I began to realise though was that I wanted a career that wasn't office-based and which got me out from behind a desk. I wanted to do something practical and hands-on, something that was useful.

I thought about plumbing because there was a lot about it in the media at the time and I thought compared to the other trades like carpentry and electricians it seemed the most diverse. The only thing which bothered me was whether, as a woman, I would have the necessary strength but that hasn't proved to be a problem. I also knew there were other female plumbers around so I wouldn't be the first. In fact there are some advantages to being female because to be a plumber it helps if you have nimble fingers and are able to get into small places.

The first thing I did once I had decided what I wanted to do was to find out as much as I could about plumbing. I contacted the Institute of Plumbing to find out what qualifications I needed and what the possible routes were. I then began to look for colleges in my area where I could study. To complete the NVQ level 2 in plumbing meant I had to study in the evenings three days a week for two years; I also had to pay for my course, which was £360 a year. As I was still in my full-time job with the charity I could afford the fees, so the money wasn't a problem. Also my job was very much 9 a.m. to 5 p.m. so I never had any difficulty getting to college on time in the evenings. It was quite tough going to college three evenings a week but it seemed the most sensible route for me because I wanted to make sure that I liked plumbing before I gave up my other job. There were other people changing careers like me on the course, mostly my age, but also a lot of people from Eastern Europe who were converting their qualifications.

The other thing I did during the two years was to take a week's holiday to do work experience as a plumber. I just wrote to a lot of plumbing companies telling them what I was doing and asked if I could have some work experience. It was really useful because I wanted to find out whether, if I did it day in day out, it was still something I wanted to do.

When I first told my family and friends that I wanted to train as a plumber they laughed, but when I explained that I was serious, and they saw that it was viable, they were quite happy to support me. When I worked for the charity I was earning £27,000, now as a trainee plumber I'm earning £8 an hour, but I'm lucky because my partner is on a good wage. Once I've finished my traineeship, and the company is confident I can work alone, I could earn between £35,000 and £55,000 with experience.

I don't have any regrets at all. I really enjoy doing something practical that is very satisfying – somebody has a problem and you sort it out for them. I feel like I'm doing something that is really useful that people are grateful for.'

JOB PROFILES

Accountant

'I wasn't the only mature trainee on the course and I think if you find the right company and set-up it can definitely work.' Trainee accountant and former council children's services manager.

The job
There are different kinds of accountants. **Accountants in private practice** work on behalf of clients. Responsibilities include preparing profit and loss accounts, helping them to make financial decisions and preparing budget reports. They can also offer advice on company law and help with statutory audits and tax accounts. **Management accountants** have slightly different roles and responsibilities. They are usually employees within an organisation devoted to developing its financial strategy and business plan and making financial projections. They often have management responsibility for a company's financial information system and its team of accounts clerks and bookkeepers. **Accounting technicians** work with qualified accountants and are usually responsible for routine daily tasks, from recording invoices and preparing ledger balances to, with more experience, preparing tax returns and accounts and helping with budget planning and controls.

The culture
Accountancy is changing. It is shedding its traditional stuffy men-in-grey-suits image and is increasingly being seen as a profession which offers equal opportunity, flexibility and a range of career paths across the business sector. As part of this metamorphosis it is keen to attract an older workforce recognising that age and experience outside the financial institutions can reap rewards. With the money markets facing increasing regulation and a continuing shortage of qualified professionals, accountancy is a real option for career changers.

Do I need a degree?
Degrees in accountancy are available which, on graduating, may exempt you from some of the professional exams needed to qualify to practise as an accountant. Details can be obtained from individual universities. See the Universities and Colleges Admissions Service (UCAS) for details of accountancy undergraduate degrees. The Chartered Institute of Management Accountants offers a postgraduate route to its CIMA professional qualification. Postgraduate students may not have to complete the CIMA certificate in business accountancy as a first step towards professional qualification. For other training options see the professional qualification entry below.

What professional qualifications do I need?

Entry qualifications to train or study to become an accountant are variable depending on training route and qualification.

To study for an **accountancy technician's** qualification good basic levels of English and maths are expected.

The **Associate Chartered Accountant (ACA)** professional qualification has a minimum entry of two A levels and three GCSEs, with maths and English at A or B grades. Alternative requirements are 220 minimum UCAS points or a 2:1 degree. Only 5 per cent of ACA trainees are accountancy degree graduates; 50 per cent have business related degrees and 45 per cent are arts, humanities, languages, law or engineering graduates.

The **Association of Chartered Certified Accountants (ACCA)** qualification has a minimum entry requirement of two A levels and three GCSEs in five different subjects but these must include English and maths. These requirements may be waived for mature students if they can prove experience in the workplace instead.

The **Chartered Institute of Management Accountants** offers both graduate and non-graduate routes to professional qualification. It offers the **CIMA certificate in business accounting** as the non-graduate route. A good understanding of maths and English is required. A postgraduate route to the full **CIMA professional qualification** is also available and often means that the certificate does not have to be studied as well.

The first step onto the accountancy ladder can be made by qualifying as an accountant technician and gaining the **Association of Accounting Technicians (AAT)** qualification. The only entry requirement is a basic level of English and maths. There are two routes to qualifying – either an NVQ-based route or the diploma route – and both can be studied part or full time. The qualification can take up to four years to complete part time, less full time, and is offered by around 400 further education colleges as well as by private providers. A year's experience after qualifying entitles you to become a member of the Association of Accounting Technicians. Many with the AAT qualification will go on to further training to become chartered accountants. The AAT entitles you to complete the Associate Chartered Accountant (ACA) professional qualification within two years rather than the usual minimum three.

Professional training schemes

Only 4 per cent of accounts trainees studying for the Associate Chartered Accountant (ACA) professional qualification are over the age of 30, according to the Institute of Chartered Accountants in England and Wales (ICAEW), with around 70 per cent starting as young graduates straight out of university. But these figures should not put you off. Both Price Waterhouse Coopers (PwC) and KPMG – two of the top four UK accountancy firms – are keen to attract older graduates to their training schemes, which provide the ACA professional qualification. PwC has around 1,200 training posts a year and attracts around 15,000 applicants, so competition is fierce. The training element alone is worth around £30,000 so you would be expected to be committed. Older graduates should not be deterred from applying, as the company says it is seeing an increasing number of applications from career changers and it looks favourably on more mature graduates who it says are often 'strong performers'. It is important to be realistic about the demands of working and training at the same time, but the opportunities are there for the taking. ACA qualification can only be achieved on an ICAEW approved training scheme, not independently. Qualification takes a minimum of three years, although that can increase to five years, and is based on exam and work practice.

The Association of Chartered Certified Accountants (ACCA) professional qualification has wide global recognition reflecting broad accountancy and business skills. The ACCA offers an alternative route to professional qualification if you have been unable to secure an ACA training place. It is possible to study for the ACCA outside the workplace. However qualification is dependent on three years' work experience. One option would be to study for the ACCA exams in the evening, on block release or distance learning, and then apply for a job as a trainee accountant or a management accountant to gain the three years' work experience needed to confirm the qualification. Although this may seem a long route, offering yourself partly trained to a prospective employer makes you an attractive candidate because you have paid for your study, have taken the financial risk and shown a personal commitment to the profession. Doors should open.

The Chartered Institute of Management Accountants offers its own professional qualification in a similar way to the other professional accountancy bodies. Following qualification, membership of CIMA is dependent on three years in work. The institute has many members who have come to the profession as career changers and from a range of different backgrounds. It recommends that any career changers planning to take a new path as a management consultant should complete the professional qualification while working so that trainees are 'earning and learning' at the same time.

What personal skills do I need?

Being an accountant is not just about being good at maths. You must have an understanding of numbers but it is just as important to have good communication skills. The essence of accountancy is not just to present numbers, but to show the meaning of the numbers, so you have to be able to express yourself comfortably and deliver presentations with confidence. Being able to share information and having good IT skills is crucial as accountancy is a technology-based profession. Commercial awareness and an interest in business is important. You have to be a team player. Personal motivation is essential because working and training at the same time is hard. Professional integrity and honesty are the top personal qualities.

Starting salary
- Qualified accountant £40,000 (London), £35,000 (outside London).
- PwC trainee £24,250 in London but salary doubles on qualification.
- Qualified accountant technician £25,000–£30,000

Jobs on qualification
Varied across finance and business but include taxation and investment advisers; auditors; insolvency experts; financial managers and analysts.

Current employment prospects ★ ★ ★ ★ ★
The market is buoyant; demand for qualified accountants is high.

Is a career change a reality? ★ ★ ★ ★ ★

Welcomes older entrants? ★ ★ ★ ★ ★

Potential high earner? £££££

Useful contacts:

Association of Accounting Technicians
154 Clerkenwell Road
London EC1R 5AD
020 7837 8600
www.aat.co.uk

Association of Chartered Certified Accountants (ACCA)
64 Finnieston Square
Glasgow G3 8DT
0141 582 2000
www.acca.org.uk

Institute of Chartered Accountants in England and Wales (ICAEW)
Chartered Accountants' Hall
PO Box 433
London EC2P 2BJ
020 7920 8100
www.icaew.co.uk

Institute of Chartered Accountants of Scotland (ICAS)
CA House
21 Haymarket Yards
Edinburgh EH12 5BH
0131 347 0100
www.icas.org.uk

Institute of Chartered Accountants in Ireland (ICAI)
Dublin
CA House
83 Pembroke Road
Dublin 4
+353 1 637 7200

Belfast
11 Donegall Square South
Belfast BT1 5JE
028 9032 1600
www.icai.ie

Chartered Institute of Management Accountants (CIMA)
22 Chapter Street
London SW1P 4NP
020 7663 5441
www.cimaglobal.com

Acupuncturist

'Earnings are low – it really is a job of love and devotion.' The British Acupuncture Council.

The job
Acupuncture is traditional Chinese medicine based on the life energy Chi, which flows through the body in channels, or meridians. An acupuncturist works holistically and relies on these channels to bring about healing by using very fine stainless steel needles inserted at points in the body to anaesthetise, bring pain relief and improve health. According to the British Acupuncture Council (BAcC) the principal aim of acupuncture is to treat the whole person so they can recover the equilibrium between the physical, the emotional and the spiritual.

The culture
Becoming an acupuncturist is often chosen as a second or third career and it is common to find people in this profession who are older than 30, which is good news if you are in this age bracket and considering a move into this area. But it will only be a realistic option if you are able to find the £15,000 it is likely to cost you over a minimum three years to complete the training, because a common route for trainees is to rely on private colleges that run accredited courses. The climate is starting to change, as more universities are beginning to offer degrees entitling graduates to go into practice. A new career as an acupuncturist is possible, with most newly qualified practitioners going into private practice. However, income is limited. Because of this many acupuncturists choose to work in part-time practice and juggle a second job to boost their income. It is the love of the job that drives most acupuncturists, and the desire to help people. This is not the job if you are keen to become a high earner.

Do I need a degree?
Minimum qualifications vary according to the college providing the training and whether it is a private provider or part of the statutory sector. Going down the university route requires a minimum of two A levels and five GCSEs grade A to C or equivalent.

Studying for a degree course, either a BA or a BSc in acupuncture or traditional Chinese medicine, offers a training route to become an acupuncturist. Look for a course that has been endorsed by the British Acupuncture Accreditation Board. Details of these degrees, with minimum entry requirements, can be found on the Universities and Colleges Admissions Service (UCAS) website.

What professional qualifications do I need?

Anybody can call themselves an acupuncturist because there is currently no statutory regulation or registration of this profession. The government does however have plans to introduce statutory regulation and registration that will bring acupuncturists into line with other health therapists. But until that happens, the professional organisation for acupuncturists in the UK is the **British Acupuncture Council (BAcC)** which voluntarily regulates the profession and holds a professional membership register. It has 2,600 members in the UK. The **British Acupuncture Accreditation Board**, affiliated to the council, monitors and accredits training courses. Completing a BAcC accredited course will entitle you to membership of the organisation but will also recognise that you have acquired a professional level of competency to practise. The BAcC has accredited courses at eight colleges in the UK which can be followed three years full time or longer part time and will include a minimum 3,600 hours of clinical practice. It can be a costly option and many trainees who go down this route will continue to work part time to fund their training.

What personal skills do I need?

Acupuncture brings together both western and eastern medicine and relies on a holistic approach to healing. With this in mind the BAcC says it can be a good choice for a career change as the better practitioners are those who bring life experience with them. Many people choose to train as an acupuncturist because of their own personal experiences of the medicine and it is not, at the moment, a common career choice by young graduates. Like other therapist roles, working as an acupuncturist is people-centred, so it is important to be able to communicate well. A desire to help people is also essential. It is a job that can be stressful so individuals must be able to work under pressure, but perhaps more importantly be emotionally 'robust' and self-assured. It is also important to have a thirst for knowledge because professional development is constant.

Starting salary

Around £12,000 to £16,000 a year in private practice but the income will depend on the level of fee charged and the number of patients.

Jobs on qualification

A self-employed practitioner in private practice often works alongside other alternative therapists like osteopaths or chiropractors. As with any other small private business expect it to take time to build up a practice. Success will be dependent on personal recommendation and individual reputation. Some acupuncturists do work in the NHS, usually attached to pain or other clinics, but these practitioners are likely to be existing health professionals such as doctors, nurses or physiotherapists who have completed a professional postgraduate qualification to allow them to offer acupuncture.

Current employment prospects ★ ★ ★ ★ ★
Alternative therapies like acupuncture are becoming more mainstream and there are shortages of trained properly qualified professionals. Job prospects are good.

Is a career change a reality? ★ ★

Welcomes older entrants? ★ ★ ★ ★ ★

Potential high earner? £ £ £

Useful contacts:

British Acupuncture Council (BAcC)
63 Jeddo Road
London W12 9HQ
020 8735 0400
www.acupuncture.org.uk

Institute for Complementary Medicine
PO Box 194
London SE16 7QZ
020 7237 5165
www.i-c-m.org.uk

British Medical Acupuncture Society (organisation for existing qualified health professionals who are statutorily regulated)
www.medical-acupuncture.co.uk

University and Colleges Admissions Service (UCAS)
Customer Services Unit
UCAS
PO Box 28
Cheltenham
GL52 3LZ
0870 1122211
www.ucas.com

Details of colleges running courses fully accredited by the British Acupuncture
Accreditation Board (August 2005)

College of Integrated Chinese Medicine (affiliated to the University of Kingston)
19 Castle Street
Reading
RG1 7SB
0118 950 8880
www.cicm.org.uk

College of Traditional Acupuncture (UK) (affiliated to Oxford Brookes University)
Haseley Manor
Hatton
Warwick
CV35 7LU
01926 484158
www.acupuncture-coll.ac.uk

International College of Oriental Medicine UK
(affiliated to the University of Brighton)
Green Hedges House
Green Hedges Avenue
East Grinstead
West Sussex
RH19 1DZ
01342 313106/7
www.orientalmed.ac.uk

London College of Traditional Acupuncture and Oriental Medicine (LCTA)
(affiliated to the University of Portsmouth)
60 Ballards Lane
Finchley
London N3 2BU
020 8371 0820
www.lcta.com

Northern College of Acupuncture
(affiliated to the University of Wales)
61 Micklegate
York
YO1 6LJ
01904 343305
www.chinese-medicine.co.uk

The School of Five Element Acupuncture
13 Mandela Street
London NW1 0DU
020 7383 5553
www.sofea.co.uk
(SOFEA are not enrolling any new undergraduate students)

University of Salford
School of Community, Health Sciences and Social Care
5th Floor, Allerton Building
Frederick Road Campus
Salford
Greater Manchester
M6 6PU
0161 295 2372
www.chssc.salford.ac.uk

University of Westminster
Department of Complementary Therapies
School of Integrated Health
115 New Cavendish Street
London W1W 6UW
020 7911 5082
www.westminster.ac.uk

Arborist/arboriculturist/tree surgeon

'We get quite a number of career changers saying "I have worked in this bank for ten years and I'm about to explode. What can I do?" ' Nick Eden, director of the Arboricultural Association.

The job

Those working in the arboricultural industry are responsible for trees. Their working week is devoted to the management and care of trees and other woody plants. This can involve tree planting, pruning, felling and, with experience and appropriate qualifications, being a specialist tree adviser. This is a highly skilled job which can be dangerous because it involves climbing trees and using potentially lethal equipment. There are minimum qualifications and training needed before you can embark on this career path (see qualifications below), but no minimum entry requirements are needed to follow this vocational route. There are job opportunities in both the public and private sector and there is the opportunity for career progression. Developing a career in arboriculture by starting as an arborist, which is a craft-based role, and moving into private consultancy and management is a common route.

A well-qualified and experienced arborist could develop a career in the public sector working as a council tree officer with responsibility for trees owned by a local authority, including those in public open spaces, country parks, conservation areas or public woodland. Tree officers are responsible for enforcing tree protection law. They also advise council departments about tree health and law and are arbitrators in neighbourhood disputes about trees, usually concerning blocked light or safety issues. Tree officers are also likely to be called in for advice around insurance claims where trees may be responsible for subsidence.

The culture

Office workers are often tempted by a career change to become an arborist or an arboriculturist because of the appeal of getting away from a desk and working outside. Many want to move into the craft side of the profession and work as an arborist – sometimes known as a tree surgeon. Others are interested in becoming an arboriculturist, developing a new career in management or consultancy advising about tree health and safety and looking at the planning issues around trees and how to incorporate them into new developments. Training for arboriculture is flexible, which makes it a good option for a career change, and it is also a growing industry, so future job prospects are very good. But being an arborist requires physical strength and is hard on the body. There are tree surgeons who are in their 50s and 60s who have been in the industry all their working lives. But the more common destination for this age group is to move into consultancy or take on a management role. However the Arboricultural Association says if you are starting out as an arborist in your mid-30s and you are fit and strong you can make it a successful long-term career change, provided you do not mind hard work and unpredictable British weather. Some people will have a greater chance of success if they are naturally good climbers and are able to work quickly.

Do I need a degree?
You do not need a degree to become an arborist.

What professional qualifications do I need?
A common practical route for career changers who want to be arborists is to study for the **Royal Forestry Society certificate in arboriculture**. This can be completed part time, one day a week at college or through distance learning. The certificate includes learning about soil formation and nutrient requirements; tree biology and physiology; causes and signs of ill health; and the selection, supply, planning and aftercare of plants. Other areas studied on the certificate are tree surgery, health and safety and equipment maintenance, how to carry out a tree survey and the law as it affects trees. Ecology, woodland and forests are also studied. Practical competencies are also included and students develop skills in maintaining a chainsaw; planting; processing brushwood and felling small trees.

The qualification is based on assessment and on examination. Once you have this minimum qualification, which is traditionally seen as a benchmark for quality in the tree industry at craft level (although there are alternative qualifications), you will have the basic skills to work in arboriculture. You would be able to work as a ground assistant to a climber working for a tree surgery contractor. In this role you would collect all the material which comes down from the tree, either putting it through a wood-chipping machine or bundling logs. After completing the **National Proficiency Training Council (NPTC) certificates of competence** in climbing trees and aerial rescue, and another NPTC certificate of competence in chainsaw and related operations – including modules in how to use a chainsaw from a rope and harness – you will be certified to climb and prune trees.

'If you are prepared to assist somebody who is climbing then it is very easy to get work; employers are looking for people who are prepared to work hard and are reliable,' says Nick Eden, director of the Arboricultural Association. With continuing professional development, it is possible to go on to complete more NPTC certificates, which will increase your range of responsibilities. These include being able to use wood chippers, stump grinders and mobile elevating work platforms.

What personal skills do I need?
You will have to have a good head for heights and be physically strong. It is hard work

and the job makes huge demands on the body. It is also important to be willing and prepared to work in all weathers, especially the rain. You must be happy to work outdoors and have an interest in the environment and conservation. Some people have a natural ability for this work as they are born good climbers, so if you fall into this category you should find it easy to find employment as you will be able to work at a quicker pace than colleagues.

Starting salary

'You will have to really love the job because the salary will never compensate for the wet days and the hard work,' says Nick Eden, director of the Arboricultural Association. Arboriculture, like other sectors of the land-based industry, is not a high earner. As a newly qualified arborist working as an assistant on the ground you are likely to earn less than £20,000. Your earning ability is, according to the Arboricultural Association, linked to your climbing ability and a good climber could earn up to £30,000. A local authority tree officer earns in the region of £20,000–£33,000 (up to around £35,000 in London). If you decide to become a self-employed tree surgeon, your annual income could be in the region of £30,000.

If you decide to establish yourself as a self-employed consultant, it can require substantial capital investment. To complete the necessary craft NPTC competencies in arboriculture to work as an arborist costs at least £15,000, according to the Arboricultural Association. There are also additional costs, for equipment such as a chainsaw (which can cost around £800) and the cost of special protective clothing and safety equipment.

Jobs on qualification

You will start as a general arboriculturist. With experience and further qualifications it is possible to become a local authority tree officer in the public sector. There are also career development opportunities in the private sector such as becoming a self-employed tree consultant or working in a consultancy.

Current career prospects ★ ★ ★ ★

This is a growing industry so career prospects are good. You will not be out of work.

Is a career change a reality? ★ ★ ★ ★ ★

Arboriculture appeals to career changers and entry qualifications and training to become an arborist are practical, flexible and reasonably inexpensive.

Welcomes older entrants? ★ ★ ★ ★ ★

There is no age limit to becoming an arborist but it is a physically demanding job that requires you to be fit and healthy.

Potential high earner? £ £

Useful contacts:

The Arboricultural Association
Ampfield House
Romsey
Hampshire
SO51 9PA
01794 368717
www.trees.org.uk

National Proficiency Training Council (NPTC)
Stoneleigh Park
Stoneleigh
Warwickshire
CV8 2LG
024 7685 7300
www.nptc.org.uk
information@nptc.org.uk

Lantra (sector skills council for land-based industry)
Lantra House
Stoneleigh Park
Coventry
Warwickshire
CV8 2LG
0845 707 8007
www.lantra.co.uk
Lantra career advice sites:
www.ajobin.com
www.afuturein.com

Institute of Chartered Foresters
7A St Colme Street
Edinburgh
EH3 6AA
0131 225 2705
www.charteredforesters.org

The Royal Forestry Society
102 High Street
Tring
Hertfordshire
HP23 4AF
01442 822028
www.rfs.org.uk

International Society of Arboriculture (ISA)
148 Hydes Road
Wednesbury
West Midlands
WS10 0DR
0121 556 8302
www.isa-uki.org

Local government careers
www.lgcareers.com

Beauty therapist

'Mature people are attracted to becoming beauty therapists because it allows them to practise holistically, which they find appealing.' Tiffany Tarrant, beauty therapy development manager at the Hairdressing and Beauty Industry Authority (HABIA).

The job

A beauty therapist is trained to offer clients treatments for the face or body. They can be specialists in skin care, make-up and facial treatments. They can also perform manicures and pedicures and be skilled in hair removal. With more training they can go on to offer body therapies such as aromatherapy, reflexology or Indian head massage. Others, with professional development, may become specialists offering advice about nutrition, diet and exercise, or be experts in electrolysis and body massage. They can work in a number of different settings such as salons; department stores; health and fitness clubs; spas; hotels and ocean liners. Some decide to be self-employed and run their own beauty therapy business. It is a career that offers opportunities to travel world-wide.

The culture

Training to become a beauty therapist is an attractive and popular option for career changers. As beauty therapies become more clinical, the level of qualification needed to work in the industry is becoming higher. There is no single qualification as a professional beauty therapist. Most of the courses on offer can be studied part time in the evenings and weekends, usually for up to two years, which makes it an attractive option for a career changer because it is possible to keep working while studying. There are also fast-track options to some qualifications, especially professional diplomas, which, in some cases, can be completed in seven to eleven months full time.

Do I need a degree?

You do not need a degree to be a beauty therapist, although there are foundation degrees available in beauty therapy, and a BSc in beauty therapy and management (see the University and Colleges Admissions Service for more details).

Once you have completed your professional training it is common practice to study for post-qualifying diplomas to increase the variety of therapies that you can offer. This not only improves your career prospects but also increases your earning potential.

What professional qualifications do I need?

There is no single qualification or route to becoming a qualified beauty therapist. Courses available include:

- NVQ/SVQ levels 1 to 3 in beauty therapy
- NVQ/SVQ level 3 in spa therapy
- BTEC/SQA national certificate/diploma in beauty therapy sciences
- City and Guilds certificate/diploma in beauty therapy
- ITEC diploma for beauty specialists
- VTCT certificate/diploma in beauty therapy
- foundation degree in beauty therapy
- BTEC HNC/HND in beauty therapy sciences.

Another route to qualification is to complete an internationally recognised beauty therapy diploma. In the UK there are two awarding bodies that offer a range of professional beauty therapy diplomas which have national and international recognition. They are the **Confederation of International Beauty Therapy and Cosmetology (CIBTAC)** and the **Comité International d'Esthétique et de Cosmétologie (CIDESCO).** CIBTAC and CIDESCO diplomas offer professional qualification and training in a range of different beauty therapy skills. They include core beautician skills in make-up, skin care, pedicure and manicure, as well as training in additional therapies such as body massage, electrotherapy, aromatherapy, Reiki, and the use of Hopi ear candles. The diplomas can be studied full or part time, and at some colleges are offered fast-track. They can be completed at some state further education colleges (see Learndirect for more details) or can be studied at private beauty colleges and schools. The education standards body for the industry, HABIA, recommends NVQ level 2 and 3 in beauty therapy as the minimum vocational qualification needed to work as a professional beauty therapist.

Be prepared to pay around £7,000 for a comprehensive beauty therapy diploma awarded by CIBTAC. Fees at private colleges to study for a comprehensive CIDESCO diploma in beauty therapy can be around £9,000 but vary according to the course studied and whether it is full time, part time or fast-track. For details of fees at FE colleges or private colleges or schools, you should contact the institutions direct.

In contrast to these professional diplomas, the cost of completing NVQ level 2 and 3 in beauty therapy – the minimum professional qualification recommended to become a beauty therapist by HABIA – is a lot lower. The NVQ level 2 qualification costs around £1,254 and can be completed in seven months full time or twelve months part time. The NVQ level 3 costs around £1,355 and is usually studied full time or two days a week for eight months.

Beauty retail companies are increasingly promoting their own beauty treatments, which has helped to create new training opportunities. The **London College of Beauty Therapy** is developing an accredited BTEC qualification for retail beauty consultants with the support of the company Elizabeth Arden. The qualification was due to be launched in 2006.

What personal skills do I need?

It is important to be well groomed and particularly to have good hands, which should be supple and sensitive. You should have a caring nature and be tactful. It is a people-centred job so you must like people and enjoy working with them. Excellent communication and interpersonal skills are essential.

Starting salary

An experienced qualified beauty therapist can expect to earn around £20,000 but the salary varies according to where they are working in the UK. There is the potential to earn a higher income. The director of a health spa, for example, could expect to earn around £50,000.

Jobs on qualification

Beauty therapist.

Current employment prospects ★ ★ ★ ★ ★

Public demand from the beauty therapy industry has increased rapidly in the last ten years. A skills survey of the health spa industry in 2006 by HABIA revealed that 96 per cent of salons predicted they would need at least the same number of employees in the following year, if not more. The London College of Beauty Therapy is regularly heavily oversubscribed. The College's chief executive, Eileen Cavalier, whose West End school offers 1,000 places every year, says: 'The demand for qualified therapists constantly outstrips available supply, with the result that faced with a booming public demand to sample the "look-good feel-good culture" and a business culture that wants to be in, or expand into that market, the lack of trained people is one factor stopping them. That may be reassuring for the public but it is frustrating for employers trying to expand their business.'

Is a career change a reality? ★ ★ ★ ★ ★

Training is flexible and can be followed while working.

Welcomes older entrants? ★ ★ ★ ★ ★

Beauty therapy attracts older entrants who are keen to offer holistic therapies. Age is no barrier to this career and some employers are keen to recruit more mature therapists.

Potential high earner? £ £ £

Useful contacts:

Learndirect
0800 100 900
www.learndirect.co.uk

University and Colleges Admissions Service (UCAS)
Customer Services Unit
UCAS
PO Box 28
Cheltenham
GL52 3LZ
0870 1122211
www.ucas.com

The London College of Beauty Therapy
47 Great Marlborough Street
London W1F 7JP
020 7208 1300
info@lcbt.co.uk

British Association of Beauty Therapy and Cosmetology (BABTAC)
Meteor Court
Barnett Way
Barnwood
Gloucester
GL4 3GG
0845 065 9000
www.babtac.com

Hairdressing and Beauty Industry Authority (HABIA)
Oxford House
Sixth Avenue
Sky Business Park
Robin Hood Airport
Doncaster
DN9 3GG
0845 230 6080
www.habia.org

International Therapy Examination Council (ITEC)
4 Heathfield Terrace
Chiswick
London W4 4JE
020 8994 4141
www.itecworld.co.uk

Vocational Training Charitable Trust (VTCT)
3rd Floor
Eastleigh House
Upper Market Street
Eastleigh
Hampshire
SO50 9FD
023 8068 4500
www.vtct.org.uk

Confederation of International Beauty Therapy and Cosmetology (CIBTAC)
www.cibtac.com

B & B business

'I'm pleased I decided to run a B & B but it has been incredibly hard work. I used to think my day would finish by noon – it's nothing like that, you are busy all the time.' Former British Airways IT manager, B & B owner Karen Thorne.

The job

It is a mistake to think that running a B & B is an easy option. It is hard work with long hours. Domestic chores – like cooking, cleaning and washing – are all part of the daily demanding routine. With guests living in your home you must be prepared to give up some of your privacy. There is a lot of paperwork and bureaucracy to deal with and the statutory regulations which govern B & Bs on health and safety issues, disability discrimination and licensing are a potential minefield. Issues that you will have to consider include whether you have to apply for change of use planning permission to run the business and also whether other planning permission is required if you want to make changes to the B & B property.

Health and safety regulations are also important. If you are going to provide food you will need to register with the local environmental health office. A number of different licences have to be applied for which can be baffling. For example, if you plan to provide radios in guest rooms, there is a licence you must apply for, and another if you intend to have music playing in the dining room. You may also find you are liable to pay local authority business rates if you plan to provide accommodation for more than six guests. Fire certificates may be needed, depending on the number of guests you plan to cater for and whether the bedrooms are above the first floor. Furniture will also have to comply with current fire regulations. If you plan to have more than four rooms for guests, you must advertise your prices, including the amount for VAT, in a place where they can be seen by the public. You will also be expected to keep accurate records of all your guests aged over 16 as well as the passport number, date of issue and further destination of any overseas guests. **VisitBritain**, the organisation responsible for marketing tourism in the UK, publishes The Pink Book – a practical guide to legislation, which gives all the details about the regulations and laws that apply to bed and breakfast premises and businesses. It is vital to read this book before you go ahead with any plans to start a business.

The culture

Running a bed and breakfast is an appealing career change for many who dream of running a business from their own home and stepping away from stressful and demanding jobs. It is a business that can attract career changers from all kinds of different backgrounds, such as former IT managers, teachers and journalists. But it is important before starting out on this new career path to understand your market and to have a thorough business plan. It is advisable to start small, maybe letting only a couple of rooms, not only to test the market, but also to find out whether this is the kind of career change which, in reality, keeps its appeal.

Do I need a degree?
No.

What professional qualifications do I need?
There are no specific professional qualifications which are recommended if you want to run your own B & B. There are scores of self-help books available, and career changer Karen Thorne has created four short learning courses, available online, aimed at people thinking of setting up in business, as well as those who are already established but want to make their business thrive. (See useful contacts below.)

A background in marketing is invaluable as this business relies on whether you can attract people through your front door.

What personal skills do I need?
You will have to be a master of all trades. You will have to be prepared to get up early. You must enjoy cooking, especially if you offer other meals in the day as well as breakfast, and there are other domestic tasks such as cleaning and tidying up. Patience and a good sense of humour are also useful. You must like meeting new people and be prepared to share some of the space in your home with them. You must be able to cope with bureaucracy because of the statutory regulations that are linked to establishing a B & B.

Starting salary
As with any small business, your income will depend on how successful you are. It is a good idea to register your B & B with the local tourist board. Registration is linked to a national independent inspection programme which is governed by national criteria and which determines how many stars your business can be awarded. If, for example, you want to aim for four stars, then at least 50 per cent of the rooms you offer have to be en suite. Alternatively if guests are expected to share a bathroom with the owners, then your business will never move above a two-star rating. The more stars you have reflects higher quality, which means you will be able to charge higher fees. It is now not uncommon for good quality B & Bs to have similar rates to hotels, which can be in the region of £90 a night for a double room. But rates will vary according to local area, demand and whether you are offering basic and cheap accommodation or something more comfortable or luxurious. The B & B industry predicts it can take three years before a new business reaches its expected business potential.

Jobs on qualification
B & B owner.

Current employment prospects ★ ★ ★
Thorough market research is crucial before setting up any small business. You must identify whether there is a need for another B & B in your district. If you can also identify a unique selling point or you can tap into a niche market such as catering for vegetarians, the gay community or families with young children, you may have greater success.

Is a career change a reality? ★ ★ ★ ★ ★

Welcomes older entrants? ★ ★ ★ ★ ★

Potential high earner? £-£ £ £ £
As with any small business your potential success will depend on the strength of your business plan and whether your marketing has hit the target.

Useful contacts:

VisitBritain
Thames Tower
Blacks Road
London W6 9EL
020 8846 9000
www.visitbritain.org

www.enjoyengland.com

Karen Thorne
Hopton House
Hopton Heath
Shropshire
SY7 0QD
01547 530885
info@shropshirebreakfast.co.uk

Black cab driver

'If you ask any taxi driver what they did before you'll discover they come from all sorts of backgrounds you would never have imagined – such as former teachers or actors. I used to be an electrician and wanted to change my trade, and becoming a taxi driver was one of the few trades I could learn while I was still working.' Black cab driver and former electrician.

The job
Most black cab or hackney carriage drivers are self-employed, working the hours they want. This is one of the appeals of the job. Some may pay a weekly subscription, usually in the region of £40, to be linked to a radio operating service so that they can take passengers referred to the service, usually company account fares. But the majority of black cab drivers will rely on fares picked up out on the road. A licensed hackney carriage driver is entitled to wait at a taxi rank for fares. Drivers can either own their own black cab or can choose to hire the vehicle by the day, week or month which can make the job very flexible; this could be another attraction.

The culture
Black cab or hackney carriage drivers are often career changers attracted by the freedom it offers. The majority are self-employed and only work the hours they want. It is a career change which can take place gradually – many work part time in their original career before taking the plunge to becoming a full-time taxi driver. This is not a cheap career move if you plan to own your own taxi, as it can cost up to £30,000 to buy a brand-new vehicle, and other costs to cover special licence fees may push start-up costs to around £35,000. But there is a cheaper route if you decide to rent a vehicle on a daily or weekly basis, and this means you can test the water before taking that giant step onto a new career path.

Do I need a degree?
You do not need a degree to become a black cab driver.

What professional qualifications do I need?
A special hackney carriage licence, known as 'the badge', is required before you can legally drive a black cab and take passengers. Each local authority has its own licensing department which is responsible for issuing the licence. Some areas will have a waiting list if the council has decided to regulate the number of black cabs in its district. In London the Public Carriage Office (PCO), which is part of Transport for London, administers the service. Each local authority will have its own conditions for granting a licence although there are common strands. These will include passing a

criminal records check; being aged over 18; passing a private medical examination to prove your physical and mental health; having a full driving licence for at least 12 months (three years in London) and passing the hackney carriage driving test.

In order to acquire a licence, you must pass a geographical knowledge test, to ensure that you are familiar with the quickest routes across the district you wish to be licensed to work in. In London this is known as learning 'the knowledge' – a blue book containing 320 different runs across the capital within a six-mile radius of Charing Cross. It can take up to three years to learn. Outside London each local authority will have its own local version of 'the knowledge'. Before being granted the licence, which entitles you to wear 'the badge', you will be tested by an examiner on 'the knowledge'. This usually involves at least one written paper, followed by a series of oral questions. You will also have to pass a driving test run by the Driving Standards Agency to ensure that you can safely drive and manoeuvre a taxi on the road. This can include a test on disability awareness and vehicle access for wheelchair users. If you intend to own your own black cab, it will have to have a hackney carriage vehicle licence. This can be applied for through the local authority licensing department or, in London, the PCO. To qualify for the licence, the vehicle has to undergo an annual check, tougher than a traditional MOT, in order to confirm that it is safe to be on the road and carry passengers. You will need special driver's insurance to allow you to drive the taxi, and this will also include public liability cover.

What personal skills do I need?
It is essential that you are a good driver but also that you enjoy driving. Excellent communication skills are crucial, and you must also have the right kind of temperament to deal with a range of different kinds of passengers and driving situations which can be stressful. Numeracy is important, as you will have to handle money and run your own accounts. A good memory is an advantage and you must be good at time management.

Starting salary
This will vary according to the number of hours you work. The average income for a self-employed taxi driver working a 40-hour week is around £16,000 but this can go up to £30,000 depending on where you work and the amount of hours you put in. Each licensing authority sets the tariff limit for its own district so this will also influence your income. Many black cab drivers choose to start by working part time and renting a licensed vehicle from a taxi fleet hire company, which costs between £160 and £260 a week, until they have the money to buy their own black cab.

The Licensed Taxi Drivers Association estimates it can cost around £35,000 to set yourself up as a self-employed black cab driver. Around £30,000 of this covers the cost of a new taxi, although there is a market in cheaper second-hand vehicles which can start at around £2,000. Other essential costs are the hackney carriage driver's licence, which is in the region of £135 if you live in the area where you are applying for a licence, or around £190 if you are non-resident. The annual vehicle licence is around £260 for a resident or around £350 for a non-resident. A medical report can cost between £50 and £200. Other costs to consider are the fee for a criminal records check, and the fee for sitting 'the knowledge' test and the cost of the DVLA hackney carriage driver's licence.

Jobs on qualification:
You will have a licence to work as a hackney carriage driver.

Current employment prospects ★ ★ ★ ★ ★
Should be plenty of work.

Is a career change a reality? ★ ★ ★ ★ ★

Welcomes older entrants? ★ ★ ★ ★ ★

Potential high earner? £ £ £

Useful contacts:

Licensed Taxi Drivers Association (LTDA)
Taxi House
Woodfield Road
London W9 2BA
020 7286 1046
www.ltda.co.uk

The Public Carriage Office
15 Penton Street
London N1 9PU
020 7941 7809
www.thelondontaxi.co.uk

The National Taxi Association
Infirmary Street
Newtown
Carlisle
Cumbria
CA2 7AA
01228 598740
www.national-taxi-association.co.uk

Driving Standards Agency
Stanley House
56 Talbot Street
Nottingham
NG1 5GU
0115 901 2500
www.dsa.gov.uk

Bookseller

'Very few people open bookshops when they are very young. It's usually older people who are looking for a career break or a completely new way of life.' The Booksellers Association.

The job

A bookseller is the link in the chain between the publisher or wholesaler and the book-buying public. It is very much a selling job although it is equally important to have a knowledge of and an interest in books. Booksellers can either work in small independent bookshops or for one of the larger book chains. These are more likely to offer good career opportunities. Another option is to run your own independent bookshop and be an owner/manager. The professional organisation for booksellers, the Booksellers Association (BA) recommends that if you choose this path you must have the necessary knowledge and experience, the right financial backing and be prepared to work hard.

Whether you decide to run your own business or work in somebody else's bookshop as a bookseller, you will be dealing with enquiries from customers and offering advice about books. You may need to trace titles for customers from existing stock or from electronic databases. You may also be asked to come up with alternative book suggestions. General housekeeping duties are common including keeping displays tidy and restacking shelves. There is a lot of lifting and carrying so the job can be physically demanding. A bookseller may also help with window displays or with book-signing events. In a large high-street book chain, a bookseller may be given responsibility for a particular section, such as children's books, and would be able to influence decisions about future stock, which would mean meeting publisher representatives and studying catalogues.

The culture

Bookselling is an industry that attracts older career changers, particularly teachers, keen to fulfil a dream to be an independent bookseller. But it is a dream that can easily become a nightmare if your passion for the written word is not matched by a keen business sense backed up with crucial commercial skills. Most people who decide to run their own bookshop will opt for buying an existing business. Around every three weeks a bookshop is advertised for sale in the trade press although there are also specialist firms that deal in selling bookshop businesses. The alternative to running your own bookshop is to work for one of the high-street bookshop chains. Although they always appear to be staffed by young people, mainly because salaries are often low, the Borders chain has taken a deliberate stand to promote age diversity in its employment policies and has signed up to the government's Age Positive campaign.

Do I need a degree?

There are no specific academic requirements to be a bookseller although many people working in the industry are graduates. A degree would however be useful if you work in a specialist bookshop such as one devoted to fine art.

What professional qualifications do I need?

The Booksellers Association (BA) used to run a diploma in professional bookselling which was the professional qualification for the industry. It consisted of 15 modules covering issues such as stock control, window displays, handling money, consumer law and health and safety. The BA says it withdrew the qualification about five years ago because of lack of interest.

Since the withdrawal of the BA diploma, there are now no professional qualifications for booksellers. Most bookshop chains will, however, provide on-the-job training. It is possible to study for NVQs in retail but these are general qualifications not specifically targeted at bookshops.

What personal skills do I need?

You must have a love of books and literature in general but you also need good selling skills. If you are to run your own bookshop you will need good business acumen and ability as well as an understanding of current market trends. You must enjoy meeting people and working with the public. You must be a good communicator and you must have researching and computer skills.

Starting salary

Salaries for booksellers are low; the average is around £16,000. If you decide to run your own business, its success would determine your personal income.

Jobs on qualification

There is a definite staff hierarchy in bookshops, starting from sales assistant to senior sales assistant, assistant manager then manager.

Current employment prospects ★ ★ ★

Variable. There has been a fall in the number of small independent bookshops because of the dominance of the large book chains and the popularity of buying books over the internet. But there may be good career prospects if you join a large bookshop chain. If you want to set up as an independent bookseller, the BA publishes its own guide which will take you through the steps of starting and running a bookselling business (see useful contacts below).

Is a career change a reality? ★ ★ ★ ★ ★

Yes – but you need more than a passion for books to succeed and it is not a high-earning profession.

Welcomes older entrants? ★ ★ ★ ★ ★

Bookshops are keen to employ older entrants and bookselling is a popular destination for career changers. The book chain Borders UK has signed up to the government's Age Positive campaign, which promotes age diversity in the workplace.

Potential high earner? £ £

Like most jobs in retail this is not a high-earning profession. Maximum earnings are around £30,000. If you run your own bookshop your income will be determined by the success of your business.

Useful contacts:

The Booksellers Association of The United Kingdom and Ireland Ltd (BA)
Minster House
272 Vauxhall Bridge Road
London SW1V 1BA
020 7802 0802
www.booksellers.org.uk

The Antiquarian Booksellers Association (ABA)
Sackville House
40 Piccadilly
London W1J 0DR
020 7439 3118
www.aba.org.uk

Book Careers
www.bookcareers.com

Skillsmart Retail
40 Duke Street
London W1A 1AB
0800 093 5001
www.skillsmartretail.com

Borders UK Ltd
Stillerman House
120 Charing Cross Road
London WC2H 0JR
020 7379 7313
www.borders.com

Charity chief executive

'If I had stayed in teaching I would have become flat and stale – no doubt a strong driver for me is leading change and making things work.' Mary Marsh, former head teacher and now chief executive of the National Society for the Prevention of Cruelty to Children (NSPCC).

The job

If you are already a chief executive in a private company or the public sector it would be a mistake to believe that moving to the charity sector offers an easier life. It can often be just as stressful, or more so, because charities have to function on limited budgets, sometimes relying on a workforce of part-time staff and volunteers. Smaller charities will also expect their chief executive to juggle a wide range of skills as well as being the public face of the organisation and its principal networker. Larger charities with an annual turnover of more than £25 million can be complex organisations. The working week can be long, more than 40 hours, with weekend working expected from time to time.

The culture

The charity sector, alternatively known as the not-for-profit or voluntary sector, is expanding as the government increasingly looks in its direction to help deliver public services. The **Association of Chief Executives of Voluntary Organisations (ACEVO)**, which has more than 2,000 members, says career changers from a public sector background may have an advantage seeking these top charity jobs over people coming from the private sector because of the contacts they can bring with them and their knowledge of how the sector works. On the other hand, charities are also keen to attract people from the private sector as they strive to become more businesslike. The organisation **Working for a Charity** estimates that around 60 per cent of people who enrol on its training courses come from the private sector and are aged between 40 and 60. The courses are popular with former health service managers and ex-BBC employees, as well as people who have left the armed forces. Chief executives have to have a multitude of different skills, especially financial acumen, so specialist charity recruitment experts say it is more likely that somebody coming from the private sector with a finance background will have a chance of becoming a chief executive than somebody with expertise in human resources or information technology. A general manager from a private company will also be a strong candidate because of the wide range of skills they are likely to have.

Age is neither an advantage nor a disadvantage in the charity sector. Older candidates wanting to become chief executives may be in a stronger position if they apply to charities that focus on older people and sometimes charities may favour candidates who possess a certain amount of gravitas, which often comes with age and experience. On the other hand, a dynamic think tank may prefer to recruit a younger, more dynamic chief executive who will more accurately match the public image it is trying to achieve. However what will really give you a head start in the charity chief executives jobs market is whether you have done your homework properly and discovered what the charity is looking for in its next chief executive – does it want somebody who is good at corporate fundraising or does it need an individual with an established network of contacts at government minister level?

Do I need a degree?

A degree may be desirable, but it is not essential. Charities and specialist recruitment agencies for the sector both recommend that anybody interested in becoming a chief executive takes part in some voluntary work or becomes a charity trustee or board member in order to gain experience of the culture and the day-to-day operation of the sector, before applying for a job. Trustee vacancies and volunteering opportunities are usually advertised in the local press or national newspapers, including the Guardian. Alternatively the website, *www.doit.org.uk*, which is supported by the Home Office, has a database of volunteering opportunities and trusteeships.

Charities are typically more interested in personal skills and experience than paper qualifications. However it is becoming increasingly more common for chief executives to have an MBA qualification.

What professional qualifications do I need?

The Institute of Directors (IOD) and ACEVO have joined forces to create the IOD/ACEVO diploma in company direction, which has been designed especially for charity chief executives. The qualification involves eight workshops, ranging from one to three days, making up 15 study days in total. They cover key areas such as legal liability, finance and strategy, and marketing skills. Acquiring the diploma entitles the chief executive to go on to gain Chartered Director status.

The organisation Working for a Charity also runs three training courses for people interested in a new career in the charity sector. These are popular with career changers. It offers a £60 short course introductory programme – covering two evenings – which gives a brief introduction to the sector, its challenges and job opportunities. The foundation course explores the sector in more detail, offering seven days of seminars and a 20-day work placement with a charity. The fee for this course is £795. A three-day executive programme, costing £595, is another option aimed at people in full-time employment who want to find out about the sector.

Research charities or medical charities may require, or prefer, a chief executive to have a relevant clinical or medical background or qualification.

What personal skills do I need?

Charity chief executives must have good networking skills because they have to work with a range of different organisations and politicians at many levels. Chief executives will often be the public face of the charity so being a good communicator with an understanding of public relations is important. The ability to communicate and feel at ease with paid staff as well as volunteers and a board of non-executive directors or trustees is also crucial, so flexibility is key. Being able to read a budget sheet and basic accounts skills, such as being able to interpret profit and loss accounts, are essential. Other skills in human resources or IT may also be valuable if the charity has few staff and the chief executive is expected to have a range of different skills.

Chief executives also need to have a passion for the charity and understand its culture and ethos. Innovation and enterprise are two of the characteristics which ACEVO lists amongst the key attributes of a charity chief executive, as well as a commitment to professional development, not only their own, but also that of the staff within the organisation. Personal drive is also important.

Starting salary

The salary of a charity chief executive varies enormously depending on the size of the organisation and its turnover. The latest annual salary survey by ACEVO for 2005/6 shows that since 2000 chief executive salaries have become more competitive, but they are still far behind comparable rates in the private sector. However they are moving closer to chief executive pay scales in the public sector. Women chief executives are also likely to be paid more than their male colleagues, the ACEVO survey based on 716 chief executives discovered. The larger charities with an annual turnover of more than £25 million paid their chief executives on average £94,000 in 2005/6. Smaller charities with an annual turnover of between £15 million and £25 million paid their top officer an average £78,300.

Jobs on qualification

A charity chief executive.

Current employment prospects ★ ★ ★

This is a growing sector so job opportunities are good. But it is also a volatile sector as charities are often dependent on local government for core funding and this source of income can change if the political landscape changes or if there is a squeeze on budgets.

Is a career change a reality? ★ ★ ★ ★ ★

> Welcomes older entrants? ★ ★ ★
>
> Potential high earner? £ £ £

Useful contacts:

Association of Chief Executives of Voluntary Organisations (ACEVO)
1 New Oxford Street
London WC1A 1NU
0845 345 8481
www.acevo.org.uk

National Council for Voluntary Organisations
Regent's Wharf
8 All Saints Street
London N1 9RL
020 7713 6161
www.ncvo-vol.org.uk

Working for a Charity
National Council for Voluntary Organisations
Regent's Wharf
8 All Saints Street
London N1 9RL
020 7520 2515
www.wfac.org.uk

Institute of Directors
116 Pall Mall
London SW1Y 5ED
020 7839 1233
www.iod.com

Rockpools
Caxton House
2 Farringdon Road
London EC1M 3HN
www.rockpools.co.uk

Charity People
38 Bedford Place
London WC1B 5JH
020 7299 8700
www.charitypeople.co.uk

www.doit.org.uk
(Website for volunteering opportunities including trustee vacancies)

Chef

'The best advice we can give is to gain some basic training and experience first – more businesses fail because people think, "right I can cook, so I will open my own restaurant".' Anne Pierce, chief executive of Springboard, the charity that promotes careers in the hospitality, tourism, leisure and travel industries.

The job

Chefs are responsible for preparing and cooking food. They may work in a variety of settings such as a restaurant, a hotel kitchen, a school kitchen or for catering contractors. Working as a chef can mean long hours in a frenetic, hot and stressful environment. Deadlines have to be met as customers expect their meals on time; this is particularly true for chefs working in restaurants or hotel kitchens. Contract catering, where chefs are employed to provide meals for business and industry for example, may offer a less stressful environment for those starting out as the hours are Monday to Friday from around 8 a.m. to 3 p.m. and are unlikely to involve weekend or night work.

There is a distinct career structure in catering, with a job as a commis chef (sometimes called a trainee chef) being the starting point for a chef's career. Roles at this level of the career ladder include food preparation and basic cooking under supervision. The next rung up is to become a chef de partie which is a senior position in the kitchen. A chef de partie is responsible for one section of the kitchen, such as the grill or pastries, and he or she has a team of commis or trainee chefs working with them. A sous chef is the number two in the professional kitchen and has key management roles, including making sure that all the meals are to the required standard and served on time, as well as having responsibility for a section of the kitchen. The most senior position in the kitchen is the head chef, who is in charge of the kitchen, plans menus, negotiates prices with suppliers and organises delivery. Staff training and development falls under the responsibilities of the head chef too. A head chef is often the public face of the restaurant or professional kitchen and can hold the reputation of the organisation in their hands. A chef patron is a small businessman who runs their own restaurant and is the head cook responsible for all the cooking. A chef patron is likely to employ a restaurant manager who is responsible for running the 'front of house' services, such as taking customer orders and serving.

The culture

A national shortage of skilled chefs means there are plenty of job opportunities in this industry for career changers who have a natural flair in the kitchen. It is an industry that offers a practical route to career changers because it is possible to work part time and shift work is also available, especially in the hotel and restaurant sectors. It is probably going to be necessary to start at the bottom of the career ladder – coming in as a trainee chef in a restaurant or hotel kitchen, or alternatively working as a catering assistant for a contract catering business. But all sectors of the industry say there is the chance of rapid career progression if you are determined, hard-working and have a natural talent for cooking. Because of the current chef skills shortages some hotels or restaurants may be more prepared to take a risk with career changers and offer a trial day in the kitchen to assess whether you have the potential to be a successful professional chef, and doors may open. Enthusiasm and a commitment to hard work may be more important than professional qualifications, according to the human resources director of a top hotel chain. She says: 'There is such a skills shortage at the moment that we really can't be closed off to any options.'

Do I need a degree?

You do not need a degree to be a chef. A degree in business would, however, be useful if you wanted to move into catering management.

What professional qualifications do I need?

Springboard, a national charity for the catering and tourism industries that offers one-to-one careers advice and support, recommends that a career changer's first step should be to try and organise some work experience in a professional kitchen or enrol in some 'tasters in industry' sessions. Either of these options would provide an understanding of the work in a professional kitchen, and at the same time would help to identify any skills weaknesses which need to be addressed through extra training. With a national shortage of skilled chefs, finding work experience should not be difficult. Springboard is able to help to find work experience, a permanent job or training schemes for career changers who want to become chefs.

NVQ work-based qualifications are the well-accepted route into chef training. The NVQs in food preparation and cooking from levels 1 to 3 are seen as the gold standard. They usually take two years of study part time which takes place alongside employment in the industry. Some employers will contribute to the cost of the study. Some businesses will offer the NVQ in-house.

Another option for career changers is to take a private cookery course such as a cordon bleu diploma or the Leiths diploma in food and wine which can be studied full time. These courses cost from £10,000 to nearly £15,000 for a three-term or six-month intensive course. They are aimed at amateur cooks who want to become professional chefs. Courses provide health and safety training as well as food hygiene, and some will offer modules in basic business skills and being self-employed.

What personal skills do I need?

A chef must be a team player, somebody who is well organised, passionate about food and creative. Personal drive and commitment is important because the hours can be long and relentless. Excellent people skills are essential as a chef is expected to manage teams of staff in the kitchen, which is a hot and stressful working environment. Being able to work under pressure is important as well as having the ability to multi-task.

Starting salary

The catering industry has a reputation for low salaries as 51 per cent of its workforce is made up of semi-skilled or unskilled staff who are likely to be on the national minimum wage or slightly above. But a skilled chef can expect to make a reasonable living with those at the top of the industry commanding six-figure salaries. A commis or trainee chef can expect to earn from £9,000 to £11,000; a chef de partie around £16,000; a sous chef up to £19,800 and a head chef or chef de cuisine around £24,000 to £29,000.

Jobs on qualification

There is distinct chef hierarchy but, according to all sectors of the industry, career progression can be swift if you have the skill and the commitment. The most junior chef is a commis or trainee chef, followed by chef de partie, sous chef, head chef and chef patron.

Current employment prospects ★ ★ ★ ★ ★

Very good. There is a national shortage of skilled chefs, so job opportunities exist for career changers who have a natural talent in the kitchen.

Is a career change a reality? ★ ★ ★ ★ ★

Welcomes older entrants? ★ ★ ★ ★ ★

Potential high earner? £ £ £ £ £

Useful contacts:

Springboard UK
3 Denmark Street
London WC2H 8LP
020 7497 8654
www.springboarduk.org.uk

People 1st
(the Sector Skills Council for the hospitality, leisure, travel and tourism industries)
2nd Floor
Armstrong House
38 Market Square
Uxbridge
UB8 1LH
www.people1st.co.uk

Leiths School of Food and Wine
21 St Alban's Grove
London W8 5BP
020 7229 0177
www.leiths.com

Tante Marie School of Cookery
Woodham House
Carlton Road
Woking
Surrey
GU21 4HF
01483 726957
www.tantemarie.co.uk

The Cordon Bleu London
114 Marylebone Lane
London W1U 2HH
020 7935 3503
www.lcblondon.com

Circus performer

'If you've got a fantastic act it doesn't matter how old you are. It's the product which is important – not your age.' Jacquie Wellbourne, aerial acrobat and circus school director.

The job

Circus performers are professional entertainers. They may work as trapeze or tightrope artists as well as acrobats and clowns. Most performers have more than one skill and should be prepared to multi-task if necessary. Circus performers are usually self-employed and work for a circus on an annual contract which runs for the season from April to October. They may spend the winter months performing in other venues, such as the theatre, or working as a children's entertainer. Some performers may prefer not to work for a touring company but instead be based in the community arts sector, which can involve physical theatre and children's workshops. The more unique your art or 'product', the greater your chance of employment and your chances of success.

The culture

Circus performers need to be fit and have lots of stamina because the job is physically demanding. If you are a member of a touring circus, you will have to be prepared to follow an itinerant lifestyle for the season, which usually runs from April through to October. If you bring a family with you, they will have to be willing to live the circus life too, and it is not always easy to maintain schooling if you have children in tow. Working well as part of a team is essential, and being prepared to help out when required is crucial. You will not survive if you are a loner. If you are keen to become a circus performer your age is irrelevant. What is more important is your commitment to the work and the community. If you do not have the courage to tour, there are other opportunities to use circus skills in the arts generally including working as a street performer or being a community artist. Actors, dancers and elite sportsmen and women are traditionally attracted to a career change as a circus performer because it offers them the opportunity to use their talent in a new way. Circus ringmaster Chris Barltrop has this advice for career changers: 'The circus is a wonderful world to be part of but you have to be prepared to commit yourself to the circus way of life.'

Do I need a degree?

Although there are no formal entry requirements, there is a two-year full-time foundation degree in circus arts, validated by the University of Kent. It is run by **The Circus Space**, which is affiliated to the Conservatoire for Dance and Drama in London.

There is the opportunity to study for another year to complete a BA (hons) in circus arts. The selection process includes an interview and audition. For further details see useful contacts below.

What professional qualifications do I need?

There is no single professional qualification for being a circus performer. Your opportunities will depend on how good your act is and how different it is from other performers. Your chances of success increase if you can show that what you bring to the circus is unique.

However, there are a number of circus schools around the UK which run a variety of classes aimed at helping you to develop the performing skills you already have to a professional level. The classes range from short part-time courses to others requiring a commitment of between one and five years. The training is demanding and requires a high level of commitment, which can make it difficult to maintain employment at the same time. It may be a good idea to attend a short summer school in circus skills first before making the decision to attend a course aimed at the professional level, so that you understand what circus performance demands. The Academy of Circus Arts is the only touring circus school where the big top is your classroom for six months while you learn all aspects of the art. Course fees at the different schools vary but costs are around £5,000 for a one-year professional diploma.

What personal skills do I need?

Obviously you must have a performing skill and talent. This could include experience in acting, dance or a professional sport such as gymnastics. It is crucial to be physically fit and have good stamina. You must be able to adapt, and be self-disciplined and highly motivated. Being self-sufficient and resourceful is also important. This is not a nine-to-five job, so you must be flexible. You will be self-employed, so you must have some business acumen. Above all, you must have a passion for what you are doing and the determination to succeed, because it is a fiercely competitive environment. But as one circus school director says: 'An accountant came to us to learn how to perform on the high wire. He took to it so much that he decided to give up everything, bought his own little big top and is still out there doing his own shows.'

Starting salary

Income varies according to individual contracts and employers. The actors' union Equity sets minimum rates for circus performers, but for most performers this is not a high-earning profession. A salary survey by Equity in 2005, based on 8,337 members working in the performing arts, revealed that half of them earned less than £6,000 from their art during the year and only 6 per cent earned more than £30,000 in the same year.

Current employment prospects ★ ★ ★

Although there are only a few UK circus companies, there are increasing opportunities for performers to take their skills outside the big top into the community arts sector, so job prospects are reasonable.

Is a career change a reality? ★ ★ ★

This is not the easiest of career moves but if you are determined, and your act is of professional standard and unique, you have a good chance of success.

Welcomes older entrants? ★ ★ ★ ★ ★

Age is no barrier but you do need to be physically fit and have stamina.

Potential high earner? £ £

Useful contacts:

Circus Arts Forum
Fulcrum
19 Great Guildford Street
London SE1 9EZ
020 7401 8866
www.circusarts.org.uk

The Academy of Circus Arts
Enborne
Newbury
Berkshire
RG20 0LD
07050 282624
http://freespace.virgin.net/zippos.circus/info.htm

Circomedia
Britannia Road
Kingswood
Bristol
BS15 8DB
0117 947 7288
www.circomedia.com

The Circus Space
Coronet Street
London N1 6HD
020 7613 4141
www.thecircusspace.co.uk

Greentop Community Circus Centre
St Thomas' Church
Holywell Road
Brightside
Sheffield
S4 8AS
0114 244 8828
www.greentop.org

Circus Maniacs
8a Kingswood Foundation
Britannia Road
Kingswood
Bristol
BS15 8DB
www.circusmaniacs.com

Sky Light Circus Arts
www.skylight-circus-arts.org.uk

Equity (London Office)
Guild House
Upper St Martins Lane
London WC2H 9EG
020 7379 6000
www.equity.org.uk

Conservator

'One conservator I know who was a career changer used to work for Marks and Spencer creating fruit fools – her background was perfect because the work was forensic, scientific and picky.' Carol Brown, training development manager for the Institute of Conservation.

The job

A conservator is devoted to restoring, repairing or preserving individual works of art or other objects of historical value. There are specialists in a whole range of different areas such as furniture, ceramics, textiles and fine art. But the majority of conservators work with paper and historical archive. Conservators increasingly focus on conservation preservation. Those working in public galleries, for example, will use their technical skills to make sure that a display or exhibition is housed in an appropriate environment, so that the risk of deterioration is minimal. Conservators can also be called upon to give advice about the safe transportation of collections.

In the private sector, conservators often belong to small or medium-sized specialist firms focusing on a particular area such as ceramics or furniture, where they are employed by clients to offer advice about the repair, restoration or preservation of an individual object. Conservators in private galleries have similar responsibilities to those working in the public sector, focusing around the maintenance or transportation of a collection.

The culture

People who change career to become conservators often come from one of the caring professions, especially nursing. It also appeals to people who have worked on the technical side of the food industry as well as those who have a background in one of the craft professions. Scientists and career changers from the general heritage sector are also drawn towards working as conservators. There is a drive to attract career changers to the profession; a third of applicants who took up paid internships offered by the Institute of Conservation (ICON) in 2006 fell into that category.

Do I need a degree?

Becoming a conservator is increasingly graduate entry which means the entry requirements for a degree course are usually A levels or equivalent. You should refer to the University and Colleges Admissions Service (UCAS) for details. A specialist degree in conservation, followed by an internship to build up work experience in the sector is the traditional route to becoming a conservator. A list of recommended degree courses including postgraduate qualifications, run at 13 higher education institutions, is available from the ICON (see useful contacts below). But you will have to be prepared to return to higher education if this new career path is for you.

However there are some areas of speciality, such as furniture, where a professional apprenticeship route is still possible.

What professional qualifications do I need?

The ICON and the Society of Archivists run a professional accreditation scheme, the **Professional Accreditation of Conservator-Restorers (PACR)**, which focuses on work-based competency. Accreditation, which is dependent on examination by peers and the production of a professional portfolio, usually requires at least three years' post-qualifying experience.

What personal skills do I need?

It is crucial to have manual dexterity: it is the single most important skill of a conservator. A knowledge of science, especially chemistry, is also becoming more important as the profession is increasingly focusing on preventative conservation. It is not always an advantage to be creative, as the job skill is in copying, rather than creating something new and unique.

Starting salary

Sixty per cent of conservators work in the private sector. They can be found working in specialist firms or are employed by private galleries. A fine arts conservator working in a top gallery in the south-east could earn up to £60,000. But most conservators will earn less, in the region of £20,000 to £25,000. In the public sector a head of conservation at a public gallery is likely to earn between £40,000 and £50,000, with assistants earning around £25,000. Carol Brown from ICON admits: 'There is a huge variation in remuneration but in general it is a profession which requires high input with low financial return.'

Jobs on qualification

A conservator or restorer.

Current employment prospects ★ ★ ★ ★ ★

Good. There is a move to attract career changers to the profession and there is a national skills shortage of professionally qualified people working in the heritage sector. It is common for people who move into the conservation profession to stay there because of the professional satisfaction it brings. It is rare for a qualified conservator to career change out of the profession.

Is a career change a reality? ★ ★ ★

The Heritage Lottery Fund has invested £1 million in internships for people who want to train as conservators and one of the target groups identified is career changers. The internships, which are being administered by the ICON, include an annual salary of £14,500. The initiative should make it easier for career changers to move into this profession. The ICON says although it feared some resistance from the heritage sector to opening the door to career changers, this has not happened.

Welcomes older entrants? ★ ★ ★ ★ ★

In 2006, a third of the applicants for paid internships run by the ICON were career changers.

Potential high earner? £ £

Experienced conservators working in the private sector for galleries in the south-east can earn as much as £60,000. Pay scales in the public sector are highest for conservators in management positions, with a head of conservation in a public gallery earning up to £50,000. Traditionally this is not a high-earning profession, with salaries on average between £20,000 and £25,000.

Useful contacts:

Institute of Conservation (ICON)
Floor 3 Downstream
1 London Bridge
London SE1 9BG
020 7785 3807
www.icon.org.uk

Society of Archivists
Prioryfield House
20 Canon Street
Taunton
Somerset
TA1 1SW
01823 327030
www.archives.org.uk

Museums Association
24 Calvin Street
London E1 6NW
www.museumsassociation.org

Guild of Master Craftsmen
166 High Street
Lewes
East Sussex
BN7 1XU
01273 478449
www.thegmcgroup.com/theguild

Creative and Cultural Skills
11 Southwark Street
London SE1 1RQ
0800 093 0444
www.ccskills.org.uk

Doctor

'What can older people bring to the profession? Well, there is the old cliché of more life experience, but I think one thing they bring is a fresh outlook.' A medical student in their 40s.

The job

There are 60 different specialities in medicine, so job opportunities are vast, but they fall into two main categories: either a hospital-based career or one in the community in general practice. A key difference between hospital doctors and GPs is their employment status. Hospital doctors are NHS employees, while GPs are independent contractors, which means they have self-employed status but are contracted to work for the NHS on a nationally negotiated contract.

Doctors' hours are long, whichever branch of medicine you choose. The hours a GP is expected to work are more predictable than those of their hospital colleagues, especially since a new contract was agreed which means they are no longer contracted to work in the evenings, at nights or weekends. It now means it is up to the individual GP if they want to be on call out of hours. Hospital doctors on the other hand are contracted to work a maximum 58-hour week, in line with the European working directive. The directive is due to change in 2009 when they will be expected to work 48 hours.

The culture

Last year (2006), medical students at their annual conference were worried that medical schools may in future impose an upper age limit on entry to applicants. Their fears were based on the arguments that it costs around £237,000 to train to be a doctor and takes at least 12 years to reach consultant status. The question at the heart of their concerns was whether, in the future, medical schools would think it cost effective to offer a place to a student in their 30s who would have fewer years to give back to the NHS than somebody who went to medical school as a teenage school-leaver. Medical students have thrown the spotlight on the issue at a time when medical schools have seen a 50 per cent increase in medical student places in the UK since 1998, with four new medical schools having opened since 2002 and an increase in applicants from older age groups. Between 2000 and 2003 the number of students aged between 25 and 39 applying for places at medical school has doubled. The number of applicants in this age group being accepted reached 43 per cent in 2002, falling back to 34 per cent a year later, according to a report by the doctors' representative organisation, the British Medical Association. However, at some universities mature students can account for up to a quarter of all medical students. At the University of East Anglia, medical school mature students make up 50 per cent of its intake.

These figures suggest that a career change to medicine is an option, but a key hurdle for making this a successful move will be money. Medical training can take up to 12 years, and long days of study, as well as weekend and night training, means it is almost impossible for medical students to take on part-time work to help fund their study. Despite extra government financial help for medical students, the British Medical Association predicted in 2005 that when university top-up fees start in 2006 a medical student could face a debt of around £64,000 on qualifying.

Do I need a degree?

A degree in medicine takes five or six years. Entry requirements to a traditional undergraduate degree are usually three A levels in maths and two sciences at grades ABB or higher. One-year **access to medicine courses** have been developed in recent years by further education and adult education colleges, aiming at offering a route into medical training for mature students who do not have science A levels. Competition for places is fierce and acceptance on the course does not guarantee a place at medical school. The curriculum is likely to include biology and chemistry to A or AS level as well as health psychology, mathematics, physics, IT and study skills.

A one-year foundation degree or a one-year pre-medical course as an introduction to medicine is another possibility and is available at some medical schools. This option is aimed at students with A levels but not in science subjects who want to study medicine. Under these schemes students complete the foundation year before continuing with the traditional undergraduate five-year medical degree programme.

Details of course requirements and medical schools are available from the University and Colleges Admissions Service (UCAS).

Medical schools are increasingly offering four-year accelerated courses in medicine to graduates with either science or arts first degrees. (See useful contacts list.)

What professional qualifications do I need?

Graduation from medical school is just the beginning of the training required to be a doctor. All graduates who want to follow a career in medicine have to complete a further two years' training on a number of clinical placements. Completion of the two-year foundation programme is similar to an apprenticeship, and at the end of the first year the graduates are entitled to full professional registration with the General Medical Council. Once qualified, a doctor has to decide which career path in medicine to follow. Training as a hospital doctor would take another six years to reach consultant status; to become a consultant surgeon takes another seven years' training, while general practice offers the shortest route to qualification, three years. For more information on funding for training, see page 246.

What personal skills do I need?

The BMA lists nine key personal attributes that make a good doctor. They are: competence; integrity; confidentiality; caring; compassion; commitment; responsibility; advocacy and the spirit of enquiry. Excellent communication skills are essential, as well as the ability to work as a member of a team and under pressure. Doctors have a duty to keep their knowledge up to date so a commitment to continuing professional development is crucial. The ability to cope with having to work to constant high professional standards is also necessary.

Starting salary

A junior doctor's salary starts at £20,295 (2006 figures) increasing to £28,307 after about five years, with a hospital consultant earning between £69,000 and £94,000. They can however boost their income through private practice. The starting salary for a GP registrar is £41,785 and the average GP income in 2005 was £87,400 before tax. GPs can also increase their income by working out-of-hours shifts or doing private work such as insurance medicals, but the opportunity for earning private income is rare compared to some hospital doctors.

Jobs on qualification

There are 60 different specialities in medicine, around 50 of them in hospital medicine. There are around 80,000 hospital doctors in the UK. Surgical medicine is another option and offers nine surgical specialities. There are around 14,000 surgeons in the UK. General practice is another possible career choice with around 40,000 GPs in the UK. Changes to the GP contract have made this an increasingly attractive career path, especially for women, because GPs are no longer contracted to work late into the evening, at night or weekends.

Current employment prospects ★ ★ ★ ★ ★

General practice career opportunities are good and are likely to be better and less competitive than those in hospital medicine. Competition for posts after completing the foundation programme can be fierce, particularly in popular specialities such as surgery.

Is a career change a reality? ★ ★ ★ ★ ★

Welcomes older entrants? ★ ★ ★

Potential high earner? £££££

Useful contacts:

Medical schools with a high percentage intake of mature students (according to BMA report Demography of Medical Schools June 2004):
Aberdeen; St Bartholomews, London; Brighton and Sussex Medical School; University of East Anglia School of Medicine; St George's Medical School, London; Southampton Medical School.

Medical schools offering foundation course (according to BMA 2006):
Bristol; Cardiff; Dundee; Edinburgh; Guy's, King's and St Thomas', London; Manchester; Newcastle; Sheffield; St George's, London; Swansea.

Medical schools that have a graduate entry programme to medicine (according to BMA 2006):
Birmingham Medical School; Bristol Medical School; Cambridge Medical School; Guy's, King's and St Thomas' School of Medicine, London; Leicester Warwick Medical School; Liverpool Medical School; Newcastle Medical School; Nottingham/Derby Medical School; Oxford Medical School; Southampton Medical School; St Bartholomews and The London Queen Mary's School of Medicine; St George's Medical School, London; University College School of Medicine, London; University of East Anglia School of Medicine; University of Wales (Swansea with final years at Cardiff) and Warwick Medical School.

British Medical Association
Tavistock Square
London WC1H 9JP
020 7387 4499
www.bma.org.uk

General Medical Council
Regent's Place
350 Euston Road
London NW1 3JN
0846 357 3456
www.gmc-uk.org

The Royal College of Physicians
11 St Andrews Place
Regent's Park
London NW1 4LE

020 7935 1174
www.rcplondon.ac.uk

The Royal College of Surgeons of England
35–43 Lincoln's Inn Fields
London WC2A 3PN
020 7405 3474
www.rcseng.ac.uk

The Royal College of General Practitioners
14 Princes Gate
London SW7 1PU
020 7581 3232
www.rcpg.org.uk

University Colleges and Admissions Service (UCAS)
Customer Services Unit
UCAS
PO Box 28
Cheltenham
GL52 3LZ
0870 1122211
www.ucas.com

NHS Careers
PO Box 2311
Bristol
BS2 2ZX
0845 60 60 655
www.nhs.uk/careers

NHS Student Grants Unit
Hesketh House
200–220 Broadway
Fleetwood
FY7 8SS
0845 358 6655
www.nhsstudentgrants.co.uk

Driving instructor

'I was made redundant at 46 and was told that I faced being on the dole for the next 19 years. I had a background in sales and management but didn't have many other qualifications. I did have a driving licence and within six months I was a fully qualified driving instructor. Now I am 59 and am a manager of a BSM branch.' Ray Billingsworth, career changer and manager of BSM centre in Enfield, Middlesex.

The job

Driving instructors teach people how to drive. They prepare them for the statutory driving test that entitles them to have a driving licence. Instructors charge an hourly fee which varies around the UK but is in the region of £20, higher in London. The majority of people who are learning to drive are older teenagers or people in their early 20s. Most driving instructors are self-employed or have a franchise with one of the large national driving schools such as the British School of Motoring or the AA. If self-employed they will own their own instructor's car, which can cost between £7,000 and £11,000 and must have dual controls. Some instructors may however decide to rent a dual-control car instead. If a driving instructor has bought a franchise then the driving school will provide the car and be responsible for its insurance and maintenance. The only expense a franchised driver faces is the cost of petrol.

The culture

Most qualified driving instructors are career changers in their 40s or 50s, according to the Driving Instructors' Association. It is becoming an increasingly popular option for older people and is attracting more women. Training to become an instructor can be completed quickly, flexibly and reasonably cheaply, which makes it a practical new career path. The job traditionally appeals to people who have left the armed forces or emergency services, such as former firefighters, policemen or policewomen. It offers the opportunity to work flexibly and most instructors are self-employed. Franchises with driving schools can be an attractive option for career changers looking for some support before becoming independent instructors.

Becoming a driving instructor may be a practical option for career changers, but it is never going to be a high earner. Full-time instructors are likely to have an annual income of around £18,000 although the amount can vary according to the local market rate for driving lessons. However if you enjoy driving and have excellent skills behind the wheel, becoming a driving instructor is a cheaper and quicker career change than becoming a black cab driver. (For more details about a career as a black cab driver see the directory entry in this section of the book.)

Do I need a degree?

You do not need a degree to be a qualified driving instructor. However in order to train as a driving instructor there are four requirements you must meet. You must have held a full driver's licence for at least four years and the licence must be clean. You must not have a criminal conviction and you must be able to read a vehicle number plate from 90 feet.

What professional qualifications do I need?

In order to become a qualified driving instructor you must be registered with the Driving Standards Agency. In order to register you must complete a recognised training course to become an **Approved Driving Instructor (ADI)**. There are three ADI exams that you need to pass in order to be professionally qualified.

The part one exam includes 100 multiple-choice questions. They cover road procedures, traffic signs and signals, car control, pedestrians and mechanical knowledge. Other areas you will be tested on are the make-up of the driving test, law, disabilities, publications and the techniques of giving driving instruction. The second part of the part one exam is a hazard perception test.

The part two ADI exam assesses your driving ability. You will be expected to be able to read a car registration number plate from 90 feet and you will be asked questions about car safety maintenance. You will have to take an advanced driving test which will assess your handling of car controls, use of correct road procedure, anticipation of other road users, judgements of distance, speed and timing and your consideration for other road users. The practical test also involves road manoeuvres. Once you have completed parts one and two of the ADI exams you are entitled to join the trainee licensing scheme which entitles you to work as a trainee driving instructor for a maximum six months. As a trainee you must be attached to an approved driving school.

The final ADI exam, known as part three, is devoted to teaching skills and tests your ability to pass on information and knowledge. It is a practical test involving role-play with an examiner.

Once you have completed all three ADI exams you can register with the DSA as a qualified instructor. The ADI exams can be taken separately but they must all be completed within a two-year timescale. Professional registration with the DSA has to be renewed every four years. A list of approved ADI training providers – called the Official Register of Driving Instructor Training or ORDIT – is available from the DSA and is included in its ADI starter pack which costs £11 (see useful contacts below).

ADI training course fees can vary but you should expect to pay in the region of £2,500–£3,500. Training is usually flexible – often offered on a one-to-one basis in the evenings – which can be appealing for career changers. Some daytime classroom tuition is also likely. The DSA says the quickest time it can take to qualify is around nine months, with most instructors reaching qualification within 18 months.

What personal skills do I need?

Patience is crucial. Most of your pupils will be young people in their late teens or early 20s so an understanding of this group would be a help. Excellent communication and interpersonal skills are essential, as well as the ability to stay calm under pressure. It is also important to be a good driver and to be able to take criticism about your driving skills. Most instructors will have to unlearn bad driving habits as part of their training so it is important that you remain open-minded about your own driving ability. If you are sensitive about your driving then choose a different career change – this one is not for you.

Starting salary

Driving instructors are not high earners. A full-time instructor working around 35 hours a week could expect to earn up to around £18,000. The majority are self-employed, so income depends on the demand of the local market and the market fee as there is no national fee structure for driving lessons. Newly qualified drivers often choose to buy a franchise with a driving school such as the AA or the British School of Motoring (BSM). Under this system the instructor remains self-employed but, in return for a weekly franchise fee, a car is provided by the driving school. The school pays for the car maintenance and insurance and will also help with finding pupils. Other administrative and professional support is also available. The franchise fee is usually worked out as a percentage of the number of instructor hours worked in a week. Different schools offer a variety of different franchise options, depending on whether you want to work full or part time. The cost for example of a franchise for a newly qualified instructor with BSM (based on a lesson fee of £24.50 and 35 hours of instruction a week) would be a maximum £367 a week out of a weekly income of £857.50.

Jobs on qualification

A qualified driving instructor.

Current employment prospects ★ ★ ★

This is an increasingly popular career choice because it offers flexible working and the option to work for yourself. Job prospects are predicted to be stable. As with any small business your success will be down to your individual reputation and the current local market.

Is a career change a reality? ★ ★ ★ ★ ★

This is a career that attracts many career changers and offers a practical and relatively cheap path to professional qualification.

Welcomes older entrants? ★ ★ ★ ★

Most driving instructors are in their 40s and 50s. There is a minimum age entry of 23.

Potential high earner? £ £

Most driving instructors are self-employed and as in any small business your success will be down to your own individual reputation and the demands of your local market. This is not a high-earning profession; most qualified instructors earn around £18,000 to £20,000 a year. Some can earn up to £25,000 but this would be the exception.

Useful contacts:

Driving Standards Agency
(Approved driving instructor branch)
Stanley House
56 Talbot Street
Nottingham
NG1 5GU
0115 901 2618
www.dsa.gov.uk
ADIReg@dsa.gsi.gov.uk

ADI starter packs available from the DSA (price £11) at:
Stanley House
56 Talbot Street
Nottingham
NG1 5GU
0870 121 4202

Driving Instructors' Association
Safety House
Beddington Farm Road
Croydon
CR0 4XZ
020 8665 5151
www.driving.org

Motor Schools Association
101 Wellington Road North
Stockport
Cheshire
SK4 2LP
0161 429 9669
www.msagb.co.uk

GoSkills (the sector skills council for the passenger transport sector)
Concorde House
Trinity Park
Solihull
Birmingham
B37 7UQ
0121 635 5520
www.goskills.org

British School of Motoring
www.bsm.co.uk

AA Driving School
www.theaa.com

Estate agent

'I feel we like more mature people in our business because they have a sense of maturity with some life and job skills and customers are more likely to listen to what they have to say.' Chief executive of a national estate agent chain.

The job

Estate agents work in the business of selling property or land. They prepare sales details used to market the property or land. They negotiate on behalf of their client, who may be the buyer or the vendor, and support them through the purchasing or sales process. There are opportunities to specialise in different aspects of estate agency such as working in the residential market, developing an expertise in commercial property or business sales, working in the lettings and property management sector of the industry or, after gaining the extra skills, becoming a property auctioneer.

The culture

The estate agency industry welcomes older entrants and values life experience as well as a career history in another sector. It often attracts career changers who have been teachers, recruitment consultants or shop managers and is a popular choice for ex-services personnel. The key to success in this sector is going to be your own personality and interpersonal skills so it is wide open to career changers. The National Association of Estate Agents, the professional organisation for people working in the industry, says every week it receives enquiries from older people looking to change careers. This is an industry where older entrants will feel comfortable. It is also a job which can be followed part time, at evenings or weekends, so it offers a practical route in as you can build up experience before making that giant leap to a new career. One high-street estate agent says that it is enthusiasm and personal temperament that count above age or qualifications.

Do I need a degree?

There are degree courses in estate agency which have been accredited by the National Association of Estate Agents and other professional organisations. Although this route may offer potential employment advantages it is not essential to have a degree in estate agency to launch yourself into a career as an estate agent. Details of estate agency degrees are available from the Universities and Colleges Admissions Service (UCAS). See list of useful contacts below.

What professional qualifications do I need?

The **National Association of Estate Agents**, which has 10,000 members, offers a range of professional qualifications, which start with technical awards in the sale of residential property or residential letting and property management. These technical courses will teach you the basic skills you require as well as bringing you up to date with property law. The qualifications are most commonly taught through distance learning, although they are also available at some further education colleges. They require up to 150 hours of study and take a minimum of three months to complete. An alternative is to take NVQ qualifications, which offer work-based learning. Those recommended by the NAEA are NVQ level 2 and level 3 in sale of residential property. The NAEA technical awards can however contribute towards the NVQs.

The NAEA also offers diploma qualifications, which are the academic equivalent of a pass degree or a Higher National Diploma (HND). The diplomas require 350 hours of study. They are available through a supported learning system, which includes a tutor, and if studied part time can be completed within a year. There are NAEA diplomas in residential estate agency, residential letting and management and commercial property agency. In order to complete the diploma you will be expected to sit four three-hour exams and complete a project. Often training is given in-house.

What personal skills do I need?

Excellent interpersonal skills are essential as this is a job based on communicating well with people from a variety of backgrounds – buyers and sellers, as well as solicitors and conveyancers. It is important that you enjoy helping people. Negotiation and persuasion skills are useful, as well as good IT skills. An outgoing, lively personality is an asset. It is also important to be a team player. A background in a sales environment would be an advantage but is not essential. Patience is also important, and the ability to persevere when things are moving slowly or the market is quiet. One high-street estate agent, whose company carries out psychometric testing on potential candidates, says, 'If we find the right person we will take them on and train them, even if they don't have any previous experience.'

Starting salary

The salary will depend on your career history and your potential. Estate agent negotiators can boost their salary by earning commission on their sales. The amount of commission you earn varies according to different company policy. It can be calculated as a percentage of the sale price, be a fixed amount per property or be based on the results of a sales team rather than the success of an individual. An average starting salary for a trainee negotiator is in the region of £15,000–£20,000, which would include a guaranteed commission. A senior negotiator can expect to earn £30,000 (which includes commission) but the salary depends on geographic location.

Jobs on qualification

There is a definite career structure if you work for a residential estate agency. You start as a trainee negotiator, going on to become a senior negotiator, with the option then of moving into branch and area management roles. Other options available, following NAEA professional qualifications or company in-house training, include specialising in residential lettings and management, which involves looking after all aspects of the let including all the legal and financial issues as well as the selection of tenants. A career path as a commercial property or business sales agent is another possibility.

There is a growing trend of estate agencies offering franchises for sale, so this is potentially another route into the industry, although it would require a capital investment and you would be best advised to achieve some personal experience in the industry before making an investment.

Current employment prospects ★ ★ ★
The job market can fluctuate, depending on the state of health of the housing market. Although it is unlikely that you would be made redundant during a downturn, it is likely that your commission would disappear.

Is a career change a reality? ★ ★ ★ ★ ★

Welcomes older entrants? ★ ★ ★ ★ ★

Potential high earner? £ £ £

Useful contacts:

The National Association of Estate Agents
Arbon House
21 Jury Street
Warwick
CV34 4EH
01926 496800
info@naea.co.uk

Asset Skills (the sector skills council for the property, housing, facilities management and cleaning sectors)
2 The Courtyard
48 New North Road
Exeter
Devon
EX4 4EP
0800 056 7160
www.assetskills.org

Royal Institute of Chartered Surveyors
Surveyor Court
Westwood Way
Coventry
CV4 8JE
0870 333 1600
www.rics.org.uk

University Colleges and Admissions Service (UCAS)
Customer Services Unit
UCAS
PO Box 28
Cheltenham
GL52 3LZ
0870 1122211
www.ucas.com

Firefighter

'We get people in their mid-40s joining us who come from a variety of backgrounds such as retail or plumbing for example. People are looking for a change of career which is more physical and which offers them something different every day.' Manjit Singh, watch manager in positive action recruitment team, London Fire Brigade.

The job

There is no national fire service; instead, separate fire brigades in England, Wales, Scotland and Northern Ireland each run independently under a chief fire officer to deliver the service. Each brigade is responsible for its own recruitment. Details of how to contact an individual brigade can be obtained from the Department for Community and Local Government, which is responsible for the service in England (see useful contact details below). Details of other UK brigades can be found on the website www.fireservice.co.uk or by contacting the Scottish Executive (www.scotland.gov.uk), the Welsh Assembly Government (www.wales.gov.uk) or the Northern Ireland Fire Brigade (www.nifrs.org).

The nature of fire fighting is changing. Today a firefighter can expect to spend a significant part of the working week in the community promoting and checking fire safety and being involved in fire prevention initiatives. Firefighters have continuous training responsibilities and are also responsible for the maintenance of equipment. Firefighters attend different sorts of emergency calls including fires, chemical spillages, road traffic accidents, minor and major emergency incidents such as terrorist attacks. It is a dangerous and hazardous job. At the scene of a fire a firefighter has to make a quick assessment of the dangers and risks and how to tackle the blaze. The impact of toxic fumes and heavy smoke has to be taken into account. As part of training a firefighter is taught how to use cutting, lifting and thermal imaging equipment.

Firefighters work a regular shift system broken down into four coloured watches – red, blue, green and white. In practice this usually means two consecutive day shifts, two consecutive night shifts, followed by four days off.

An alternative option to becoming a full-time firefighter is to become a retained firefighter, which is a paid voluntary post. Retained firefighters have to live near to a fire station and are called out if needed in times of emergency.

The culture

Becoming a firefighter is traditionally a popular career choice for any age or background. Recruiters running a campaign for the London Fire Brigade in 2005 expected to send out around 1,000 enquiry forms but received requests for 5,000. There is no longer an upper age limit to join the service and it is common to find new recruits in their 40s. You are still likely to find more men than women training to be

119

firefighters, although the government is campaigning to attract more women and others from minority ethnic backgrounds in order to create a more diverse workforce. This is a job where a high level of personal fitness and health, as well as good communication skills, will increase your chances of success.

Do I need a degree?

You do not need a degree to be a firefighter, although it may help with career progression and promotion to management roles. There is discussion in the service about bringing in a two-tier entry system which would include a graduate entry route but this is not yet happening.

What professional qualifications do I need?

Training to be a firefighter is open entry so you do not need any prior qualifications to apply. Everybody who joins the service to become a firefighter has to undergo the same training, regardless of qualifications or experience. The selection process to be accepted onto a firefighter training course is rigorous. You will have to have a medical, take part in physical fitness assessments, written tests and attend an interview. Health exemptions that in the past would have prevented you from training as a firefighter have been dropped following the introduction of the Disability Discrimination Act in 2005. Each application is considered independently on medical grounds. However, you must have good vision without the use of glasses or contact lenses, and you can expect to have your colour vision tested. There are no longer restrictions on entry linked to how tall you are.

Training to become a firefighter takes up to 16 weeks and takes place at local or regional fire service training centres. A firefighter's basic training includes skills in ladder safety, hose laying, and the use of breathing equipment. A first-aid qualification is also part of the training package. Learning about fire safety and how to teach others in the community the importance of fire safety is a crucial part of the course. Firefighters who get through the training are attached to a fire station and face a probationary period before being fully qualified. Firefighters are expected to commit to continuing professional development and must sign up to the national programme of continuing in-service training, the Integrated Personal Development System.

What personal skills do I need?

You must be fit and have a high level of stamina. The ability to carry out instructions and take orders is crucial. You need good communication skills and must be a good listener and be able to empathise with a range of different people. Firefighters come into contact with diverse communities so you must be non-judgemental. You must have good composure and be understanding. The ability to react quickly in a crisis is crucial. Being a good team player is essential and you should be considerate, resourceful, innovative and decisive within a team. It is important to be able to solve problems and be a logical thinker. You are expected to be able to cope with pressure and must be interested and keen to follow continuing professional development.

Starting salary

The starting salary in 2006 was around £19,000 outside London or £24,000 in the capital. After three years' experience it is possible to earn around £30,000 in London or around £25,000 elsewhere.

Jobs on qualification

There is a distinct hierarchy in the fire service. Roles range from firefighter to crew manager, watch manager, station manager, group manager, area manager and finally brigade manager. There are other firefighter career opportunities with the British Airports Authority or the Defence Fire Service, the fire service of military and ministry of defence sites.

Current career prospects ★ ★ ★ ★ ★ (for women and minority ethnic groups)

This is a competitive market, but there is a national campaign to recruit more women and people from minority ethnic backgrounds into the service, so career prospects are good if you fall into these categories.

Is a career change a reality? ★ ★ ★ ★ ★

Yes. With open entry and no upper age limit, this is a practical option for a career change.

Welcomes older entrants? ★ ★ ★ ★ ★

There is no longer an upper age limit for applicants and it is increasingly common to find new recruits in their 40s.

Potential high earner? £ £

Pay scales for firefighters are set nationally. This is not a high-earning career, but the predictable shift system can create time to pursue other employment which can boost income. If you work as a retained firefighter you will receive an annual payment between £1,293 and £2,585 depending on what hours you are available to be on call. Retained firefighters are also paid an additional fee for every incident they attend. For a retained firefighter the call-out fee is £3.39 with an additional fee of up to £11.80 for every hour worked.

Useful contacts:

The Department for Communities and Local Government
Eland House
Bressenden Place
London SW1E 5DU
020 7944 4400
www.communities.gov.uk

Fire Brigades Union
Bradley House
68 Coombe Road
Kingston Upon Thames
Surrey
KT2 7AE
www.fbu.org.uk

UK fire service resources website
www.fireservice.co.uk

Integrated Personal Development System
IPDS
www.ipds.co.uk

The Fire Service College
Moreton in Marsh
Gloucestershire
GL56 0RH
01608 650831
www.fireservicecollege.ac.uk

Headhunter/executive recruitment consultant

'Becoming a headhunter offers people from a variety of senior backgrounds the opportunity to change direction in their career.' Paul Harper, chairman of the Association of Executive Recruiters.

The job

Headhunters, or executive recruitment consultants, often work as part of small specialist consultancies. They are employed by clients who are looking to fill executive posts. The headhunter will be responsible for taking a brief from the client. Researchers who work with the headhunter will then discreetly discover who might be suitable to fill the vacancy and also who is interested in the post. It is then up to the headhunter to carry out an in-depth confidential interview with prospective candidates and to draw up a short list for the client. The headhunter will then work with the client on the selection process, which can include arranging and managing candidate assessment days and carrying out psychometric testing. The priority of the headhunter is to make sure the client gets the best person available to fill the position. Summing up the essence of the work an experienced recruiter says: 'The job is to get the right person and find out if they are interested by selling them an idea and giving them the opportunity to mull over that idea.'

The culture

A career change to become a headhunter or executive recruitment consultant can be a very successful, and potentially lucrative, move if you are prepared to specialise in the sector you are moving from. It can be an attractive option if you are an experienced top executive from the private or public sectors who wants a career change, having progressed as far as you can within your existing career. If you have years of experience in a sector and have spent recent years moving in and out of a network of top executives you will be in a strong position to become an executive recruiter. Headhunting is client-driven and having the right connections is an invaluable asset. But at the same time you must have strong 'influencing' skills so a background in sales, retail or customer services is an advantage, One recruitment expert warns: 'What you know about the industry you are recruiting to is irrelevant if you don't have the skills to reach the person you are headhunting in the first place.' Anybody interested in becoming a headhunter should first approach one of the specialist executive recruitment agencies in their chosen field to find out what employment opportunities there are, and to discuss what it is you can bring to the consultancy. The professional organisation for headhunters, the Association of Executive Recruiters (AER), estimates half of its members have a background in the sector they recruit to. This is a career move where your contacts and networking experience could open doors.

Do I need a degree?

It is not necessary to have a degree to work in executive recruitment although a degree in business, marketing or finance may be useful. In September 2005 the Recruitment and Employment Federation and Middlesex University Business School launched the first BA in recruitment practice, which is aimed at people working in the recruitment industry. Details are available either from Middlesex University or the REC (see professional qualifications and useful contact entries below).

What professional qualifications do I need?

The professional qualification, the **certificate in recruitment practice** accredited by the professional association, the Recruitment and Employment Confederation (REC) is aimed at people in the industry who have no formal qualifications. If you are not a graduate but have professional qualifications from the sector you are coming from, they will be invaluable in helping you to launch your new career. If you have studied to at least A level standard you may want to study for the REC's **diploma in recruitment practice**, the advanced professional qualification for those working in this sector.

If you decide to specialise in recruitment in the sector you have moved from, then the professional qualifications you have from your previous career will also give you increased professional status with clients. In the world of headhunting your personal skills and how competent you are in the workplace are more important than qualifications.

Details of the three professional qualifications offered by the REC are as follows. The **certificate in recruitment practice** covers the basic skills required to work in recruitment, including employment law, and is aimed at those people new to the sector who have no formal qualifications. It can be studied through a distance learning package over 15 weeks or fast-track on a three-day course. The REC also offers the more advanced **diploma in recruitment practice** which is a specialist qualification aimed at people who have studied to A level standard or who are graduates wanting to develop skills in recruitment assessment and selection. The diploma is modular and can be studied by distance learning with tutor support and weekend workshops. Modules can be taken separately, but all four modules, which complete the diploma, must be taken within four years. Alternatively the diploma can be studied at London-based evening classes over 11 weeks. More than 3,500 people working in recruitment have either the REC certificate or diploma.

People who have the diploma can go on to study for the **BA in recruitment practice.** Having the diploma means they may be exempt from the first year of the three-year degree course, which includes a mix of work-based learning and business projects. For more details, contact REC or Middlesex University (see useful contacts below).

The AER also runs short courses as part of ongoing professional development.

Details are available from its website (see useful contacts entry below).

The professional body for people working in people management, the Chartered Institute of Personnel and Development, also has its own accredited recruitment and selection training programmes. Details of these can be found on its website (see useful contacts below).

What personal skills do I need?

Self-confidence is crucial and you must have excellent communication skills, including the ability to listen and to work to a brief. Discretion and personal integrity are essential, as a lot of your negotiations will be carried out on the basis of confidentiality. You must have empathy with both the client and the candidate, so a personal background in the speciality or sector you are recruiting to is invaluable. You must be able to work under pressure, be flexible and be prepared to work in the evening. But one of the key attributes is the need for influencing skills – without those you will struggle.

Starting salary

The salary varies according to the consultancy. If you are a career changer the breadth of the contacts that you can bring to the business will influence your starting salary. Headhunters are usually paid a basic salary plus commission or bonus. With experience you may earn an average £55,000. But income levels vary, with some successful consultants earning more than £100,000.

Jobs on qualification

A headhunter or executive recruiter for a specialist recruitment agency. Some headhunters go on to run their own recruitment agencies after gaining some experience in the sector. Details of how to do this are available on the REC website (see useful contacts below).

Current employment prospects ★ ★ ★ ★ ★

This is a profession which is becoming increasingly important because of the shortage, in both the private and public sectors, of people with the necessary experience and of the right calibre to take on these top jobs. Companies or public sector organisations cannot afford to make mistakes and they are increasingly looking to headhunters to help them fill vacancies. The climate is not expected to change, so job prospects are good. This is a growing market.

Is a career change a reality? ★ ★ ★ ★ ★

Welcomes older entrants? ★ ★ ★ ★ ★

Potential high earner? £££££

Useful contacts:

Association of Executive Recruiters (AER)
36–38 Mortimer Street
London W1W 7RG
020 7462 3260
www.rec.uk.com

Chartered Institute of Personnel and Development (CIPD)
151 The Broadway
London SW19 1JQ
020 8612 6200
www.cipd.co.uk

Employment National Training Organisation (ENTO)
Head Office
4th Floor
Kimberley House
47 Vaughan Way
Leicester
LE1 4SG
0116 251 7979
www.ento.co.uk

Middlesex University Business School
Middlesex University
The Burroughs
London W4 4BT
020 8411 5000
www.mdx.ac.uk

Recruitment and Employment Confederation (REC)
36–38 Mortimer Street
London W1W 7RG
020 7462 3260
www.rec.uk.com

Heritage craftsperson

'Career changers are just the kind of people who we want to attract into heritage skills because they bring with them a devoted interest and skills from their past career, such as patience, which is very valuable.' Beverley Peters, manager of the National Heritage Training Group.

The job

There are a number of different heritage craft skills:

● A steeplejack inspects, tests and repairs spires, turrets and chimneys and other high architectural features of listed buildings, ancient monuments and churches. Work includes coating, re-pointing and repairing masonry. Steeplejacks usually work in pairs.

● A leadworker is trained to work with lead and other metals which are used to protect roof slates, chimney stacks and dormer windows. They are also skilled in metalwork on domes, turrets and spires. They often work with lead but are also trained to work with other metals such as copper, zinc and stainless steel.

● A roof slater and tiler is skilled at identifying problems with roofing slates and tiles and is trained to carry out repairs using traditional methods and materials.

● A historic buildings painter and decorator is able to reproduce designs from across the ages. They may have additional skills in gilding, marbling and graining.

● A carpenter/joiner is usually based in a workshop and works with a different range of woods. They are trained to carry out repairs to wood used in the structure of buildings, such as floors or roofs, as well as working on internal wooden features including skirting boards, doorframes and cupboards.

● A plasterer works on external and internal walls, floors and ceilings, either rendering the outside of buildings or screeding inside features. They are often involved in repair and restoration work as well as creating ornamental decorations like domed ceilings or elaborate mouldings.

● Stonemasonry offers a variety of career opportunities in the construction heritage sector. There is a banker mason who crafts and shapes blocks of stone to replace worn out or damaged stones on buildings and a fixer mason who works on site using the stone created by the banker mason to repair and conserve building stone.

● Dry stone wallers are skilled at using local stone to build walls without using cement or mortar.

● A bricklayer is trained to repair and replace bricks in historic buildings and relies on traditional bonding methods that match the age of the building. They are skilled at 'cutting and rubbing' bricks and using pointing methods that reflect the original style of the building.

● A thatcher works at roofing, re-roofing and repairing a property's thatch. There are

1,000 of them working in the UK and most are self-employed.

The culture
The heritage sector is suffering from an acute shortage of skilled craftspeople to help restore, repair and maintain the UK's historic buildings. Government departments and organisations that have joined forces to try to fill the skills gap are keen to attract career changers to the sector because of the experience they can bring with them from previous careers. They are after craftsmen and women who work in the modern construction industry and who are interested in using their skills in the heritage sector, but they are equally enthusiastic about reaching career changers from completely outside the construction industry. Career changers with no previous craft experience must be prepared to start learning the trade from scratch. According to the National Heritage Training Group, the organisation devoted to boosting heritage craft skills in the UK, it can take up to two years of work-based training to become a competent heritage craftsperson.

Do I need a degree?
You do not need a degree to work in the heritage construction industry.

What professional qualifications do I need?
Work-based qualifications in heritage craft skills at NVQ level 3 are encouraged. For more details contact the **National Heritage Training Group**, which has a database of all qualifications and courses available for the heritage construction industry. The data can be searched by qualification or craft and has contact details of course providers. In 2006 the Heritage Lottery Fund launched a £1 million fund for bursaries towards the cost of training heritage craftspeople at NVQ level 3 or equivalent in England and Wales. Career changers were identified as one of the target groups eligible to apply for bursary support. The trades where bursaries were being offered were: blacksmithing, brick masonry, carpentry and joinery, dry stone walling, earth building, fibrous plastering, flint working, ironwork, lime mortar, lime plaster, painting and decorating, stone conservation, roofing and wheelwrighting. There are expected to be around 80 bursary places available under the scheme, which is being run jointly by English Heritage, the National Trust, the Construction Industry Training Board (CITB), ConstructionSkills, the National Heritage Training Group and Cadw – the heritage agency of the Welsh Assembly. The bursary scheme runs until 2010 and includes work-based placements ranging from one month to two years as part of the package. Details of the bursary initiative are available from the National Heritage Training Group.

What personal skills do I need?
Bricklayers should enjoy working outside and be happy working on scaffolding. They

should also have an eye for detail because historic building brick is often not uniform. Plasterers working on historic buildings should be good at maths because of the amount of measuring required to do the job. They should be happy working up a ladder and have a creative flair, especially if employed on fibrous plastering and decorative features. Painters and decorators should also have a creative spirit and be inspired by their working environment. Carpenters and joiners must be good at maths because of all the calculations required. Roof slaters should, like other heritage craftspeople, enjoy working outside and have a head for heights.

Whichever craft you opt for it is crucial that you are patient, because you could find yourself working months at a time on a single project such as a solitary brick wall. It is also important to have an interest in the historic environment. Says Beverley Peters from the National Heritage Training Group: 'The career changers we have attracted so far are perhaps more literate than the other guys who have come up through the ranks, but what they all have in common is that they can talk for hours about a single brick or a particular piece of stone.'

Starting salary
With experience, a craftsperson could expect to earn in the region of £30,000.

Jobs on qualification
There are job opportunities with specialist heritage construction companies and also sub-contractor work for English Heritage, which no longer has its own direct labour workforce. The National Trust employs around 160 heritage craftspeople in England and Wales, but most of its maintenance and conservation work is outsourced to specialist contractors.

Current employment prospects ★ ★ ★ ★ ★
Very good. There is a national heritage construction skills shortage. The National Heritage Training Group has warned that the future of Britain's heritage is under threat because of a 6,500 shortfall of skilled craftsmen and women. Research published by the National Heritage Training Group, supported by English Heritage, highlighted the lack of specialist bricklayers, carpenters, roofers, stonemasons and thatchers. The study revealed there is a need for 500 specialist bricklayers, carpenters and slate and tile roofers; 400 joiners, leadworkers and stonemasons; and 200 painter and decorators and thatchers in order to meet the present demand from the built heritage industry. It warned that in the next 20 years, skills such as dry stone walling, thatching and earth walling could disappear altogether if nothing was done to help fill the skills gap.

Is a career change a reality? ★ ★ ★ ★ ★

Career changers are one of the groups that are being targeted by the Heritage Lottery Fund traditional building skills bursary scheme. The money, up to £1 million, is being made available to provide work-based training in heritage construction skills. The National Heritage Training Group also confirmed it is keen to reach career changers – both those from outside, and those already working in, the construction industry.

Welcomes older entrants? ★ ★ ★ ★ ★

The above initiatives and the national skills shortage of skilled craftspeople should make it easier for older career changers to make a move into this sector.

Potential high earner? £ £ £

With experience it is possible for a heritage craftsperson to earn in the region of £30,000.

Useful contacts:

The National Heritage Training Group
Carthusian Court
12 Carthusian Street
London EC1M 6EZ
01159 217 562
www.nhtg.org.uk

English Heritage
Customer Services Department
PO Box 569
Swindon
SN2 2YP
0870 333 1181
www.english-heritage.org.uk

Cadw
Welsh Assembly Government
Plas Carew
Unit 5/7 Cefn Coed
Parc Nantgarw
Cardiff
CF15 7QQ
01443 336000
www.cadw.wales.gov.uk

CITB-ConstructionSkills
Bircham Newton
King's Lynn
Norfolk
PE31 6RH
01485 577577
www.citb.org.uk

The National Trust
PO Box 39
Warrington
WA5 7WD
0870 458 4000
www.thenationaltrust.org.uk

Homeopath

'Many people train in homeopathy because they feel stuck in a career and want to do something which is more worthwhile and meaningful for them.' Former teacher Linda Wicks, who is a practising homeopath and senior educational adviser for the Society of Homeopaths.

The job

A homeopath takes a holistic approach to healing. A practitioner takes into account physical, emotional and mental health symptoms when treating patients and uses homeopathic remedies to improve health. Homeopaths work on the principle that 'like treats like'.

They rely on homeopathic remedies, given in highly diluted form, which are the closest match to the patient's individual picture of symptoms. These are natural remedies that are expected to boost the individual's health and immune system without damaging side effects. The majority of homeopaths are self-employed, working on their own in practice or within complementary health centres. Some are employed by GP practices and work in the NHS, while others work for charities or in hospices. Homeopathy has been available in the UK for more than 200 years and has its roots in ancient Greece. The Society of Homeopaths has more than 1,200 registered homeopaths in the UK and there are about 3,500 qualified professionals working in the UK.

The culture

A career change to become a homeopath is a popular choice for people in their 30s and 40s looking for a profession where they feel they can make a meaningful difference to people's lives. Qualified homeopaths come from a variety of backgrounds but the profession particularly attracts teachers and health professionals such as nurses, although it also has its fair share of ex-city workers and accountants. At the moment it is an unregulated health profession, although this is likely to change in the future, so in theory anybody can call themselves a homeopath and set themselves up in practice, regardless of their training.

There are four main homeopathy associations or societies which have their own independent professional register and which give their approval to different homeopathy training courses. The organisation with the largest membership and professional register is the Society of Homeopaths, while the British Homeopathic Association runs a register of existing medical professionals who are also qualified to practise as homeopaths. If you are thinking of becoming a homeopath, it is advisable to enrol in a course that has been approved by one of these organisations, as they are working towards creating a central register for practising homeopaths.

Training in homeopathy requires a big commitment as the study, which includes hours of essential clinical practice, can take up to five years if followed part time. Most professionally qualified homeopaths are self-employed although some do work in the NHS, for charities or in hospices. It is also common for homeopaths to work part time. They do this for two reasons: the work is very demanding, but also this is not a lucrative profession and homeopaths often have to juggle two jobs to make a reasonable living. If you have a good business sense and financial acumen, however, you can make it your main source of income, but you would be unlikely to earn more than £30,000. Your chances of running a successful practice will often depend on the disposable income of your patient population, so private practices are likely to be more profitable in affluent parts of the UK, particularly London and other major cities.

Do I need a degree?

Universities run full-time and part time courses in homeopathy. There are five-year part-time courses at four universities – University of Lancashire, University of Westminster, University of Middlesex and University of Thames Valley. For degrees that are recognised by the Society of Homeopaths, refer to their website (see useful contacts entry below) and the University and Colleges Admissions Service (UCAS) for further entry details (see useful contacts entry below).

A life science degree is useful but not essential. Qualified doctors, dentists, veterinary surgeons, nurses, midwives, podiatrists and pharmacists can take shorter qualifying courses, which bring professional recognition and either membership of the Faculty of Homeopathy or entitlement to be a licensed associate of the faculty. Details of training courses and qualifications available to qualified health professionals are available from the British Homeopathic Association and the Faculty of Homeopathy (see useful contacts entry below).

It is not necessary to have a degree before you can train to become a homeopath. There are also diploma or licence courses that can usually be completed within four years on a part-time basis. Part-time courses usually involve home study but also require a weekend (two-day) attendance every month at a university or college. Up to 200 hours' clinical practice is expected and the amount of clinical casework, under supervision, increases in the final two years. The Society of Homeopaths does not recognise distance learning.

What professional qualifications do I need?

Graduation from an approved homeopathy course which has been recognised by one of the homeopathy organisations will entitle you to practise as a homeopath and bring you professional registration with the same body. Courses at private colleges have annual fees in the region of £1,500 a year.

What personal skills do I need?

This is a caring profession so you must be a good listener, be non-judgemental and have excellent communication skills. Consultations can be emotionally draining, so you must be emotionally 'robust'. You must have an in-depth knowledge of the various remedies as well as an understanding of disease. As most homeopaths are self-employed, it is an advantage if you have some financial acumen and business skills.

Starting salary

This is not a high-earning profession. The average income for a full-time self-employed homeopath is in the region of £20,000, although the majority will work part time.

Jobs on qualification

A professional homeopath. The majority work in private practice although there are also career opportunities working with charities or in hospices. There are also five NHS homeopathic hospitals which offer another career option.

Current employment prospects ★ ★ ★

Employment prospects depend on demand. Patient demand is usually higher in affluent areas where there is disposable income. Demand is generally higher in London and other large cities.

Is a career change a reality? ★ ★ ★ ★ ★

Welcomes older entrants? ★ ★ ★ ★ ★

Potential high earner? £ £

Useful contacts:

Alliance of Registered Homeopaths
Millbrook
Millbrook Hill
Nutley
East Sussex
TN22 3PJ
08700 736339
www.a-r-h.org

British Homeopathic Association incorporating the Homeopathic Trust
Hahnemann House
29 Park Street West
Luton
LU1 3BE
0870 444 3950
www.trusthomeopathy.org

Homeopathic Medical Association (HMA)
Administration Office
6 Livingstone Road
Gravesend
Kent
DA12 5DZ
01474 560336
www.the-hma.org

Society of Homeopaths
11 Brookfield
Duncan Close
Moulton Park
Northampton
NN3 6WL
0845 450 6611
www.homeopathy-soh.com

Universities and Colleges Admissions Service
Customer Services Unit
UCAS
PO Box 28
Cheltenham
GL52 3LZ
0870 1122211
www.ucas.com

Horticulture therapist

'This career choice is more about the passion for the job than it is about generating income. The rewards come in different ways.' Kim Pierpont, training and education manager for the charity Thrive.

The job

A horticulture therapist relies on activities focusing on plants and horticulture to improve an individual's general wellbeing, emotional and physical health and behaviour. They are usually employees and can work in a variety of settings including hospitals, the prison service or in special schools, working with a wide range of patients or clients. Their patients or clients are likely to include people with disabilities or learning difficulties, prisoners or people with mental health problems. But a horticulture therapist can also use their horticultural skills to help people who have poor literacy and numeracy, and can help individuals to improve their social skills including team working and patience. According to the charity Thrive there are around 1,000 garden projects in the UK helping more than 21,000 people who are either disabled or socially excluded. The setting for these projects varies from walled gardens and smallholdings to prison gardens and allotments.

The culture

The idea of using gardening and horticulture to help people with a disability has been around for more than 30 years. But the development of the professional role of a horticulture therapist is relatively new in the UK although it is well established in the USA. The majority of people who are attracted to this new profession are career changers, according to Thrive, the charity that is devoted to promoting gardening and horticulture for people with disabilities. Teachers, policemen and nurses are especially drawn to this career. But it is also a good option for others like occupational therapists, physiotherapists and social workers who are looking to diversify. The learning route to the professional qualification for a horticulture therapist is very flexible and has been designed with the career changer in mind, which means it is possible to stay in your current job while studying to become qualified before switching careers. This is also a cheap option for career changers as the fees to study for the professional qualification are only £1,000. The biggest drawback to those considering a move will be your likely salary on qualification. Horticulture therapy is never going to provide a high income, but the professional satisfaction the work can bring could be compensation enough.

Do I need a degree?

There are foundation degrees which include horticulture therapy. The foundation degree in social and therapeutic horticulture first became available in 2005 and is run by Nottingham Trent University. The qualification can be studied full time (up to three days a week) over two years or part time (up to two days a week) over three years. This is an A-level or equivalent entry course although mature students without formal qualifications will be considered. Another option is to study the foundation degree in animals and horticulture as therapy at Myerscough College in Preston, which is a specialist college for the land-based industries. This qualification can be studied over three years and the entry requirement is a minimum one A level. The foundation degree route is recommended for people who have no previous experience, either as a volunteer worker or as an unqualified paid employee, in horticulture therapy.

The University of Reading offers a BSc (Hons) in horticulture which includes a module in horticultural therapy. Entry requirements are usually two A levels and five GCSEs. You can check details with the university or with the University and Colleges Admissions Service (UCAS).

What professional qualifications do I need?

The professional qualification for horticulture therapists is the **professional development diploma in social and therapeutic horticulture**. This diploma, run by Thrive and Coventry University, can be studied by distance learning and is divided into modules. Although the course can take a year to complete, there is the option to take individual modules over a number of years, which makes the course a very flexible and popular route for career changers. Entry requirements are usually a higher education certificate in nursing, teaching, horticulture, occupational therapy, physiotherapy or social work. There is some flexibility and if you have solid experience of working as a volunteer for gardening projects you will have a good chance of being accepted onto the course. Each application is treated on its own merits, but Coventry University says it is especially keen to recruit mature students.

If you do not already have a professional qualification in one of the caring professions, such as nursing, physiotherapy or social work, you may still be able to study for the professional development diploma in social and therapeutic horticulture if you have extensive experience of working as a volunteer in garden projects. Anybody interested in a career change in this direction should gain experience as a volunteer first. There are around 1,000 different projects in the UK. Details of the projects and volunteer opportunities are held by Thrive on a database which it makes available to anybody interested in becoming a horticulture therapist.

What personal skills do I need?

It is important to have an interest in plants, horticulture and people. Excellent communication skills are needed as well as patience and tolerance as the therapists work with client groups who may have low motivation or specific learning difficulties.

Therapists have to be versatile and be able to respond to individual needs, so you will have to be a good listener.

Starting salary

This is not a high-earning career but, as a caring profession, the professional satisfaction is high. Salaries start at around £16,000 and with experience can rise to around £20,000.

Jobs on qualification

Horticulture therapists can be found mainly in the public or voluntary sectors and most commonly work in hospitals, special schools, the probation service, hospices, residential homes, rehabilitation units, charitable organisations and the prison service. A horticulture therapist is sometimes alternatively known as a horticultural trainer.

Current employment prospects ★ ★ ★ ★ ★

This is a growing profession as garden projects are continuing to expand with, according to latest figures, around 1,000 schemes up and running in the UK. Although the profession is in its infancy here, it is already well established in the USA.

Is a career change a reality? ★ ★ ★ ★ ★

Welcomes older entrants? ★ ★ ★ ★ ★

Potential high earner? £

Useful contacts:

Thrive
The Geoffrey Udall Centre
Beech Hill
Reading
RG7 2AT
0118 988 5688
www.thrive.org.uk

Cultivations
Head Office
Nant yr Helyg Maentwrog
Blaenau Ffestiniog
Gwynedd
LL41 4HF
01766 590480
www.cultivations.co.uk

Coventry University
Priory Street
Coventry
CV1 5FB
024 7688 7688
www.coventry.ac.uk

Nottingham Trent University
School of Animal, Rural and Environmental Sciences
Brackenhurst
Southwell
Nottinghamshire
NG25 0QF
01636 817099
www.ntu.ac.uk

Myerscough College
Myerscough Hall
St Michael's Road
Bilsborrow
Preston
PR3 0RY
01995 642211
www.myerscough.ac.uk

University of Reading
Whiteknights
PO Box 217
Reading
RG6 6AH
0118 987 5123
www.rdg.ac.uk

Lantra (the sector skills council for the environment and land-based industries)
Lantra House
Stoneleigh Park
Coventry
Warwickshire
CV8 2LG
0845 707 8007
www.lantra.co.uk

Lantra career advice line for career changers
www.afuturein.com

Universities and Colleges Admissions Service
Customer Services Unit
UCAS
PO Box 28
Cheltenham
GL52 3LZ
0870 1122211
www.ucas.com

Interior designer

'I don't think ageism is an issue in this industry. People are judged on the skills they have and what they can offer.' Clare Keil, course leader spatial design, Herefordshire College of Art and Design.

The job

Interior designers can work in a multitude of different environments – offices, shops, hotels, factories and people's homes. Their main role is to plan and carry out the design of a space relying on light, colour, textures and fittings. They produce outline sketches, which they turn into detailed, often computerised, drawings, and they will also produce models to support their work. Interior designers are usually employed by design companies or consultancies, or are self-employed. When starting off in this career it is advisable to get a few years' experience working for a company before launching as a self-employed designer. Interior designers often work out of a studio, working with individual clients or architects. Some interior designers will diversify and become television and theatre designers working on sets, lighting and costumes, or focus on outdoor space and become landscape architects or landscape designers. Some may also take on the responsibility for interior decoration, if they have the necessary skills, or will pass on this element of the work to a qualified interior decorator. The interior decorator will focus on interior surfaces including the colour schemes, soft furnishings and layout of the furniture.

The culture

The design industry is flourishing, especially in the area of interior design, and it is an industry that is increasingly attracting older entrants. Job prospects are good because of the current climate that favours sustainable environments, outside space and urban design. Career changers who take this path and invest in further training and qualifications are likely to find employment on graduating. It is also an industry which welcomes late entrants and which judges people according to their commitment, enthusiasm and personal skill.

Do I need a degree?

Most interior designers will have a degree or Higher National Diploma.

A BA in spatial design, which can be completed in one year as a 'top-up' honours degree, is one route for graduates who want to career change into interior design. This kind of degree offers a broad design curriculum. As well as covering interior design and decoration, it can also focus on architectural design, exhibition design, film and set design, and open spaces. But the degree will not equip you with the practical skills you need to become an interior decorator. As one course director says, 'This degree is more "Grand Designs" than "Changing Rooms".' If you want the practical skills to work as an interior decorator, you will also need to complete a short course in interior decoration which can often be studied full or part time at a number of different colleges.

What professional qualifications do I need?

A **diploma in interior decoration** will entitle you to become an interior decorator. **City and Guilds** design and craft qualifications offer another qualifying route to becoming an interior decorator (see contact details below).

Completing a short intensive course in interior decoration is one route into the interior design industry. Some of these courses can be studied part time at evening classes. There are no minimum qualifications and the course will give you the practical skills you need to become an interior decorator. If your heart is set on becoming an interior designer it is likely you will have to study for a degree. However if you have built up an impressive portfolio of your work, some post-degree design courses may accept you. There is some flexibility in the system but you will have to show you have the intellectual rigour to complete a degree course. Details of all these courses are available from Learndirect and the University and Colleges Admissions Service (UCAS) (see useful contacts below).

Another option for graduates who want to move into interior design is to take a **diploma in interior design and decoration**. These can be intensive one-year courses run by specialist design colleges, specifically aimed at graduates. They can charge in the region of £17,000 for a one-year course, but the advantage of this kind of diploma is that it offers a fast-track route into two potential careers: interior decoration and interior design.

What personal skills do I need?

Although the skills needed to work in design can be taught, it is essential that you have some natural creative flair at the outset. You must have good administration and business skills and be able to cost a project and work to budget. Excellent communication skills are essential as the work is very client-based. You must be a good listener and be able to deliver a brief. You must also be able to work under pressure.

Starting salary

The starting salary for an assistant interior designer in a private firm is around £18,000–£20,000. The average salary for a successful interior designer can be around £60,000, but income varies and can depend on the individual reputation of the practice.

Jobs on qualification

An interior designer or an interior decorator or both. Some qualified designers will work as television or theatre designers or become landscape architects or designers.

Current employment prospects? ★ ★ ★ ★ ★.

Is a career change a reality? ★ ★ ★ ★ ★

Welcomes older entrants? ★ ★ ★ ★ ★

Potential high earner? £ £ £ £

Useful contacts:

The British Interior Design Association (BIDA)
3/18 Chelsea Harbour Design Centre
Chelsea Harbour
London SW10 0XE
020 7349 0800
www.bida.org

The Chartered Society of Designers
Bermondsey Exchange
179–181 Bermondsey Street
London SE1 3UW
020 7357 8088
www.csd.org.uk

The Design Council
34 Bow Street
London WC2E 7DL
020 7420 5200
www.design-council.org.uk

The Design Trust
41 Commercial Road
London E1 1LA
020 7320 2895
www.designtrust.co.uk

Creative and Cultural Skills
11 Southwark Street
London SE1 1RQ
020 7089 5866
www.ccskills.org.uk

University and Colleges Admissions Service (UCAS)
Customer Services Unit
UCAS
PO Box 28
Cheltenham
GL52 3LZ
0870 1122211
www.ucas.com

Learndirect
0800 100 900
www.learndirect.co.uk

City and Guilds
1 Giltspur Street
London EC1A 9DD
020 7294 2800
www.cityandguilds.com

www.ideasfactory.com (career advice website for the creative arts)

Journalist

'Employment prospects are really dependent on what these older entrants can bring with them to the job which will get the interest of the editor.' The National Council for the Training of Journalists (NCTJ).

The job

A journalist is responsible for news-gathering and turning that information into stories or features to appear in print, in newspapers, magazines, on TV or radio, or online. Journalists who decide to stay in news can either be general news reporters or can go on to specialise in an area that interests them such as health, education or sport. Some journalists will opt to move into the production side to become a sub-editor (responsible for editing the copy, fitting stories onto the page and writing the headlines) or a production editor (responsible for drawing up the pages and layout). A newspaper editor (responsible for the style and content of the publication) can come from either a production or a writing background.

The culture

Breaking into journalism is always going to be difficult whether you start as a school leaver, graduate or career changer. Competition is fierce. However, if you are prepared to start off on trade magazines or professional journals linked with your previous work, coming into the profession from another career can have its advantages. Editors in this sector are more likely to take you on because of the professional contacts you would be bringing with you, as well as your understanding of the issues in which their readers are interested. But they would still expect you to have excellent English writing skills and be meticulous about spelling and the use of language. The trade press should also train you in the core journalistic skills you need to do the job – shorthand, law and news and feature-writing skills.

If you have ambitions to work in newspapers, then retraining is going to be your best option. The profession's training body, the National Council for the Training of Journalists, offers a range of options from short crash courses to distance-learning packages and postgraduate diplomas, which will give you the basic skills you need to do the job. With a recognised qualification behind you, you are going to be in a stronger position to find that first job. The traditional route into newspaper journalism is via local papers, but if you decide to go down this road, be prepared to see your pay drop. The average starting salary for a local newspaper reporter is up to £14,000, the hours will be long and the quality of journalism on local papers varies considerably. An alternative way into newspaper journalism as well as magazine journalism is to become a self-employed freelance journalist. Around 30 per cent of all journalists are freelance. When starting out as a freelance you could offer news stories or features on spec to news desks as a way of getting yourself known. It would be advisable to work as a freelance alongside your current job until you feel confident it can provide you with a living income. But if you want to be a successful freelance you will have to be persistent and thick-skinned because rejection, especially in the early days, is common. The mushrooming of online journalism, which can only grow, and the recognition by editors in this sector of the power of the internet blogger offers another route in. An entertaining and informative blogger can get noticed and this can provide a less conventional opening.

Do I need a degree?

Journalism degree courses, accredited by the **National Council for the Training of Journalists (NCTJ)**, will prepare you for sitting the preliminary exams for the NCTJ. Details of these accredited undergraduate degrees are available from the NCTJ website.

What professional qualifications do I need?

The NCTJ has been running training courses for entry into journalism since 1951. It offers more than 30 accredited courses for training as a journalist at different levels of entry. The minimum entry requirements are five A–C grades at GCSE which must include English, and two A levels. If you decide to follow one of the three NCTJ distance-learning courses, the organisation recommends you complete its self-test pack, available on its website, before signing up, to judge whether you are academically capable of following the course. Further details can be found below.

Postgraduate NCTJ accredited courses that offer diplomas or Masters degrees in journalism are available and usually take a year. There are also fast-track postgraduate courses that take 41 weeks part time or 21 weeks full time. Graduates from these courses will be equipped to sit for the preliminary exams needed as the first step towards gaining the NCTJ professional qualification, the **National Certificate Exam (NCE)**. These preliminary exams cover practical journalism, media law, public affairs and shorthand, where students have to achieve 100 words a minute. Graduates of the preliminary qualifications need two years' paid work in journalism before they are eligible to sit the NCE, which is made up of four exams and a logbook including examples of copy and cuttings of published articles.

The NCTJ pre-entry course is the route to training for non-graduates. Students must have at least five A–C GCSEs including English, and two A levels. The course can be taken in a year or through day or block release if you are already a working journalist. Graduates from this course will have to achieve two years' paid work in journalism before they can sit the NCE.

The NCTJ also offers a distance-learning course in newspaper journalism which equips the student with the knowledge and skills needed to be able to sit the preliminary NCE exams. This course, based on self-assessment, is a popular option for career changers because students can study at their own pace, in their own time, while still working in their first career. The course can be completed in six months but more often takes two years. Study is based on learning from books and tapes. The National Certificate Exam is the professionally recognised qualification that shows employers you are competent in the basic skills needed to do the job.

What personal skills do I need?

A sense of curiosity and a passion for language are crucial if you want to be a journalist. Self-confidence is a must, as well as tenacity and determination. Excellent communication skills are important and the ability to get on with a range of people from different backgrounds is essential. An ability to work under pressure and to deadlines is vital as well as the ability to take criticism and learn from it. The hours can be unsocial and unpredictable so you must be prepared to be versatile. An ability to write clear copy that is grammatically correct and spelt properly will be expected. According to the NCTJ you must also 'possess enough idealism to get indignant about the unjust but still see both sides of an argument, have a healthy distrust of officialdom, [be] sceptical but not cynical when people tell you they're being absolutely truthful.'

Starting salary

The starting salary of a trainee reporter on a local paper is historically low, starting around £13,000 to £14,000, rising to £16,000 to £17,000 with the NCE professional qualification. Salaries on national newspapers vary hugely depending on the paper and the journalist's experience. But on average a national newspaper reporter starts on a minimum £30,000 rising to £80,000 on some titles. Freelance journalists are paid a rate for the work they do. The rate varies according to the publication and the journalist's experience. The National Union of Journalists has minimum recommended fee rates for freelances.

Jobs on qualification

Journalist. With experience journalists can go on to become specialist writers or correspondents or move into production roles including sub-editing. Some journalists may use their experience to cross over into public relations, which often pays higher salaries.

Current employment prospects
Variable. Be prepared to face tough competition.

Is a career change a reality? ★ ★ ★ ★ ★

Welcomes older entrants? ★ ★ ★ ★ ★

Potential high earner? £ £ £

Useful contacts:

National Council for the Training of Journalists (NCTJ)
Latton Bush Centre
Southern Way
Harlow
Essex
CM18 7BL
01279 430009
www.nctj.com

National Union of Journalists
Headland House
308–312 Gray's Inn Road
London WC1X 8DP
020 7278 7916
www.nuj.org.uk

Newspaper Society
Bloomsbury House
Bloomsbury Square
74–77 Great Russell Street
London WC1B 3DA
020 7636 7014
www.newspapersoc.org.uk

Society of Editors
University Centre
Granta Place
Mill Lane
Cambridge
CB2 1RU
01223 304080
www.societyofeditors.co.uk

University and Colleges Admissions Service (UCAS)
Customer Services Unit
UCAS
PO Box 28
Cheltenham
GL52 3LZ
0870 1122211
www.ucas.com

Landscape architect

'Landscape architecture attracts people with a maturity of purpose. It's an easier profession to move into than architecture where there is a much younger culture.'
Qualified and practising landscape architect running own practice.

The job

Landscape architects are experts in space and place. Like traditional architects they work in three dimensions – height, depth and breadth. But what distinguishes them from architects is that their work considers the passing of time. For example, they bring living things like plants to a landscape. They argue that a new building created by an architect probably looks its best on the day it is opened, but an open space that has been developed by a landscape architect will look its best a decade after the work is first completed. The core principles of the job are to design, plan and manage open spaces in cities and rural areas. This can include a wide variety of open spaces, from local parks and areas of outstanding natural beauty to urban regeneration schemes and historic gardens. A landscape architect is an expert in assessing the environmental impact of changes to landscape as well as the conservation and ecological issues of outdoor space. The job often involves public consultation, so good communication skills are important. Landscape architects are mainly office-based with much time spent on the computer, but the role does involve some outdoor site work.

The culture

Landscape architects are often career changers, and the profession has traditionally attracted older entrants, including former garden or interior designers, as well as others who have moved from completely unrelated careers. It is a profession that is popular with mature entrants who, as they have grown older, have developed a personal passion for, and a commitment to, their environment and its design. According to some career changers, life experience is recognised as a valuable asset within the profession, and it has a culture which might give a more mature person the edge over a younger newly qualified graduate in the jobs market. Career changers say this is a career that can become all-consuming. It presents constant challenges and it helps, they say, to be open to new ideas.

Do I need a degree?

The Landscape Institute, the professional organisation for landscape architects, does not offer a non-graduate route to its professional qualification although it says this could change in the future. So if you are really keen to career change and are not a graduate, the simplest option would be to take a first degree and then study for a postgraduate professional qualification.

Degrees in landscape architecture, landscape design, land planning and land management would be a good first step on the career ladder in landscape architecture. Entry requirements are usually a minimum of two A levels and five A–C GCSEs. More details about the necessary qualifications and the degrees available can be found by contacting the Universities and Colleges Admissions Service (UCAS).

Graduates will need to take a year's conversion course and then go on to study a postgraduate diploma or MA in landscape architecture. The qualifications, including conversion, can be studied full or part time and can take up to three years to complete. Details of courses accredited to the Landscape Institute are available from the Institute's website (see useful contacts below).

What professional qualifications do I need?

A postgraduate diploma or MA in landscape architecture entitles you to **associate membership** of the **Landscape Institute**, which means you are professionally qualified. Most associate members will go on to work towards and gain chartered status which, apart from allowing you to put letters after your name, also means your earning potential increases. To become a chartered landscape architect you must undertake the Institute's **Pathway to Chartership**. This includes completing a logbook based on reflection and experience in practice with the support of a professional mentor, followed by an oral exam. The length of time taken to reach chartered status will depend on an individual's work experience.

What personal skills do I need?

A constantly enquiring mind is valuable and an interest in the environment around you is crucial. If you are the person on the bus who prefers to have their head stuck in a book rather than being drawn to look out of the window at your surroundings, then this would be the wrong career change for you. It is a career path that will appeal 'if you get annoyed about cracked paving stones,' as career changer Deborah Nagan puts it. Much of the work is computer-based so you must have good IT skills beyond knowing how to use Word and sending email. Having some idea about computer-aided design (CAD) would be an advantage. A good imagination and a creative mind are key. Good design and drawing skills would be useful. Communication skills are crucial, as a lot of landscape architects work in the community with local groups, helping to create the open spaces that meet their needs. But the overriding personal credential for a successful career as a landscape architect is to have a passion about open space.

Starting salary

This is not a high-earning profession. Salaries for junior newly qualified landscape architects in private practice start at around £20,000. Most practising landscape architects with some experience will earn under £30,000. Directors or principals in top firms with chartered status will have higher earning potential, between £45,000 and a maximum £80,000 for a leading and large practice. Salaries in public sector organisations tend to be lower but then they have the advantages of a public sector pension and flexible working.

Jobs on qualification

A landscape architect. There are opportunities in both the public and private sectors. In the public sector landscape architects work for local authorities. They might find themselves working in a planning department, or 'green space' or regeneration teams. Other opportunities are available in government agencies such as English Nature, Scottish Natural Heritage or the Countryside Council for Wales and within organisations in the not-for-profit sector like Groundwork. However 50 per cent of qualified landscape architects work in private practice.

Current employment prospects ★ ★ ★ ★

Very good. The emphasis on all things green and the built environment means job opportunities are increasing all the time. Demand for well-qualified professional landscape architects outstrips supply.

Is a career change a reality? ★ ★ ★ ★ ★

Welcomes older entrants? ★ ★ ★ ★ ★

Potential high earner? £ £

Useful contacts:

The Landscape Institute
33 Great Portland Street
London W1W 8QG
020 7299 4500
www.l-l.org.uk

British Association of Landscape Industries (BALI)
Landscape House
Stoneleigh Park
Warwickshire
CV8 2LG
0870 770 4972
www.bali.co.uk

Landscape Design Trust
Bank Chambers
1 London Road
Redhill
Surrey
RH1 1LY
01737 779257
www.landscape.co.uk

Society of Garden Designers
Katepwa House
Ashfield Park Avenue
Ross-on-Wye
Herefordshire
HR9 5AX
01989 566695
www.sgd.org.uk

Universities and Colleges Admissions Service
Customer Services Unit
UCAS
PO Box 28
Cheltenham
GL52 3LZ
0870 1122211
www.ucas.com

Lantra (the sector skills council for the environment and land-based industries)
Lantra House
Stoneleigh Park
Coventry
Warwickshire
CV8 2LG
0845 707 8007
www.lantra.co.uk

Groundwork
85–87 Cornwall Street
Birmingham
B3 3BY
0121 236 8565
www.groundwork.org.uk

Landscape designer

'It's a good move for somebody considering a career change; there are lots of people in their 30s and 40s. There are so many people coming into the profession at the moment that one would imagine there is only a finite amount of work, but having said that I have never been busier.' Caroline Davy, career changer from marketing to landscape designer.

The job

It is a mistake to decide to become a landscape designer simply because you enjoy gardening and the great outdoors. At least 60 per cent of time as a landscape designer is spent in front of a desk or a drawing board working on the elements of design. Only 40 per cent is spent outdoors and some landscape designers may never get their hands dirty, preferring instead to offload the construction or plant-laying elements of the job to subcontractors.

Landscape designers devote their time to transforming gardens, which are often privately owned. This is one of the key differences when the job is compared to landscape architects, who are more likely to work on larger commercial projects in the private sector or on public open spaces – it is often the scale of the job that distinguishes them from landscape designers. Landscape designers have to be multi-talented, as the work requires a range of skills and knowledge. A key part of the work is to survey and measure the site to be landscaped and carry out soil analysis. The landscape designer has to develop a brief for the client that reflects what the client wants to use the land for, and then has to return to the drawing board and computer to create a design that fits the brief and is practical for the site. Once the client accepts the brief, the landscape designer has the option of carrying out the hard landscaping work themselves to create the physical framework for the garden. This would include, for example, erecting fencing, or building patios or walls. Alternatively this work could be sub-contracted to other specialist contractors. Once the physical framework is completed the landscape designer will become more involved again, usually buying and planting the plants to complete the job.

The culture

A career as a landscape designer can be a lonely one because the majority are self-employed, and like many design-based careers it can be very competitive. But it is a profession that traditionally attracts career changers in their 30s and 40s and older. A survey in 2005 initiated by English Heritage revealed that 55 per cent of respondents working in the horticulture sector were career changers coming from diverse backgrounds such as banking or mining.

Do I need a degree?

Training opportunities to become a landscape designer are varied and flexible. Courses are offered at postgraduate, undergraduate or non-graduate level, and the volume of courses on offer can appear to be overwhelming. Full-time courses are an option, but the majority of career changers opt to study part time, while building up new skills and knowledge, before launching themselves into their new career as full-time landscape designers. Courses can focus on the design side or the horticultural side of the job, or they can cover both aspects.

BA or BSc three-year full-time degrees in landscaping and garden design are available. A BSc is likely to be a more technical degree than a BA. Masters degrees in garden design and landscaping and design are available. Details, including entry requirements, are available from the University and Colleges Admissions Service (see useful contacts below).

Diplomas and certificates in garden design are available at further education colleges. These can be studied part time and are an alternative route to acquiring the basic skills for the job. Students choosing this route often study for a Royal Horticultural Society qualification as well to boost their plant skills and knowledge.

Foundation degrees in landscape and garden design are a popular route for career changers. The flexibility of the courses often means that students can juggle the study alongside continuing employment. A foundation degree takes two years to complete and requires two days a week in college. A typical course would include small-business skills, marketing and business law, as well as horticultural science and hard landscaping skills, and design skills including computer-aided design. Many landscape designers feel they have enough knowledge and skill after completing a foundation degree to launch themselves as landscape designers.

What professional qualifications do I need?

The **Royal Horticultural Society** offers its own professional qualifications, the RHS level 2 certificate in horticulture and the RHS level 3 advanced certificate in horticulture. The RHS level 3 diploma in horticulture is aimed at professional horticulturalists, but it is also an option for students who have studied the lower certificates. The most senior award from the RHS is its Master of horticulture (RHS) award, which is equal to a degree and is usually studied full time for three years.

What personal skills do I need?

Landscape designers require a range of personal skills. An ability to work flexibly and in all weather conditions is crucial. Good maths skills are needed, as well as the ability to communicate well – good people skills are essential, especially if you are self-employed. Design skills are also important as well as commercial and business acumen.

Starting salary

The majority of landscape designers start out as self-employed, and as with any small business, it can be tough at the outset. It is important to set fees at the appropriate market level. The **Society of Garden Designers** has a recommended fee structure, which is available to members. Non-members might rely on **Spons Landscape and External Works Price Book**, published annually, which lists price guidelines for landscape design work. An average income in the first year can be around £20,000, but will depend on where you are working in the UK. There are landscape hotspots like parts of Cheshire and the south-east, while other parts of the UK may not prove so lucrative. The potential to become a high earner exists, with some garden designers demanding fees of around £15,000 per project.

Jobs on qualification

Landscape designer. Most landscape designers work alone and are self-employed. Some start off by working in garden maintenance as well as design in order to have a more secure income.

Current employment prospects ★ ★ ★ ★ ★

Horticulture is an employment sector where there is a lack of skilled and qualified professionals so there are good job opportunities. Landscape designers are also predicting a greater interest in landscaping and gardening across the UK, triggered by the 2012 London Olympics.

Is a career change a reality? ★ ★ ★ ★ ★

Welcomes older entrants? ★ ★ ★ ★ ★

Potential high earner? £ £ £ £ £

Useful contacts:

The Society of Garden Designers
Ashfield Park Avenue
Ross-on-Wye
Herefordshire
HR9 5AX
01980 566695
www.sgd.org.uk

Royal Horticultural Society
80 Vincent Square
London SW1P 2PE
020 7834 4333
www.rhs.org.uk

RHS qualifications:
The Qualifications Office
RHS Garden Wisley
Woking
Surrey
GU23 6QB

Institute of Horticulture
14–15 Belgrave Square
London SW1X 8PS
020 7245 6943
www.horticulture.org.uk

Writtle College
Chelmsford
Essex
CM1 3RE
01245 424200
www.writtle.ac.uk
www.growing-careers.com

Reaseheath College
Nantwich
Cheshire
CW5 6DF
01270 625665
www.reaseheath.ac.uk

Guildford College
Merrist Wood Campus
Stoke Road
Guildford
GU1 1EZ
01483 884000
www.guildford.ac.uk

Hadlow College
Hadlow
Tonbridge
Kent
TN11 0AL
01732 850551
www.hadlow.ac.uk

Kingston Maurward College
Dorchester
Dorset
DT2 8PY
01305 215000
www.kmc.ac.uk

Universities and Colleges Admissions Service
Customer Services Unit
UCAS
PO Box 28
Cheltenham
GL52 3LZ
0870 1122211
www.ucas.com

Lawyer/solicitor

'I would say there is no bar to anyone coming into the profession late by virtue of their age. In fact age and experience would be looked at positively by most law firms.'
Colin Hunter, partner in high-street law firm Coodes Solicitors, which has branches in Devon and Cornwall.

The job
A solicitor provides clients with expert legal advice and help, and is skilled at interpreting and explaining the law. The type of legal work a solicitor is involved in depends on the firm they work for. They can become a commercial solicitor, where salary potential is very high, or a non-commercial solicitor, where the top salaries are generally lower. Solicitors can represent their clients in magistrates' and county courts and they can, with extra qualifications, represent clients in the higher crown courts, although it is more likely in these cases that they will brief barristers who will appear on their client's behalf instead.

The culture
Large city law firms say they are noticing more applications for trainee solicitor posts from 'second jobbers' and older career changers in recent years, although the majority of trainees are still likely to be those who have followed the traditional undergraduate route straight from school. But there is a recognition amongst employers of the added advantages of taking on an older trainee. This is especially true in the bigger firms, who may welcome a trainee who is, for example, a former doctor or banker, if the firm specialises in these areas of law. Older entrants are also in a strong position because they already understand the culture and etiquette of office life. As Colin Hunter puts it, law can throw up complex problems where common sense, life experience and personal confidence can make a major contribution to finding the solution. There is still a culture of long hours in some firms, especially the larger ones specialising in corporate law who work according to a global clock with an international client base, which may deter some career changers. But there are also other successful large firms which offer flexible working, part-time working and workplace support groups for new parents. The biggest obstacle to a career change into becoming a solicitor is going to be funding. The trainee solicitors group warns that a trainee, who can expect to earn an average starting salary of around £19,000, can start their career with debts of between £29,000 and £44,000.

Do I need a degree?
The traditional first step on the road to becoming a qualified solicitor is to study for an undergraduate law degree. Because of the high interest from potential law students

some law schools have introduced entrance exams for undergraduates in an attempt to sift out the most able students.

It is possible to become a qualified solicitor if you have a degree but not in law. In this case, you must study for the **common professional examination** or the **graduate diploma in law**. These can be studied either part time or full time and once passed are valid for seven years. Course fees vary from £1,125 to £5,400 depending on where you study. Once the course is completed you can follow the route to professional qualification (see entry below).

A law degree, which must be approved by the Law Society and the Bar Council, takes three years full time. Because of the fierce competition for places, in 2006 11 universities and law colleges asked undergraduate candidates to sit a national admissions test for law in order to select the most able students. An alternative undergraduate route is through the **Open University** which, in partnership with the College of Law, offers a bachelor of laws (LLB) degree which is recognised by the Law Society and the General Council for the Bar as meeting the academic requirements needed before vocational training to become a lawyer.

After graduation, the law degree is only valid for seven years if you want to use it as the first step towards becoming a practising solicitor. If you decide to qualify as a solicitor, it is at this point that you must apply to the Law Society for student membership and a certificate which confirms you have completed your academic training. Once you have done that you will need to undertake vocational work-based training, then further professional qualifications before you complete your professional training and are entitled to register on the roll of solicitors at the Law Society. This can take another three years, bringing total study and training to six years.

However, there is an option available to non-graduates, which is to apply directly to the Law Society for a **certificate of academic standing**, which will entitle you to study for the common professional examination or the graduate diploma in law. You will then be able to follow the professional qualification route to becoming a solicitor (see entry below). A criterion for this certificate is a minimum age of 25, and you must also have considerable experience in a professional, academic or administrative field. Qualification certificates at A level and beyond must also be supplied as well as employment references for the last 10 years. You will be expected to have reached at least a middle-management role in your current career. In 2005, the Law Society granted 1,512 certificates of academic standing – slightly more than the previous year.

What professional qualifications do I need?

On completing a law degree (or the common professional examination or the graduate diploma in law) you must go on to complete the **legal practice course**. This course teaches you how to apply the law in practice. This can be studied one year full time or two years part time or by distance learning. There is no student loan for this course. There are around 10,000 full and part-time places on offer but fees can vary from £5,200 to £8,500.

On completion of the legal practice course, you then face two years of on-the-job training where you are employed as a trainee solicitor. In 2003/4 there were 5,708 training contract places available. At this point, for the first time, you will begin to earn a salary, which according to the latest figures for 2003 was on average £19,748. As part of your training contract you will be expected to complete the professional skills course which entitles you to apply to join the Law Society's roll of solicitors, confirming your professional qualification and your right to practise.

Sponsorship from some law firms is available for students completing the vocational part of their training. Packages vary, covering some or all of the costs of the legal practice course or the common professional examination or graduate diploma in law. Sponsorship might also include money to cover maintenance and course fees. These financial packages are often offered as part of a training contract and are traditionally aimed at younger students coming into the profession immediately after graduating with a law degree. It would be exceptional, though not impossible, for a mature entrant to be successful in securing this source of funding.

Older entrants may be in a stronger position to qualify for a Law Society bursary, which is available to students who can prove financial hardship and who are completing the common professional examination or graduate diploma in law or the legal practice course. Another potential pot of money is via the Law Society's diversity access scheme. Charities and grant-making trusts are another possible source of income and details can be sought from the Charities Commission for England and Wales. The Inderpal Rahal memorial trust, in memory of a female barrister, is a possibility for women from an immigrant or refugee background who want to continue their legal career or study law.

Working and training as a **legal executive** offers an alternative route to qualification as a lawyer. Qualified legal executives are professional lawyers who work alongside solicitors and barristers. They usually specialise in a particular area of the law but their day-to-day work is similar to that of a solicitor. This can include the legal aspects of property transfer, drafting wills, criminal cases and establishing a company under the law. The **Institute of Legal Executives (ILEX)** provides a work-based route to becoming a qualified lawyer. Once ILEX-qualified you can also go on to further training to become a qualified solicitor. The advantage of taking this route is that training and qualification is provided on the job and employers, who are usually either legal firms or legal departments, are encouraged to provide funding and time off for study. This is a cheaper route of entry to the legal profession. The ILEX professional qualification in law takes up to four years part time and can be followed through day release, evening classes or distance learning. Full professional qualification, which entitles you to be a fellow of the ILEX; confirming your status as a qualified lawyer, is dependent on five years' work-based experience – two of which must take place after passing the ILEX professional qualification in law. To go on to become a qualified solicitor, candidates must have completed the academic stage of training of the Law Society, enrolled as a student member and completed the legal practice course. However, ILEX professionally qualified lawyers may be exempt from the two years' work training contract because of the work experience they have already undergone. They, like other trainee solicitors, must also complete the professional skills course in order to be included on the Law Society's roll of solicitors.

What personal skills do I need?

Intellectual ability is a must because the law is a complex beast. The ability to be versatile is useful, as every day is different. An analytical aptitude is essential, and being able to think logically and write and express yourself clearly is crucial. Discretion is also called for, but probably most important is a personal commitment to training as whichever route to qualification you choose it is going to be a long process – and expensive.

Starting salary

The minimum starting salary for a commercial lawyer is around £16,450 but it will depend on the size and reputation of the practice. It can go up to around £30,000 for one of the big London city firms. With around 15 years' experience, a partner in a commercial firm can expect to earn well into six figures. Annual bonuses are also payable. Salaries for non-commercial lawyers tend to be lower, starting at around £14,000 and rising to £21,000. With experience a partner in a small private firm or a local authority solicitor could expect to earn up to £55,000. The salary would however depend on the size of the organisation or public authority.

Jobs on qualification

Qualified solicitors tend to fall into two categories: commercial or non-commercial. Those who are commercial lawyers work for large private practices. They will usually specialise in an area of law such as property, tax, employment, finance, intellectual property or competition law. Non-commercial lawyers are more likely to work in smaller high-street firms offering a wide range of legal services to clients, which will include individuals and small businesses. They may also become involved in legal aid cases.

Current employment prospects ★ ★ ★ ★ ★

Is a career change a reality? ★ ★ ★ ★ ★

Welcomes older entrants? ★ ★ ★ ★ ★

Potential high earner? £ £ £ £ £

Useful contacts:

The Law Society of England and Wales
113 Chancery Lane
London WC2A 1PL
020 7242 1222
www.lawsociety.org.uk

Society of Asian Lawyers
Gray's Inn
4-5 Gray's Inn Square
London WC1R 5AH
www.societyofasianlawyers.com

Society of Black Lawyers
Winchester House
11 Cranmer Road
London SW9 6EJ
020 7735 6592

Trainee Solicitors Group (TSG)
The Law Society
113 Chancery Lane
London WC2A 1PL
020 7320 5794
www.tsg.org

Institute of Legal Executives (ILEX)
Kempston Manor
Kempston
Bedfordshire
MK42 7AB
01234 841000
www.ilex.org.uk

Government Legal Service
Chancery House
53–64 Chancery Lane
London WC2A 1QS
020 7649 6023
www.gls.gov.uk

Law Centres Federation
Duchess House
18–19 Warren Street
London W1T 5LR
020 7387 8570
www.lawcentres.org.uk

Law Society of Ireland (Republic of Ireland)
Blackhall Place
Dublin 7
00353 1672 4800
www.lawsociety.ie

The Law Society of Northern Ireland
98 Victoria Street
Belfast BT1 3JZ
028 9023 1614
www.lawsoc-ni.org

Law Society of Scotland
26 Drumsheugh Gardens
Edinburgh EH3 7YR
0131 226 7411
www.lawscot.org.uk

Law Careers.net
www.lawcareers.net

Charity Commission for England and Wales
Harmsworth House
13–15 Bouverie Street
London EC4Y 8DP
0845 300 0218
www.charity-commission.gov.uk

The Inderpal Rahal Memorial Trust
Irmt@2gardenct.law.co.uk

Nurse

'Nursing hasn't actively gone out to attract older people to the profession, it's just that it seems to appeal to people who are looking for something more fulfilling than their current career can offer. They want to give something back.' Howard Catton, head of policy at the Royal College of Nursing.

The job

Professionally qualified nurses can work in a range of different places. They can be found in hospitals, GP surgeries or health teams in the community, such as those working with patients with drug abuse problems or others with mental health needs or a disability. They can also be found in residential homes or working in education as a school nurse. Their core responsibility is to care for patients. They must observe and assess what is happening to their patient and then select the most appropriate course of action. Nurses are trained to check a patient's temperature, blood pressure and respiratory rate and they sometimes help doctors with physical examinations. They are also trained to give drugs and injections and treat wounds. But as the profession takes on more responsibility for patients, some of the duties which have traditionally fallen to doctors in the past are now performed by nurses, such as the prescribing of medicines. Nurses often work as part of multi-disciplinary teams which can include other health professionals and those from other caring agencies, such as social workers. Hospital nurses work according to a shift rota which includes weekend and evening work, while nurses in the community, especially those in GP practices or attached to out-patient clinics, can expect to work more regular daytime hours.

There are four branches of nursing:

• Adult nurse: these are nurses specialising in the adult branch and are trained to look after patients aged over 16 who have acute health needs or are suffering from chronic conditions. Adult nurses work in a hospital ward, in a specialist clinic or out in the community visiting people at home. They can also work out of a health centre. Adult nurses can become specialists working in intensive care, theatre, cancer care or care of the elderly.

• Children's nurse: a children's nurse cares for children under the age of 16 – from newborn babies to teenagers. In child patients the onset of symptoms can be sudden and extreme and can also impact on their future development so the job can be very stressful and demanding. It involves working closely with the child's family – both the parents and siblings. It is a key part of the job to make sure that the child's carers have the knowledge and the skills to care for the child when they are discharged. Children's nurses help the whole family.

• Mental health nurse: mental health nurses work with GPs, psychiatrists and social workers to help coordinate the care of patients with mental health problems. They work in people's homes, in small residential units and in health centres, and as government policy shifts towards moving people out of hospital into the community their responsibilities have increased. They are trained in identifying when a patient is at risk of harming themselves or others. They work with people of all ages and from all backgrounds and with extra training can go on to specialise in working with, for example, patients with drug misuse problems or patients who are ex-offenders.

• Learning disability nurse: the key role of a learning disability nurse is to use their skills to help people with a learning disability to maintain and improve their lifestyle and enhance the role they have in society. The demands of the job can vary from helping people develop their manual and recognition skills so that they can live safely and independently to being a professional support if they are bringing up a family or looking for employment. Learning disability nurses work in a variety of settings such as people's own homes, residential care homes and schools.

The culture

Nursing is increasingly becoming a career of choice for older people. Research highlighted last year by Nursing Standard magazine showed that 45 per cent of student nurses are aged over 30, and a third of those over the age of 26 are parents. So age and family commitments are no barrier to a career move into nursing. However, as with entry to other medical professions, it will require a commitment to retraining. A number of different government grants and allowances are available to help to make that transition back into learning more financially comfortable. Students who have a place on an NHS-sponsored nurse diploma course will benefit from an annual non-means-tested bursary, while those on degree courses can apply for a means-tested bursary. But despite this support many student nurses struggle financially when training and often have to juggle another job, such as working as a healthcare assistant, in order to meet their financial commitments. The role of nurses has changed dramatically over the last 20 years, with today's nurses often expected to deliver some of the services that have traditionally been provided by GPs or junior doctors.

Do I need a degree?

Nursing is a statutorily regulated profession. You will need to have a recognised nursing diploma, degree or postgraduate qualification, any of which will entitle you to register with the **Nursing and Midwifery Council**.

If you have at least two A levels then you are eligible to study for a nursing degree. This takes three years full time or longer, possibly up to five years, part time. All student nurses have to complete a core common foundation programme year before deciding to specialise in one of the four different branches of nursing.

However, there are other routes into nursing. If you have a minimum of five GCSEs (or equivalent) then you may apply to study for a diploma in higher education (nursing) at a university. The diploma course is three years full time or can be longer, possibly five years, part time. There is the option to complete the diploma of higher education (nursing) in either adult or mental health nursing through the **Open University** in a partnership developed between the OU, the NHS, UK governments and health employers including private providers. Students on this course must be employed by one of the partner organisations in order to be eligible for the scheme. The OU route allows students to complete the diploma through flexible study within six years, although most take between four and five years.

A non-means-tested bursary is paid every year to students studying for the nursing diploma. The bursary is paid for every year of study and is not linked to family income. In London the annual non-means-tested bursary was £6,859 in 2006, or £5,837 outside the capital and £5,837 if you are still living with parents. Students on part-time courses can receive a proportion of the annual bursary. If you are on a diploma course and receiving a non-means-tested bursary you are not entitled to apply for a student loan.

A means-tested bursary is available to students on degree-level NHS courses and those on postgraduate courses. The amount of bursary you receive is dependent on income, so it will vary from student to student. Students on part-time degree courses will be eligible for 75 per cent of the full bursary. The bursary available for 2006 was £2,837 per year in London or £2,309 per year outside London, £1,889 if you are still living with your parents. If you are on an NHS degree course you will also be able to apply for a reduced student loan to help towards your maintenance costs.

Students on diploma courses who are aged over 26 when they enrol are eligible for an older students' allowance of £682 per year. They are also entitled to the single parent allowance of £1,001, but they are not entitled to claim both.

Students on NHS degree and postgraduate courses are also eligible for an older students' allowance if aged over 26 before the first academic year of starting the course. This allowance is from £406 for 26-year-olds, up to a maximum £1,381 for the over-29s. If you are a single parent you are eligible for an allowance called a single parent addition, which is £1,181 for a year. If you are over 26 and claim this benefit you forfeit the older students' allowance, as do diploma students (above).

There are also other discretionary means-tested grants available whether you are on a degree or diploma course. See the chapter on funding for more details.

What professional qualifications do I need?

Nursing is a regulated profession and a nurse degree or diploma will allow you to register with the Nursing and Midwifery Council, which entitles you to practise.

What personal skills do I need?

The ability to juggle different priorities and to be able to communicate with a range of different people is essential. You must be understanding, tactful and sensitive to other people's needs. It is important that you remain well informed because you are the patient's most frequent point of contact. You are also their advocate and must make sure that their needs are recognised and met by other members of the care team. You have to be quick-witted. In children's nursing in particular, you must have an open mind about parents' different ways of caring for their children and be non-judgemental. Mental health nurses especially must be able to listen to their patients and help to find the best solution to their problems, while nurses working with people with a learning disability should be resourceful and adaptable. It is a demanding job with huge responsibility, but there can be great professional satisfaction.

Starting salary

The government has moved to bring nursing salaries in line with other public sector pay through its overhaul of NHS salaries, which culminated in the publication of the document Agenda for Change. So nurses are not as poorly paid today as they have been in the past. A newly qualified nurse in 2006 had a starting salary of £19,166. A top nurse consultant can earn around £51,000 while nurses who go down the management route can earn more: from around £60,000 if they are in charge of nursing services for a small primary care trust, up to £100,000 or more if they decide to become a director of nursing for a large teaching hospital trust.

Jobs on qualification

A qualified nurse can work in one of the four fields mentioned above. A qualified nurse can also go on to train as a health visitor or a midwife, and another option would be to study for a specific degree or diploma in midwifery instead. Nurses who have qualified in the adult branch are eligible, once they have two years' experience post-qualification, to train to become a district nurse.

Continuing professional development is essential in nursing as in other medical professions and there is a wide variety of postgraduate qualification options. The clinical responsibilities of nurses are being increased all the time as the government is keen to boost their professional status and give nurses responsibility for some of the patient care which has traditionally been delivered by GPs and other doctors. With postgraduate training, nurses now have the authority to prescribe drugs, and the formulary that determines which drugs they can prescribe is growing. This development has been a breakthrough in expanding their clinical responsibilities and roles and it is now common to find experienced senior nurses running minor ailment or injury clinics in walk-in centres or GP surgeries. Nurses can also become specialists in the management of chronic disease such as asthma, diabetes or coronary heart disease and are increasingly working autonomously in GP surgeries, clinics or within the community. Some also train in alternative therapy such as homeopathy and acupuncture.

Current employment prospects ★ ★ ★ ★ ★

Last year (2006) news headlines were dominated by cuts in NHS jobs as hospitals and primary care trusts attempted to balance their books and clear financial deficits. The organisation which represents NHS employers and is responsible for workforce issues, NHS Employers, was keen to stress at the time that every day there are 3,000 vacancies in the NHS. It argued the NHS would always need new staff to help deliver the services it was creating and meet the government's health policy to move health care out of the hospital into the community. The nurses' professional organisation, the Royal College of Nursing, also predicted that the need for nurses in the NHS was not going to diminish as the demand for care was always going to exist. The RCN's long-term prediction is that health services will be delivered in a different way, in people's homes rather than hospital-based, and by nurses increasingly being employed by voluntary organisations rather than the NHS. The nursing population is also an ageing population, and a quarter of the workforce is due to retire in the next five to ten years, which in turn creates more career opportunities. So if this is a career change that you want to follow, do not be put off by the newspaper headlines. You are not going to be out of work.

Is a career change a reality? ★ ★ ★ ★ ★

Welcomes older entrants? ★ ★ ★ ★ ★

Potential high earner? £ £ £

Nursing pay scales have been increased by the government as part of its Agenda for Change reforms, which brought an overhaul of NHS pay scales across a range of professions. The changes mean that a student nurse can expect to start on £19,166. Nurse consultants can expect to earn £51,000, and top nursing managers up to £100,000.

Useful contacts:

NHS Careers
PO Box 376
Bristol
BS99 3EY
0845 606 0655
www.nhscareers.nhs.uk

Nursing and Midwifery Admissions Service (NMAS)
Rosehill
New Barn Lane
Cheltenham
Gloucestershire
GL52 3LZ
0870 112 2206 for general enquiries
0870 112 2200 for application packs
www.nmas.ac.uk

Universities and Colleges Admissions Service (UCAS)
Rosehill
New Barn Lane
Cheltenham
Gloucestershire
GL52 3LZ
0870 112 2211
www.ucas.ac.uk

Nursing and Midwifery Council
23 Portland Place
London W1B 1PZ
020 7637 7181
www.nmc-uk.org

Royal College of Nursing
20 Cavendish Square
London W1G 0RN
020 7409 3333
www.rcn.org.uk

NHS Education for Scotland
Careers Information Service
66 Rose Street
Edinburgh
EH2 2NN
0131 225 4365
www.nes.scot.nhs.uk

Health Professions Wales
2nd Floor, Golate House
101 St Mary Street
Cardiff
CF10 1DX
029 2026 1400
www.hpw.org.uk

Queen's University Belfast
School of Nursing and Midwifery
Medical Biology Centre
97 Lisburn Road
Belfast
BT9 7BL
028 9097 2233
www.qub.ac.uk

University of Ulster at Jordanstown
School of Nursing
Shore Road
Newtownabbey
Co Antrim
BT37 0QB
08700 400 700
www.ulster.ac.uk

Paramedic

'A lot of people, especially those in their 30s, want to change direction and train as a paramedic. I get a couple of calls a week from people looking for a career change.'
Roland Furber, chief executive of the British Paramedic Association.

The job

A paramedic is highly trained in all aspects of pre-hospital emergency care. They are skilled to deal with a range of different clinical emergencies from crush injuries in major motorway pile-ups, to dealing with a patient who has had a cardiac arrest at home. They are trained to use heart defibrillators, administer oxygen and set up intravenous drips. They also know how to use spinal and traction splints, and have the authority to administer drugs for medical and trauma emergencies. The key responsibility of a paramedic is to make an assessment of the patient and ensure they are stable before being transferred to hospital. However, the role is changing. Paramedics are increasingly being given more clinical responsibility and are being asked to carry out more diagnostic tests and procedures on patients in the home. A paramedic will often be accompanied by an ambulance technician and will work a shift system which covers 24 hours. Apart from their clinical competence, paramedics are also trained in advanced driving skills and may have the opportunity to train to pilot rescue helicopters. Paramedics are a statutorily regulated health profession and in order to practise as a paramedic it is necessary to register with the Health Professions Council.

The culture

Working as a paramedic has always been a popular career choice, and it is common for ambulance trusts to receive more than 100 replies for every advertised vacancy. Although it is a competitive job market it is a career that welcomes older entrants because of the maturity they can bring to the role, which can be both physically and emotionally demanding. Each individual NHS ambulance trust is responsible for its own recruitment. Unlike in other parts of the NHS, there is no national recruitment programme and, unlike other health careers, such as nursing, there is also no automatic right to government financial help to support training. However, many of the university degrees and diplomas are developed in partnership with local ambulance trusts and there are opportunities for students to be employed by the trust and receive a salary while they study. Although the profession is moving towards graduate entry, there is still a work-based route to becoming a professionally qualified paramedic. Pay scales for paramedics are not high, despite the government's recent overhaul of NHS salaries through Agenda for Change. The British Paramedic Association describes the salary as a 'living wage' but its chief executive Roland Furber says: 'The main reward from being a paramedic is that every day you make a difference to somebody's life.'

Do I need a degree?

There are currently two paths to professional qualification: either via the undergraduate degree or higher education diploma programme, or via the work-based direct entry route.

Paramedics are statutorily regulated, which means you can only practise as a paramedic if you are registered with the Health Professions Council (HPC). In order to be entitled to register with the HPC you must make sure that the paramedic degree or diploma course you are studying has been recognised by the HPC. A list of the degrees and diplomas that entitle you to professional registration are available from the HPC (see useful contacts below). Entry requirements for degree courses are usually five GCSEs grades A to C and two A levels. Diploma and foundation degrees have lower entry levels, usually five GCSEs in A to C grades and a single A level. In 2006 seven universities in England offered full or part-time degrees or higher education diplomas for paramedics. The degree path can take from three years full time up to five years part time.

The diploma courses provide a shorter route to professional qualification and can be completed in two years full time. It is possible to be funded by an ambulance trust to complete a higher education qualification, but as each trust is responsible for its own workforce training it is best to contact individual trusts and individual universities to discover what financial support is available. NHS Careers confirms that any funding help for studying to become a paramedic is up to individual trusts. It advises anybody interested in training as a paramedic to contact their own individual ambulance trust for more information.

There is no postgraduate route to becoming a paramedic although this is expected to change in the future.

What professional qualifications do I need?

There is a work-based route to becoming a professionally qualified paramedic. It is possible to apply to become an ambulance technician or emergency medical technician for an ambulance trust. Each of the individual ambulance trusts in the UK handles its own recruitment. Contact details of ambulance trusts are available from the Ambulance Services Association (see useful contacts below). Trainee technicians are given 12 weeks induction before being attached to an ambulance station, which will provide more on-the-job training. There are also clinical assessments and further study to be completed. After a year as a trainee a technician is professionally qualified. It is then possible, with at least one year's experience as a qualified technician, to apply to your employing trust to train you as a paramedic.

Paramedics are a statutorily regulated health profession. In order to practise as a paramedic you must be registered with the HPC. A list of qualifications that includes the entitlement to professional registration is available from the HPC (see useful contacts below).

What personal skills do I need?

It is important, according to the British Paramedic Association, to be a good listener. You must have excellent communication skills. It is crucial to have the ability to handle an emergency with what the BPA calls 'strong nerve'. Some people will have this skill as a natural ability, for others it can come with training and experience. It is also important to be a clear decision-maker because you will daily be required to make life-or-death decisions. A caring personality and a commitment to continuing professional development are also vital.

Starting salary

A qualified paramedic's starting salary is from £19,166 to £24,803. With experience annual income can rise to £31,004. An ambulance technician's salary is from £16,405 to £19,730.

Jobs on qualification

A qualified paramedic. It is possible with further training for a qualified paramedic to become an emergency care practitioner (ECP). The ECP is a new NHS role and in 2005 there were approximately 600 employed nationally, mainly by ambulance trusts. An ECP has a range of responsibilities, which can include carrying out and interpreting diagnostic tests, undertaking basic procedures on patients in their own home and assessing patients with long-term conditions in their home. An ECP also has the authority to refer patients to social services and can directly admit patients to specialist NHS units. Most ECPs work as members of an ambulance crew or in hospital minor injuries units. Many are also on call in the evening or through the night as part of the GP out-of-hours service.

Current employment prospects ★ ★ ★ ★ ★

Competition for paramedic posts is fierce – there are usually more than 100 applications for every advertised vacant post. But older applicants can bring a necessary maturity to the role and this is recognised by ambulance trusts.

Is a career change a reality? ★ ★ ★ ★ ★

If you are able to persuade an ambulance trust to pay for your higher education training, or you become an ambulance technician trainee and gain financial backing to become a paramedic, then it can be a practical, and cost-effective, career change. Funding decisions vary according to the different trusts so it is advisable to contact the ambulance trusts directly to discover what options are available.

Welcomes older entrants? ★ ★ ★ ★ ★

The British Paramedic Association says the NHS recognises the benefits that older entrants can bring to the profession. It is increasingly attracting career changers in their 30s.

Potential high earner? £ £

This is not a career change to make if you are looking to be a high earner. However the professional rewards are great as you will be making decisions every day which can potentially save a life.

Useful contacts:

British Paramedic Association
28 Wilfred Street
Derby
DE23 8GF
01332 746356
www.britishparamedic.org

NHS Careers
PO Box 376
Bristol
BS99 3EY
0845 606 0655
www.nhscareers.nhs.uk

Health Professions Council
Parl House
184 Kennington Park Road
London SE11 4BU
020 7582 0866
www.hpc-uk.org

Ambulance Services Association
Friars House
157–158 Blackfriars Road
London SE1 8EZ
020 7928 9620
www.asa.uk.net

University and Colleges Admissions Service (UCAS)
Customer Services Unit
UCAS
PO Box 28
Cheltenham
GL52 3LZ
0870 1122211
www.ucas.com

Personal trainer

'Often the self-employed personal trainers who do really well are those who are dedicated, who are older and who bring with them transferable skills from a former career.' Fitness Industry Association.

The job
Personal trainers work with groups or individuals in gyms, health and fitness centres and leisure centres in both the private and public sectors. They supervise and support users to make sure they are exercising safely and using the equipment properly. With extra training they can go on to run exercise classes such as aerobics, Pilates and circuit training and work with particular client groups such as people with a disability or those recovering from a stroke or other illness. Personal trainers must be prepared to work weekends and evenings as well as early mornings as their working week is usually divided into shifts.

The culture
Becoming a personal trainer is an increasingly popular choice for career changers, according to the **Register of Exercise Professionals (REP)** and some training course providers and health clubs such as Fitness First which has around 400 clubs in the UK with more than one million members. It appeals, they say, because the job can offer flexible working and the professional qualifications needed can be studied part time around existing employment. Although age is not a barrier, you are expected to have a good level of personal fitness. And, according to one provider of training qualifications, age can even be an advantage as older gym users may feel more at ease taking instruction from somebody in their own age group rather than a younger trainer. The latest annual survey of people working in the fitness industry, 'Working in Fitness 2005', carried out by SkillsActive (the sector skills council for the fitness industry) and REP, says 57 per cent of personal trainers are self-employed – making them the largest group of fitness professionals in the sector. The percentage of male personal trainers is 58 per cent compared to 42 per cent female. The average age of people registered with REP, the industry's regulator, is 34. Personal fitness is a growth industry in the private sector, but there are also increasing opportunities in the public sector. Both are growing because of an increased public awareness about keeping fit and healthy but also as a result of the government's public health white paper 'Choosing Health'. This is committed to improving the fitness levels of the population. GP fitness referral schemes, where patients are referred to personal trainers, are expected to increase alongside other NHS initiatives to boost fitness. According to the Fitness Industry Association, which represents fitness centre and club operators, the continuing trend of more older people becoming interested in fitness means there will

be a greater need for personal trainers who reflect this age group.

Do I need a degree?

You do not need a degree to be a personal trainer. See options for professional qualifications below.

What professional qualifications do I need?

The fitness industry is self-regulated. Four years ago the industry, with encouragement from the department of health, decided to set up the Register of Exercise Professionals (REP) in an attempt to introduce regulation and establish minimum professional standards and a code of practice for people working in fitness. By 2007, REP expects to have 25,000 registrants. In order to stay on the register, registrants have to commit to continuing professional development and achieve a minimum number of credits each year.

The REP recognises a number of different qualifications in personal training from a range of awarding bodies. These include NVQs, central YMCA qualifications, OCR certificates, and those awarded by Premier IQ. A PT1 class 3 certificate (issued by the armed services) is also recognised as reaching the required standard as well as other fitness awards run in-house by private clubs.

Some of the qualifications can be studied in the evenings and weekends, can be worked around current employment and can take up to 18 months to complete. Some of the awarding bodies offer the opportunity of crash courses. The REP recommends taking qualifications gradually and making informed choices, rather than investing thousands of pounds in one kind of fitness training programme only to discover you do not enjoy it. It is likely that you will be expected to fund your own study, as most of the statutory financial support for these kinds of courses goes to the under-24s. This is not always the case so it may be worth approaching some of the larger fitness groups to see if funding is available. The cost of the courses varies, depending on whether they are being delivered by a statutory or private provider. The prices can range from around £150 to more than £3,000. Details of REP accepted qualifications are available on the REP website (see contact details below).

What personal skills do I need?

Having the right practical and technical skills for the job is essential, but there is also the need to be a good communicator and have an outgoing and approachable personality. Good computer and problem-solving skills are also valuable. It is important to be able to motivate people, to be patient and to be able to work on your own as well as within a team. Being up to date with health and safety issues is critical according to those working and running the industry. The Working in Fitness Survey 2005 revealed that all professions within the fitness industry believe personal appearance and attitude are also important.

Starting salary

The salary will vary according to whether you are an employee or self-employed. The average fitness instructor's salary is around £17,000 to £19,000. If you are self-employed it is possible, with appropriate qualifications and experience, to earn between £25 and £70 an hour. A successful self-employed personal trainer can earn around £90,000.

Jobs on qualification

Personal trainer. It is common practice for trainers to qualify in other areas of fitness, such as circuit training or aerobics, to create and expand their own personal professional fitness portfolio.

Current employment prospects ★ ★ ★ ★ ★

This is a growth industry. Employment prospects are good.

Is a career change a reality? ★ ★ ★ ★ ★

Welcomes older entrants? ★ ★ ★ ★ ★

Potential high earner? £ £ £ £

Useful contacts:

Register of Exercise Professionals
3rd Floor
8–10 Crown Hill
Croydon
Surrey
CR0 1RZ
020 8686 6464
www.exerciseregister.org

Fitness Industry Association
4th Floor
61 Southwark Street
London SE1 0HL
020 7202 4700
www.fia.org.uk

SkillsActive
Castlewood House
77–91 New Oxford Street
London WC1A 1PX
020 7632 2000
www.skillsactive.com

Central YMCA Qualifications (CYQ)
112 Great Russell Street
London WC1B 3NQ
020 7343 1800
www.cyq.org.uk

Premier Training International
Premier House
Willowside Park
Canal Road
Trowbridge
Wiltshire
BA14 8RH
01225 353535
www.premierglobal.co.uk

Premier International Qualifications
Unit 2
Willowside Park
Canal Road
Trowbridge
Wiltshire
BA14 8RH
01225 717256
www.premieriq.co.uk

City and Guilds
1 Giltspur Street
London EC1A 9DD
020 7294 2800
www.cityandguilds.com

OCR
02476 851509
www.ocr.org.uk

Physiotherapist

'Increasingly we are getting more people who are making big career changes, people who have worked in the City and now want a caring and more worthwhile position.'
Chartered Society of Physiotherapy.

The job

Physiotherapists are concerned with human function and movement, and maximising potential. They treat patients with physical problems caused by injury, illness and old age, especially those that are associated with the neuromuscular, musculoskeletal, cardiovascular and respiratory systems. Physiotherapists are experts in a number of different techniques such as manipulation and mobilisation, massage, hydrotherapy, exercise and electrotherapy such as ultrasound. Some may also be trained in complementary therapies and may be professionally qualified acupuncturists. They can be involved with helping a patient's mobility after surgery, for example, or with rehabilitation after an injury. Physiotherapists may also work with children with disabilities and older people who have problems with their mobility. The majority of newly qualified physiotherapists will work in the NHS, moving into private practice once they have built up some experience. One physiotherapist can run a private practice single-handedly, but some choose to work in partnerships of two or more.

Large private practices are increasingly becoming involved in training and supervising student physiotherapists, and if this trend continues it is likely that some may have openings for newly qualified basic-grade physiotherapists interested in starting out in private practice. But at the moment this is not the norm. Most newly qualified physiotherapists will start their career in the NHS.

The culture

Becoming a physiotherapist is an increasingly attractive option for career changers. But it has its downsides – it requires at least three years of full-time studying, more if you do not have an up-to-date A level in biology or human biology. And even after all that training the employment prospects for newly qualified physiotherapists in the NHS are currently looking very bleak. Although there are lots of work opportunities in the private sector, this is not a normal route for a newly qualified physiotherapist. The employment situation is not expected to change in the short term.

Do I need a degree?

Physiotherapy, like other branches of medicine, is a degree-entry profession. A physiotherapy degree will provide you with the training you need to become registered to practise in the UK. If you already have a degree in another subject, you are still going to have to go back to university to study for a second degree in physiotherapy.

Physiotherapy is a profession that is statutorily regulated and in order to practise as a physiotherapist you must register with the Health Professions Council. But in order to register you must graduate from a degree course which has been endorsed by the HPC. It is advisable to study for a degree that has also been approved by the Chartered Society of Physiotherapy – the professional organisation for physiotherapists. Graduates of CSP-accredited courses are automatically members of the CSP and have chartered physiotherapy status.

Minimum qualifications for the physiotherapy degree course are three A levels at minimum C grade, including one in a biological science, and five GCSEs in grades A to C including mathematics, English and science. There are also some **access courses** that can open the door to a physiotherapy degree. Details are available from individual universities.

An A level in human biology is becoming essential for all career changers hoping to become physiotherapists, even those who are graduates from other disciplines. Universities are increasingly realising that a good grade at A level, an A or B, is needed by mature students if they want to be capable of understanding the science in the first year of the degree. The **Open University foundation course in science** level 2 in either human biology and health or health disease is an alternative option to human biology A level. Some career changers may prefer this course because it offers a more practical route if they want to carry on in full-time employment while they study to complete the entry qualifications.

Although physiotherapy is a degree-entry profession, you could start as a physiotherapy assistant, which does not require a degree, and gain NHS sponsorship for a degree place. This is a common route into physiotherapy. You may be able to get onto a physiotherapy degree course if you are already working as a hospital physiotherapy assistant by seeking sponsorship from your NHS employer to fund study on a part-time physiotherapy degree course. Sponsored NHS places are available at five universities but competition for places will be tough. It is unlikely that a hospital trust would sponsor more than one physiotherapy assistant per academic year. The details are available on the NHS careers website.

An NHS bursary, which is means tested, is available to student physiotherapists in addition to other normal undergraduate funding for students on NHS-funded places. Tuition fees are paid.

What professional qualifications do I need?

Training is degree-based and takes three years full time or four as a part-time student. Some places on part-time courses are open to non-NHS-sponsored students so it is worth approaching the university course directors individually to assess what the chances are.

The Professional Footballers Association, the players' trade union, sponsors 10 places a year on the part-time physiotherapy degree course at Salford University, which takes four and a half years. The PFA has been running the initiative since 1992. To be considered for a place an applicant must be a member of the PFA. Past students include existing professional footballers who have the academic ability to study for the degree, players in their 30s in the twilight of their career and former players who have left the sport but are looking for a new career. The PFA sponsorship, which meets all the costs of the degree, is unconditional – there is no obligation on graduation to work for a football club or stay within the sport.

What personal skills do I need?

It is important to care about people and have an interest in health sciences. This is very much a people job, working sometimes with patients who are very stressed, so good communication skills are crucial. Being patient and understanding are also valuable personal skills. This is a profession where life experience counts. An older person may find that the demands of working as part of a multi-disciplinary team come more easily than they would to a younger graduate.

Starting salary

Pay scales for NHS physiotherapists are set nationally. A newly qualified physiotherapist, according to 2006 figures, starts on £19,166 and at the top of the profession a consultant physiotherapist can earn £88,397.

There are no set fees for physiotherapists in private practice. How much you charge very much depends on where you practise. A successful practice in central London for example might set fees at £50 per consultation or per assessment, but the fees might be half this amount elsewhere in the UK.

Jobs on qualification

The NHS is an obvious destination where physiotherapists can work in a range of different health environments. These include hospitals, GP practices and community clinics. Opportunities also exist in nursing homes and hospices working with the terminally ill. The private sector also offers other options with physiotherapists in private practice attached to private sports clinics or fitness centres. Private physiotherapists can either be employees or be self-employed. But both the CSP and the organisation which represents private physiotherapists, the Organisation of Chartered Physiotherapists in Private Practice, recommend NHS experience before establishing yourself as a private practitioner. It is common for NHS physiotherapists to work sessions in private practice as freelance physiotherapists to boost their income and experience.

Current employment prospects ★

Newly qualified physiotherapy students have recently found it difficult to find a job in the NHS. At the end of 2005, 50 per cent of newly qualified graduates were still looking for their first NHS post. The future employment prospects are not looking good, according to NHS Employers, the organisation that represents all NHS employers and which focuses on workforce issues. It believes some parts of the UK, such as Hull and East Anglia, are having less difficulty finding jobs for newly qualified physiotherapists, while other parts of the country, including the north-east, are struggling. It is warning mature students to be 'cautious' if they are considering switching careers in the near future.

The Organisation of Chartered Physiotherapists in Private Practice says employment opportunities in different kinds of practices are buoyant, but again recommends that it is desirable to gain NHS experience first. The Organisation of Chartered Physiotherapists in Private Practice, which has 3,300 members who also have to be members of the CSP, offers advice and support to members who are starting out in private practice. It also helps with continuing professional development.

Is a career change a reality? ★ ★ ★ ★ ★

Welcomes older entrants? ★ ★ ★ ★ ★

Potential high earner? £ £ £ £

Useful contacts:

Chartered Society of Physiotherapy
14 Bedford Row
London WC1R 4ED
020 7306 6666
www.csp.org.uk

NHS Careers
PO Box 376
Bristol
BS99 3EY
0845 606 0655
www.nhscareers.nhs.uk

Health Professions Council
Park House
184 Kennington Park Road
London SE11 4BU
020 7582 0866
www.hpc-uk.org

Organisation of Chartered Physiotherapists in Private Practice
PhysioFirst
Cedar House
The Bell Plantation
Watling Street
Towcaster
Northamptonshire
NN12 6HN
01327 354441
www.physiofirst.org.uk

PFA Education
2 Oxford Court
Bishopsgate
Manchester
M2 3WQ
0161 236 0637
education@thepfa.co.uk

Plumber

'Career changers don't stick out now in the trade, it's no longer unusual as it was a few years ago. It's an advantage being older because they are likely to be more serious about their training – especially if they have had to take a huge cut in salary.'
Charlie Mullins, managing director Pimlico Plumbers.

The job

There are three potential routes that a qualified plumber can take. A domestic plumber is responsible for installing and maintaining heating and hot and cold water systems as well as sanitation in houses and other residential properties. Plumbers can also choose to work in industrial and commercial workplaces, concentrating on designing, installing and maintaining complex sanitation systems and providing hot and cold water services to large buildings such as offices or schools. A third, more specialist route is to work as a sheet weathering plumber – developing and installing intricate weather systems to protect historic or listed buildings from the damage caused by rainwater. As the technology plumbers work with has become more complex, the academic requirements expected of plumbers have risen.

The culture

A national shortage of plumbers six years ago led to an abundance of stories about career changers, many of them trying to escape the demands of a high-flying City job, turning to this craft and pulling in £90,000 salaries. The high salaries were dismissed as 'myths' by those running the industry, but there were many columns in national newspapers and magazines about the benefits of swapping an office desk and a computer for a spanner and a blocked sink.

But today there are signs that the bubble in plumbing employment may have burst. The Association of Plumbing and Heating Contractors, an organisation that represents plumbers including sole traders, says that every year 1,500 new plumbers are needed to fill the gaps created through natural wastage and demand in the industry. But in January 2006 it reported there were 26,000 trainees on NVQ plumbing and heating courses, the nationally recognised training route into plumbing. Supply is outstripping demand, it says. At the same time SummitSkills, the sector skills council for the building services engineering sector, including plumbing, highlights another problem that could affect career changers considering plumbing. SummitSkills says there is an employment bottleneck in the industry for people who want to become plumbers, as there are not enough employers to offer places for trainees or apprentices in the work-based training they need to complete their NVQ qualification. With this in mind SummitSkills advises career changers to find an employer willing to offer them a trainee post before they enrol on their NVQ course.

The boss of one London plumbing company says half the letters he gets every week are from career changers offering to work for nothing in order to achieve the crucial work-based training they require to complete their NVQ.

SummitSkills is also warning would-be career changers, and others interested in training as plumbers, to be wary of rogue trainers who promise to train you to become a qualified plumber in just a few weeks. It cites the case of two adult trainees in West Yorkshire who took out a bank loan and handed over £10,000 for a plumbing course that promised they would be qualified in four weeks. Despite these potential problems, plumbing is a trade where career changers will not feel out of place. One central London plumbing company said recent trainees included career changers from such diverse backgrounds as journalism, banking, the charity sector and the army. But the clear advice to career changers from the industry is: find a company prepared to offer you an apprenticeship or training position first, before you give up your current job. And don't expect to earn a six-figure sum – £50,000 is more likely to be the top salary.

Do I need a degree?

You do not need a degree to be a plumber. It is a trade dependent on gaining work experience and undertaking work-based qualifications (see the entry under professional qualifications below).

What professional qualifications do I need?

The NVQ qualification is the most common route to becoming a qualified plumber. It is also the only qualification recognised by the industry and the government for plumbing, according to SummitSkills. The NVQ qualification is work-based learning offered in tandem with theory taught either on day or block release. But be aware that a certificate confirming a pass in the theory alone does not mean you are a qualified plumber. The theory has to be supported by on-the-job training so that you can prove you are competent at putting the theory into practice. The time it takes to qualify varies according to the work/college balance, but it can take three to four years.

The City and Guilds (6089) NVQ level 2 and 3 in mechanical engineering services: plumbing, and the City and Guilds (6129) technical certificate level 2 in basic plumbing skills and level 3 in plumbing studies are the gold-standard qualifications which will qualify you as a plumber. The City and Guilds certificates can be studied at further education colleges, at private training colleges or through distance learning, and will give you underpinning knowledge to join the trade. But on their own the certificates do not qualify you as a plumber – you have to find work-based experience in order to complete your NVQ qualification and prove your competency to work as a plumber. If you need to check whether your course is accredited, you should contact City and Guilds before enrolling on the course. It is worth checking with SummitSkills as well if you have any doubt about the course, or the provider, as it is compiling a list of rogue trainers.

What personal skills do I need?

Good customer relations are essential if you want to be a successful plumber. It is a job that requires you to be physically fit with the ability to work in confined spaces. You must also have a good head for heights. Good practical skills and the ability to solve problems are critical and you must be able to read technical drawings and plans.

Starting salary

A trainee plumber can earn between £10,000 and £25,000. The starting salary is really dependent on the employer – it is worked out according to how long they think it will take to train you. In some cases being a career changer is an advantage because taking you on as an adult apprentice may pose less of a risk – employers may think you are less likely to skip college than a school leaver and will qualify more quickly than somebody younger. The average income for a self-employed plumber is around £30,000; this can rise to around £50,000 in some parts of the UK after five years' experience.

Jobs on qualification

Plumbing is not a regulated industry so anybody can call themselves a plumber. However with the NVQ qualifications behind you the industry recognises you as a competent qualified tradesman.

Current employment prospects ★ ★ ★
Not as good as they were six years ago.

Is a career change a reality? ★ ★ ★ ★ ★

Welcomes older entrants? ★ ★ ★ ★ ★

Potential high earner? £ £ £

Useful contacts:

SummitSkills
Vega House
Opal Drive
Fox Milne
Milton Keynes
MK15 0DF
01908 303960
www.summitskills.org.uk

Institute of Plumbing and Heating Engineers
64 Station Lane
Hornchurch
Essex
RM12 6NB
01708 472791
www.plumbers.org.uk

Association of Plumbing and Heating Contractors
14 Ensign House
Ensign Business Centre
Westwood Way
Coventry
CV4 8JA
024 7647 0626
www.aphc.co.uk

City and Guilds
1 Giltspur Street
London EC1A 9DD
020 7294 2800
www.cityandguilds.com

Podiatrist/chiropodist

'The profession attracts career changers. Mature students make up about half the undergraduate intake. I think it appeals because it is a flexible profession which allows you to work in the NHS and the private sector.' The Society of Chiropodists and Podiatrists.

The job

A podiatrist is an alternative word for a chiropodist, and is the internationally recognised title for a specialist health professional trained to diagnose and treat abnormalities or disease of the foot and the lower leg. A podiatrist is skilled in giving advice about preventing foot problems and care of the foot. Podiatrists work with patients of all ages from children to older people. They also work with patients who have chronic conditions such as diabetes and arthritis and who are at risk from amputation. Podiatrists work in a variety of settings in the NHS including hospital departments or clinics, a GP surgery or health centre. Some may work in schools or nursing homes. After training podiatrists can choose to specialise, for example focusing on biomechanics (relying on mechanical methods in the diagnosis and treatment of the foot and lower limb) or working with children. Some go on to develop a career in surgery or sports injuries. There is also the option of working in private practice.

The culture

The profession is a common destination for career changers – around half of all undergraduates on podiatry degree courses are mature students. There is the option to study flexibly, so it can be an attractive choice if you want to stay in employment and study for your new career at the same time. Registered podiatrists can work both in the NHS and in private practice, so this career offers a variety of employment options. It is one of the few allied health professions offering a career in private practice. This might be especially appealing at a time when the NHS is facing widespread job cuts and vacancies are being frozen.

Do I need a degree?

Podiatry is a degree-entry profession so you will need A-level qualifications or equivalent in order to train. However, if you are interested in foot health it is possible to train as a **foot health practitioner** (see professional qualifications below), which does not require a degree, but you will not be entitled to call yourself a podiatrist or chiropodist as these are protected titles.

If you already have a degree in another subject you are going to have to complete another undergraduate degree in podiatry in order to practise as a podiatrist. There are 13 schools of podiatry where you can complete a podiatry degree that has been validated by the Society of Chiropodists and Podiatrists, entitling you to professional registration and allowing you to practise. The courses include 1,000 hours of clinical study. Graduation from an accredited degree entitles you to membership of the Society of Chiropodists and Podiatrists. The full-time degree course takes three years but there are options to study part time at Salford and Huddersfield Universities, based on two days a week attendance over four and a half years. Another option is to take the 'flexi-route' to qualification offered by Southampton University, where students can complete the degree in three years studying three days a week. The lengths of academic terms on the flexi-route at Southampton are longer than those of the traditional three-year full-time degree course. Entry requirements vary and it is best to contact individual schools for details or the University and Colleges Admissions Service (UCAS). Mature students are encouraged to apply but they will be expected to have evidence of some recent academic study. They are also usually expected to have the equivalent of A level biology and it is common for schools to request a C grade.

If you are accepted onto one of the courses at the 13 schools of podiatry, the NHS will pay your course tuition fees. You will also be eligible for a means-tested bursary to help fund your study. The amount of bursary you receive is dependent on income, so will vary from student to student. Students on part-time degree courses will be eligible for 75 per cent of the full bursary.

What professional qualifications do I need?

A degree in podiatry which is recognised by the HPC and validated by the Society of Chiropodists and Podiatrists brings professional registration with the HPC, which entitles you to practise and call yourself a podiatrist or chiropodist.

To become a foot health practitioner you should complete the **diploma in foot health practice** run by the College of Foot Health Practitioners. The diploma, based on 10 modules and 11 days' clinical practice, is delivered through distance learning. The course fee is £1,950 and the qualification can be completed in a year. Foot health practitioners are trained in basic foot care, focusing on common conditions affecting the foot and leg such as verrucas, corns, hard skin and callous. They often work in private practice. Completion of the College of Foot Health Practitioners diploma entitles you to put your name on the voluntary register for foot health practitioners which is held by the Alliance of Private Sector Chiropody and Podiatry Practitioners.

What personal skills do I need?

Like other allied health professions, working as a podiatrist is a people-oriented profession, so you must have excellent interpersonal and communication skills. It is important to have a caring nature and to be sensitive. You must be able to work on your own as well as in a team. If you work in private practice, you must have an understanding of business skills.

Starting salary

An NHS graduate podiatrist salary starts at £19,166. Podiatrists who work in private practice can earn around £40 an hour.

Jobs on qualification

A professionally qualified podiatrist or chiropodist.

Current employment prospects ★ ★ ★

Historically the career prospects for qualified podiatrists have been good. The Society of Chiropodists and Podiatrists says around 75 per cent of student graduates who want to go straight into employment find work within four months of qualifying. There is a 100 per cent employment rate within nine months of graduation. In 2006/7 career prospects are unpredictable because of the deficits that NHS trusts are facing. However, unlike some other allied health professions, there is the opportunity in podiatry to move into private practice to boost income and many podiatrists develop a career in both the public and private sectors.

Is a career change a reality? ★ ★ ★ ★ ★

Although the profession is graduate entry there are flexible study options. As an undergraduate on an NHS-funded degree course your tuition fees are paid and you are also eligible for a means-tested bursary which can help soften the financial blow of returning to study.

Welcomes older entrants? ★ ★ ★ ★ ★

Half the students on podiatry degree courses are mature students and the schools encourage applications from older entrants.

Potential high earner? £ £ £

With experience a principal NHS podiatrist can earn from £35,232. More senior NHS clinical roles can command salaries of between £49,381 and £88,000. Podiatrists who work in private practice earn an average £40 an hour, but as in any small business, success and income is determined by local demand and personal professional reputation.

Useful contacts:

NHS Careers
PO Box 376
Bristol
BS99 3EY
0845 606 0655
www.nhscareers.nhs.uk

The Society of Chiropodists and Podiatrists
1 Fellmonger's Path
Tower Bridge Road
London SE1 3LY
020 7234 8620
www.feetforlife.org

Health Professions Council
Park House
184 Kennington Park Road
London SE11 4BU
020 7582 0866
www.hpc-uk.org

The Alliance of Private Sector Chiropody and Podiatry Practitioners
01492 535795
www.thealliancepsp.com

The College of Foot Health Practitioners
Market Chambers
Blackheath
Rowley Regis
B65 0HP
01225 590180
www.collegefgp.com

Universities and Colleges Admissions Service (UCAS)
Customer Services Unit
UCAS
PO Box 28
Cheltenham
GL52 3LZ
0870 1122211
www.ucas.com

Publican

'If you are thinking of running your own pub then get some experience of the trade first – it's not as rosy as everybody thinks from the other side of the bar.' Tony Payne, chief executive of the Federation of Licensed Victuallers Associations.

The job

Being a publican is a 365-day-a-year job. According to Tony Payne, the chief executive of the Federation of Licensed Victuallers Associations (FLVA), anybody keen to run their own pub should see it as a way of life rather than a job.

There are four options if you want to run a pub. The first option is to work for a brewery, or for a pub management company as a pub manager. If you decide to go down this route, you remain an employee and you would be paid a salary linked to your pub's profits. The company is responsible for decisions around how the business is run and looks after things such as stocktaking, deliveries, auditing, accounts and promotions. Mitchells and Butlers, which manages around 1,400 pub restaurants and bars across the UK, says it is increasingly getting enquiries from career changers – often businessmen or women or those with a background in retail – who want to manage their own pub.

Your second career option is to become a pub tenant, renting a pub from a brewery or a pub management company on a short-term contract, usually for two or three years. You would be interviewed by the brewery or pub management company and would be expected to come up with a good business plan to support your application. The rental terms vary but you would pay a price that included the pub's fixtures and fittings and its stock. You should expect to part with at least £10,000. The amount will be higher if it includes an amount for any business 'goodwill' the pub has built up. As a tenant you will be responsible for the upkeep of the pub and you will have some freedom in developing the future shape of the business.

Alternatively, you might decide to become a pub leaseholder. Although this is similar to a tenant arrangement the main difference is that the agreement would be for a longer period – commonly between 10 and 20 years. The minimum capital investment for a leasehold pub would be around £20,000.

The final option open to you – which requires the biggest capital investment and brings the highest risk, but gives you total control over the business – is to buy a pub freehold. Prices vary across the UK, according to where the pub is and the success of the business. Few freehold pubs come onto the market but if you are keen to go down this road it would be best to contact a specialist agent (see useful contacts below).

The best advice for career changers thinking of going into the pub trade comes from the FLVA – whichever option you choose, it recommends that you build up experience behind a bar first before switching careers.

The culture

It is common for people in their 40s or 50s to enquire about running their own pub and, according to one brewery, it especially appeals to parents once their children have left home. There are four career paths you can take if you want to run your own pub. Only one option - being employed as a manager by a pub managemnt company - does not require capital investment and personal financial risk. The risks are highest if you decide to go down the freehold route. There are national specialist business agents like Fleurets and Christie and Co. which sell leasehold and freehold pubs; their details are listed below. Contact information for other regional specialist agents can be found in trade magazines. If you do not want to go through an agent it is also possible to apply directly to a brewery if you are keen to run one of its pubs as a tenant or leaseholder. The professional and financial rewards from running your own pub can be great but, like any other small business, those in the trade warn that it requires hard work and personal commitment around the clock.

Do I need a degree?

You do not need a degree to become a licensed publican.

What professional qualifications do I need?

Under the Licensing Act 2003, in order to become a licensed publican you need to obtain a personal licence. In order to qualify for a licence you must pass the **National Certificate for Personal Licence Holders (NCPLH)** qualification. Training is provided by private or college providers and takes a day to complete. Fees are in the region of £145 to £225. The qualification is based on a written exam lasting 40 minutes. Once you have the qualification you can apply for a personal licence from your local council. A criminal records check is also part of the application process. The licence is valid for 10 years. All freeholders and some leaseholders and tenants, depending on the terms of their agreement, will also need to apply for a **premises licence** in their name.

What personal skills do I need?

Excellent people and communication skills are essential. Your personality can determine the success – or failure – of your business. You must be prepared to work hard. Unless you are in a manager role, as a self-employed publican you are responsible for the business 365 days of the year. You must have good people management skills, as you will be responsible for staff. Your numeracy skills should be excellent and you should have good general small-business skills. Knowledge of alcohol and the law is also essential. You must be able to work under pressure and stay calm in a crisis. You should have strong leadership skills and it helps to have an interest in food and drink. Tolerance is valuable, as well as an element of understanding, but it is also important to be firm, otherwise according to the FLVA 'the customers will run the pub – not you.' It is also important, says the FLVA, to be 'personally disciplined' about your own alcohol habits.

Starting salary

A pub manager's salary is usually a basic amount plus a share of pub profits. A successful pub manager can earn from £35,000 and boost their income with bonuses. The salary of a tenant or leasehold publican depends on the profits of the pub and the terms of the lease or tenancy agreement but they can expect to clear an annual profit of more than £30,000 and up to around £80,000. A freehold publican has the potential to earn more, but again, as in any small business, the profits can vary.

Jobs on qualification

A pub manager; a pub tenant; a pub leaseholder or a pub freeholder.

Current employment prospects ★ ★ ★ ★

Changes to the licensing laws which have increased licensing opening hours have in turn boosted job and career opportunities in this sector. Career prospects are good.

Is a career change a reality? ★ ★ ★ ★ ★

As in any other small business, running your own pub, as a manager, tenant or freehold landlord, requires a tremendous amount of hard work. It also requires significant capital investment if you choose to become a tenant, leaseholder or freeholder.

Welcomes older entrants? ★ ★ ★ ★ ★

It is a common choice for people in their 40s and 50s to decide to run their own pub.

Potential high earner? ££-££££

Unless you work as an employed pub manager, where you will be paid a salary, your income will be directly determined by the success of your pub. The trade is potentially a high earner, with annual profits of around £80,000 in some cases. But, according to one brewery, the average profit is more likely to be in the region of £30,000 a year.

Useful contacts:

The British Institute of Inn Keeping
Wessex House
80 Park Street
Camberley
Surrey
GU15 3PT
01276 684449
www.bii.org

Federation of Licensed Victuallers Associations
126 Bradford Road
Brighouse
West Yorkshire
HD6 4AU
01484 710534
www.flva.co.uk

British Beer and Pub Association
Market Towers
Nine Elms Lane
London SW8 5NQ
020 7627 9199
www.beerandpub.com

Campaign For Real Ale (CAMRA)
230 Hatfield Road
St Albans
Hertfordshire
AL1 4LW
01727 867201
www.camra.org.uk

Christie and Co.
39 Victoria Street
London SW1H 0EU
020 7227 0700
www.christie.com

Fleurets
4 Roger Street
London WC1N 2JX
020 7280 4700
www.fleurets.com

Schoolteacher

'Being paid while you train certainly makes a difference to a career changer like me.'
Secondary school science teacher career changer.

The job

Schoolteachers can either work as primary teachers with children aged 5 to 11 or with secondary schoolchildren aged between 11 and 19. Secondary schoolteachers will usually specialise in one or two subjects, teaching them to classes of children of different ages and abilities. Primary schoolteachers will deliver lessons which reflect the national curriculum but may also have a specialist subject which they will coordinate throughout the school.

Whatever school teachers work in, their working day continues after the school day ends with time spent preparing lessons and marking work. Teachers also have to liaise with other professionals from different agencies, and commit to in-service training and continuing professional development. According to the teacher trade unions, it is a job that requires commitment and a lot of hard work. It is a myth to believe it offers short days and long paid holidays and is an easy option for a part-time job leading into retirement, they say. The main drawbacks to teaching, according to the profession, are constant government-led changes, and indiscipline of students. But 90 per cent of teachers put the reward of seeing childrens' achievements as the biggest benefit of the job.

The culture

More than a third of newly qualified teachers are aged over 30, according to the Training and Development Agency for Schools, and a third of all secondary teachers who are career changers come from a background in senior management, while another 22 per cent have held other middle-ranking management or professional roles. The statistics suggest that teaching is a common destination for career changers. The government has also tried to make it financially attractive to mature entrants by offering non-means-tested bursaries, unlike bursaries for NHS students, which are means-tested. 'Golden hellos' are also available to all newly qualified teachers in subjects where there are skills shortages.

There are three training routes into teaching with career changers in mind: the registered teacher programme, the school-centred initial teacher training, and the graduate teacher programme. They offer a salary while training and there is no obligation to stay on with the school after qualifying. However, none of these training options comes with a guaranteed job at the end of training. Once qualified it will still be up to you to find a job, although it is common for career changers on these courses to find permanent employment with the school that trained them.

Do I need a degree?

The most common route into teaching is to study for a degree, either a BEd or a BA or BSc with Qualified Teacher Status, which can take between two and four years. The minimum entry requirements for anybody wanting to train as a teacher are a grade C in GCSE maths and English (or equivalent). Anybody born after 1979 who wants to train to teach 7–14-year-olds must also have a GCSE (or equivalent) grade C in science. There is however some flexibility; if you do not have these qualifications you may be able to enrol on a training course if you pass a pre-entry test set by the course provider.

The traditional route is to go back to university and study for a postgraduate certificate of education which usually takes a year. The PGCE will give you **Qualified Teacher Status (QTS)**, which you require in order to be able to teach in a maintained school.

However, there are two other training routes for graduates who want to maintain an income while they retrain. They are the **graduate teacher programme (GTP)** and the **school-centred initial teacher training (SCITT)** programme. Competition for both these schemes is fierce. The GTP leads to QTS and takes from three months, if you have some past teaching experience, up to a maximum one year if you are completely new to teaching. You will first have to find a school that is willing to take you on and support your training. This can be achieved either by replying to a training post advertised as part of the GTP scheme or by applying through your local Designated Recommended Body (details of DRBs can be found on the Training and Development Agency for Schools website). GTP schemes provide on-the-job teacher training in the classroom with the support of other qualified teachers who act as mentors and trainers. As part of the GTP initiative you will also be expected to complete some of your studying at a teacher training college or university. While you are training, the school will pay you at least £14,040. Like other NQTs you will have to complete a year-long induction before your professional training is complete. If you are already working as a teaching assistant you may be able to persuade your school to put you on a GTP, provided you have a degree, so that you can go on to qualify as a teacher.

The SCITT initiative is also aimed at graduates and is provided by a consortium of schools and colleges working together. Unlike the GTP scheme, training is delivered exclusively in schools with teachers acting as mentors and trainers. While training you are likely to be based in a 'lead school' with practice placements taking place at other schools in the consortium. SCITT training runs for one academic year. A tax-free non-means-tested bursary of between £6,000 and £9,000 is available. Applications and more details about SCITT should be made through the Graduate Teacher Training Registry (see below for contact details).

If you are thinking of completing the postgraduate certificate in education as the first step in your career change into teaching, then the OU is a possibility if you live in England or Wales. It offers the PGCE in six subjects – a modern foreign language (specialising in German, French or Spanish); geography; mathematics; music; science; and design and technology. The programme is recognised by the Department for Education and Skills and the Training and Development Agency for Schools. Most students who take this route have their tuition fees paid by the TDA, according to the OU. There is also the possibility of training bursaries, up to a maximum £9,000. More details are available from the OU and the TDA.

What professional qualifications do I need?

Teaching is a graduate-entry profession, and you must have achieved Qualified Teacher Status before you are entitled to teach in a state school. However, a non-graduate career changer who wants to become a qualified teacher and who has some higher education training or qualifications can still enter the profession if they take the **registered teacher programme (RTP)** route. This scheme has been developed by the government, and is aimed specifically at career changers, but you must be working in a school as an unqualified teacher in order to be considered for a place. You must also have the statutory minimum requirements at GCSE level (or equivalent) and have completed two years of higher education such as a Higher National Diploma (HND) or the first two years of a bachelor's degree. To obtain QTS on this programme will take at least a year, if you have some previous teaching experience, or two years if you are a novice. Like the GTP scheme, it offers entrants a guaranteed salary of at least £13,599 while training. To get onto an RTP you have to find a school that is willing to take you on as an unqualified teacher and to support you through the programme. You can do this either by approaching a school directly or looking for job advertisements that promote the RTP. Alternatively contact your local education authority to see if any RTP opportunities are available. Once you have found a school to take you on under the RTP, you then have to apply to your local Designated Recommended Body (DRB). Details of your local DRB can be found on the Training and Development Agency for Schools website (see useful contacts listed below). The DRB will assess your application and decide what further academic study you require to meet QTS standards. It is also possible that if you cannot find a school that will offer you an RTP training place, the DRB may be able to find a placement for you instead. Competition for these places is fierce.

If you want to specialise and become a special educational needs (SEN) teacher, you need two years' post-QTS experience and you must then take a Masters degree or a postgraduate diploma in special educational needs. If you specifically wish to teach children who are visually or hearing impaired or have multiple sensory deprivation you will also have to study for a specific postgraduate diploma or Masters degree. The Department for Education and Skills currently has eight approved universities for delivering these specialist teaching qualifications, which can be studied either one year full time or three years part time. Skills in sign language or braille are also compulsory for specialist teachers where appropriate.

To become a music teacher you will need the QTS qualification to teach in a state school, and you are also likely to be expected to have achieved at least a grade 6 in your chosen instrument.

What personal skills do I need?

It is important to have an interest in education, and to like children and be able to empathise with them. Enthusiasm for the subject or subjects you teach is also important. Good management skills are critical, as well as good communication skills and patience. Personal skills are more important than previous experience.

Starting salary

A newly qualified teacher can earn a minimum £19,023 outside London and £22,611 in the capital. With experience the salaries rise to £32,391 outside London to £38,634 in London. Additional payments are made for additional school or teaching responsibilities. A secondary head teacher can earn more than £90,000 depending on the size of the school.

'Golden hellos' worth between £4,000 and £5,000 are also available to postgraduate NQTs who are trained to teach maths, science, modern languages, English and drama, design and technology, religious education, music and ICT.

Jobs on qualification

You will be qualified to teach in a maintained (i.e. state) primary or secondary school.

Current employment prospects ★ ★ ★ ★

High in some subjects where there are shortages, such as maths and science.

Is a career change a reality? ★ ★ ★ ★ ★

Welcomes older entrants? ★ ★ ★ ★ ★

Potential high earner? £ £ £

Useful contacts:

Training and Development Agency for Schools
Portland House
Bressenden Place
London SW1E 5TT
www.tda.gov.uk

Teaching Information Line (information advice line for anybody interested in becoming a teacher)
0845 6000991

Department for Education and Skills (DfES)
There are offices in London, Sheffield, Darlington and Runcorn.
www.dfes.gov.uk

Graduate Teacher Training Registry
Rosehill
New Barn Lane
Cheltenham
Gloucestershire
GL52 3LZ
0870 112 2205
www.gttr.ac.uk

General Teaching Council for England
Whittington House
19-30 Alfred Place
London WC1E 7EA
0870 0010308
www.gtce.org.uk

General Teaching Council for Scotland
Clerwood House
96 Clermiston Road
Edinburgh
EH12 6UT
0131 314 6000
www.gtcs.org.uk

General Teaching Council for Wales (GTCW)
4th Floor
Southgate House
Wood Street
Cardiff
CF10 1EW
029 2055 0350
www.gtcw.org.uk

National Association of Schoolmasters and Union of Women Teachers (NASUWT)
Hillscourt Education Centre
Rose Hill
Rednal
Birmingham
B45 8RS
0121 453 6150
www.teachersunion.org.uk

National Union of Teachers (NUT)
Hamilton House
Mabledon Place
London WC1H 9BD
020 7388 6191
www.teachers.org.uk

Education website for teachers and schools
www.teachernet.gov.uk

Northern Ireland Department of Education
Rathgael House
43 Balloo Road
Bangor
County Down
BT19 7PR
www.deni.gov.uk

Universities and Colleges Admissions Service (UCAS)
Customer Services Unit
UCAS
PO Box 28
Cheltenham
GL52 3LZ
0870 1122211
www.ucas.com

Enquiries about Open University study and help with registering for your course:
Student Registration & Enquiry Service
The Open University
PO Box 197
Milton Keynes
MK7 6BJ
general-enquiries@open.ac.uk
0870 333 4340 (Monday to Friday 08.30 to 21.00 and Saturday 09.00 to 17.00)

OU headquarters:
The Open University
Walton Hall
Milton Keynes
MK7 6AA
01908 274066
www.open.ac.uk

Social worker

'Mature applicants are welcome to study social work and many thousands of mature students have successfully qualified.' The General Social Care Council.

The job

Social work is a people-centred profession. It is also demanding and can be emotionally draining, but it can bring huge professional satisfaction. Social workers can work for a local authority, for a charity or other voluntary organisation, or for a private provider of social care. They can choose to work with a range of different clients: children and families, adults, offenders, people with mental health problems, and those who have learning difficulties or a disability. They often work as part of a multi-professional team in partnership with voluntary organisations and other statutory agencies such as the health, probation or youth justice services, as well as schools. Roles include carrying out client assessments, organising and managing packages of care and, where necessary, writing reports, sometimes linked to court action, as well as keeping up-to-date client records. Social workers split their time between working in an office and visiting clients at home or in a number of other locations such as health centres, court or day centres. The working hours can be irregular.

The culture

Both the government and the professional organisation, the British Association of Social Workers (BASW), are keen to attract people into social work from diverse backgrounds, age groups and cultures. But anyone considering moving into this profession will have to go to university, because in 2003 it became a degree-entry profession. The degree entitles you to register with the regulatory body, the General Social Care Council (GSCC) in England or the equivalent body in the other UK countries, which in turn entitles you to practise as a social worker. Without registration you are unable to work. The BASW says it is difficult for career changers to move into the profession because of the commitment to study and because, on graduation, salary levels are not high. Career changers are going to have to be determined and be prepared to see their income fall, especially at the beginning of their new career, if they want to become qualified social workers. But career changers will be welcomed by BASW because it believes a more diverse social care workforce enriches the profession, which in turn benefits those most vulnerable people who are being cared for.

Do I need a degree?

The social work degree takes three years full time and students are entitled to an annual non-means-tested bursary towards the cost of study. For 2006/7 the bursary was £4,000 for those studying outside London or £4,400 if you are a London student.

Unlike in previous years, from 2006 social work undergraduate students have to pay their tuition fees. If you study part time you are entitled to 50 per cent of the bursary. You should contact the GSCC for more details if you plan to study in England, or the equivalent organisations in other UK countries. The degree must be endorsed by the GSCC in England (or equivalent bodies in other UK countries) so that it entitles you to professional registration, which means you can practise as a social worker. The GSCC has details of recommended degrees on its website (see useful contacts below). An employment-based route to the social work degree and professional registration is another option (see details under professional qualifications).

A social work degree is not necessary in order to become a professional social worker. However, you must complete either a **postgraduate diploma in social care** or an **MA in social care**, which can be studied two years full time, or three years part time. The postgraduate qualifications must be endorsed by the GSCC in England or the equivalent bodies in the other UK countries. A non-means-tested bursary, a contribution towards tuition fees and a means-tested maintenance grant are available to help towards the cost of studying. For 2006/7 in England the non-means-tested bursary available if you are studying outside London on a full-time course is £2,500, or £2,900 in London. There is an additional £3,162 tuition fee contribution available, wherever you are studying, and a means-tested maintenance grant to the value of £2,450 outside London or £3,745 inside London. A proportion of the financial support is available if you are studying part time, but you will not be entitled to a maintenance grant. For more details you should contact the GSCC or equivalent organisation in other UK countries. Details of postgraduate diplomas and MA courses are available from the GSCC website. An employment-based route to the social work degree and professional registration is another option for graduates.

What professional qualifications do I need?

A number of local authorities offer an **employment route** into professional social care by running sponsored trainee social worker schemes. Under this initiative, the council pays trainees a salary while they are studying for the social work degree. It is usually tied to a commitment to work for the council during university vacations and after graduation for a specified number of years. This is a popular option, especially for people already working in social care, such as a social care assistant who wants to progress, but it is also an option for career changers who want to maintain a source of income while studying. All sponsorship packages differ slightly, so it is best to contact local authorities direct to see if they offer this route into the profession or keep a lookout for trainee social worker posts in advertisements in newspapers, for example in Society Guardian every Wednesday or the Guardian's jobs website (www.guardian.co.uk). If you are sponsored to study for the social work degree you are not entitled to the non-means-tested bursary that is available to other social work degree students. The **Open University** offers a BA honours in social work degree which has to be completed in at least three years. It is a work-based learning route to the professional social work qualification but is only open to students who are already working in social care. If you want to take the OU route to professional qualification, the application for the course has to come from the employing authority.

What personal skills do I need?

A caring, non-judgemental personality is important. Excellent communication skills are essential so you can put people at their ease. You must be a good listener and be able to explain complex information simply. The ability to work as part of a team is essential, as most social workers belong to multi-disciplinary teams and care packages are likely to be dependent on contributions from different agencies. Patience is important, and the ability to cope with bureaucracy and not baulk at report writing and other essential administration. Good time-management and organisational skills are also key.

Starting salary

Salaries will vary depending on the needs of different parts of the UK and where the skills shortages are. Some local authorities, especially those in London and the metropolitan areas, offer 'golden hellos' in an attempt to attract newly qualified staff. But on average the starting salary for a newly qualified social worker is in the region of £18,000.

Jobs on qualification

One of the biggest attractions of becoming a social worker is that the profession offers a wide range of possible career paths across the public and voluntary sectors. Qualified social workers are often employed by local authorities, but there are also social work career opportunities in the NHS, both in hospitals and in the community. You could work as part of a community drugs and alcohol team, or have links with schools working with the education authority. The youth offending service, which works with young offenders or those at risk of offending, is particularly keen to attract staff from diverse backgrounds and offers another possible career option on qualifying. Charities also employ qualified social workers. As multi-agency team-working increases and the barriers between different statutory and non-statutory organisations breaks down, career movement between the different agencies and sectors is becoming easier.

Current employment prospects ★ ★ ★ ★ ★

Good. The government has a continuing recruitment campaign for social workers and local authorities frequently report difficulty in recruiting qualified social workers. The government is also committed to moving care out of hospital into the community, which should bring an increase in demand for community-based social care and healthcare professionals.

Is a career change a reality? ★ ★ ★ ★ ★

Although social work is a degree-entry profession, there are flexible routes to qualification and funding packages are available whether you take the postgraduate or undergraduate route. With employment-based routes to qualification available as well, it is a career change that could appeal to many people.

Welcomes older entrants? ★ ★ ★ ★ ★

Both the government and the British Association of Social Workers, which represents the profession, are keen to see people from diverse backgrounds and of different ages and cultures come into social work.

Potential high earner? £ £

Useful contacts:

British Association of Social Workers
16 Kent Street
Birmingham
B5 6RD
0121 622 3911
www.basw.co.uk

General Social Care Council (GSCC)
Goldings House
2 Hay's Lane
London SE1 2HB
020 7397 5100
Bursaries helpline: 020 7397 5835
www.gscc.org.uk

Scottish Institute for Excellence in Social Work Education (the Institute)
University of Dundee
Gardyne Road Campus
Dundee
DD5 1NY
01382 464980
www.sieswe.org

Social Care Association
Thornton House
Hook Road
Surbiton
Surrey
KT6 5AN
020 8397 1411
www.socialcaring.co.uk

Universities and Colleges Admissions Service (UCAS)
Rosehill
New Barn Lane
Cheltenham
Gloucestershire
GL52 3LZ
0870 1122211
www.ucas.com

Social Work and Care Careers
0845 604 6404
www.socialworkcareers.co.uk

Skills for Care (England)
Albion Court
5 Albion Place
Leeds
LS1 6JL
0113 245 1716
www.skillsforcare.org.uk

Scottish Social Services Council (SSSC)
Compass House
11 Riverside Drive
Dundee
DD1 4NY
01382 207101
www.sssc.uk.com

Care Council for Wales (CCW)
South Gate House
Wood Street
Cardiff
CF10 1EW
029 2022 6257
www.ccwales.org.uk

Northern Ireland Social Care Council (NISCC)
7th Floor Millennium House
Great Victoria Street
Belfast
BT2 7AQ
028 9041 7600

Community Service Volunteers (CSV)
237 Pentonville Road
London N1 9NJ
020 7278 6601
www.csv.org.uk

Teacher of English as a foreign language

'It's becoming increasingly more common to have students in their 30s and 40s and even in their 50s either looking for a new career or for something which they can do additionally which allows them to work and travel at the same time.' Max Loach, St George International School London.

The job

Teaching English as a foreign language (Tefl) involves teaching English to students whose first language is not English, using English as the language of instruction and delivery. Lessons focus on four key areas: understanding, speaking, writing and reading.

There are three career paths for specialist English language teachers. Teachers who teach English as a foreign language (Tefl) can work in the UK or abroad. Their students are often seeking to prepare for exams or perhaps improve their language to gain entry to a UK university. There may also be other students who need to use the language in their job and to improve their career prospects. Secondly, it is possible to become a teacher who teaches English to speakers of other languages (Tesol). In this case your students would be adults or children whose first language is not English. Traditionally you would be teaching adults and children who need to improve their language skills in order to apply for residence or remain resident in the UK. This group of students could include asylum seekers and refugees and you would be likely to work in the public or voluntary sectors, in state schools or adult education centres or institutions. Thirdly you could qualify as a teacher of English for a specific purpose (TESP) where you teach English with a particular focus, such as English for medicine, business or law. Whichever kind of English language teacher route you decide to take, you are likely to be working with small groups or individual students in the private or public sector in the UK or abroad. Teachers are expected to prepare lessons and activities to be taught in English. They may develop their own teaching resources or use established ones.

The culture

A professional qualification that entitles you to teach English as a foreign language may be your passport to global travel and, although it was a traditional career option for new graduates, it is becoming an increasingly popular choice for older career changers. The career path appeals because of the flexibility it offers, as teachers can work in private language schools, as home tutors or, with additional qualifications, in other settings including further education colleges. But perhaps its biggest draw is that it creates the chance to work and travel the world at the same time. Qualification is quick – the two most common professional teaching courses can be completed in four weeks full time. It is also a reasonably cheap career change, as the most you will be expected to pay is £1,000, with some courses on offer at around £650.

Do I need a degree?

It is not necessary to have a degree to be a teacher of English as a foreign language. The minimum academic requirements for completing the most common Tefl or Tesol courses in the UK, which are seen as the minimum professional standard required, are two A levels or equivalent. However, if you want to be a Tesol teacher and teach in a state school or further education college you will have to obtain Qualified Teacher Status (see directory entry on Schoolteacher for more information). All new teachers in FE are also expected to complete a level 4 certificate in FE teaching at stage 3 and a certificate for ESOL subject specialists. There is the option of studying Tefl or Tesol at degree level. (Contact the University and Colleges Admissions Service for more details.)

What professional qualifications do I need?

There are two widely recognised minimum qualifications in the UK with global recognition which will put you on the first step of your new career as a Tefl, Tesol or TESP teacher. They are the **Cambridge certificate in English language teaching to adults (CELTA)** or the **Trinity College London certificate in teaching English to speakers of other languages (CertTESOL)**. If you are keen to teach younger students then you should also complete the **Cambridge certificate in English language teaching to young learners (CELTYL)** – a qualification which will give you the skills to teach children up to the age of 16. But if you plan to teach children in a state school or intend to work in a further education college you will also need to complete a qualification which gives you Qualified Teacher Status (see directory entry on Schoolteacher for more information about QTS). All new teachers in FE are also expected to complete a level 4 certificate in FE teaching at stage 3 and a certificate for ESOL subject specialists.

The CELTA qualification can be completed fast-track, four weeks full time, while it can take between four and ten weeks full time for the CertTESOL. Alternatively both qualifications can be studied part time over a year. Courses are run by private providers as well as some state colleges or universities. Details of providers and centres are available from the examination boards (see useful contacts below). The general advice from the British Council is to complete a Tefl certificate if you plan to teach English abroad or a Tesol qualification if you want to work in the UK. The **Trinity licentiate diploma** in TESOL and the **Cambridge diploma in language teaching to adults** are also available as qualifications for professional development. They are aimed at ambitious teachers, usually with at least two years' experience, who want to move into top management posts or write course material. The British

Council is a useful resource if you are interested in a career change in Tefl or Tesol. The organisation accredits English language schools in the UK in both the private and state sectors. The British Council has accredited more than 400 UK schools.

What personal skills do I need?

It is essential to have a good level of spoken English as well as good grammar. As in any teaching role your communication skills should be excellent. Patience and enthusiasm for language are essential and a good sense of humour would be useful. It is important to be confident and to have an understanding of different cultures and nationalities. It is not essential to have a second language although this is useful because it gives you an understanding of the difficulties or issues people face in learning a language that is not their native one.

Starting salary

Teachers of English as a foreign language in the UK could earn from £12,000, but the work is usually on a short-term contract or paid by the hour or week. Working outside the UK the salary varies enormously. Rates of pay are usually lower than in the UK and can be in the region of £5,500 in Bosnia, £7,500 in China. If you work in the EU you might earn up to £18 an hour. However these figures are only a rough guide and you must bear in mind that packages may include accommodation and flights. Professionally qualified teachers of English as a second language in schools and colleges in the UK can earn from £15,000 to £23,000, rising to £36,000 with 10 years' experience.

Jobs on qualification

With appropriate professional qualifications you will be able to teach English in a variety of settings within the UK and abroad. This could be as a teacher in a private language school, language centre or state further education college. There are also opportunities to work as a home tutor or with international businesses or government departments. As a teacher of English as a second language you are more likely to work in the state sector or for voluntary organisations with students who are asylum seekers or refugees.

The British Council employs 2,000 teachers of English in 90 language centres across the world. They are established in European cities including Paris, Barcelona and Madrid, but there are others in China, Asia and South America.

Current employment prospects ★ ★ ★ ★

The number of people across the world who want or need to use English is growing. Career prospects are good.

Is a career change a reality? ★ ★ ★ ★ ★

This is a practical career change that can be made quickly with little expense and open the door to work opportunities across the world.

Welcomes older entrants? ★ ★ ★ ★ ★

Language colleges and examination boards say it is becoming increasingly common for older people to train to become teachers of English as a foreign language. It is particularly appealing to people approaching retirement who see it as a way of combining travel with the opportunity to work around the world.

Potential high earner? £ £

This is not a high-earning career but it does create the opportunity for travel if you decide to teach English as a foreign language.

Useful contacts:

University of Cambridge ESOL Exams
1 Hills Road
Cambridge
CB1 2EU
01223 555355
www.cambridgeesol.org

Trinity College London
89 Albert Embankment
London SE1 7TP
020 7820 6100
www.trinitycollege.co.uk

International Association of Teachers of English as a Foreign Language (IATEFL)
Darwin College
University of Kent
Canterbury
Kent
CT2 7NY
01227 824430
www.iatefl.org

British Council
10 Spring Gardens
London SW1A 2BN
020 7939 8466
www.britishcouncil.org

Information on qualifications:
www.britishcouncil.org/teacherrecruitment-tefl-qualifications-tefl-or-tesol.htm

EnglishUK
50 Buckingham Gate
London SW1E 6AG
020 7802 9200
www.englishuk.com

National Association for Teaching English and other Community Languages to Adults
(NATECLA)
South Birmingham College
Room HB110
Hall Green Campus
Cole Bank Road
Hall Green
Birmingham B28 8ES
0121 688 8121
www.natecla.org.uk

University and Colleges Admissions Service (UCAS)
Customer Services Unit
UCAS
PO Box 28
Cheltenham
GL52 3LZ
0870 1122211
www.ucas.com

Tourist guide

'As a tourist guide you are meeting different people every day, you are not answerable to anybody and if you are independent-minded it would appeal. It's a popular career change because you can train reasonably inexpensively and quickly and there are no overheads.' Qualified tourist guide and former fashion accessory buyer, Jackie Stater.

The job

Tourist guides are employed to escort groups or individual visitors from abroad or from the home countries around cities, historic buildings, museums, galleries and other places of interest. They are experts in cultural, natural and environmental heritage. They have a broad knowledge covering history, geography, art and architecture, economics, politics and religion. They are expected to use their knowledge to inform, inspire and entertain their group – the job is much more than just passing on information. Most guides are self-employed and work as freelances for a variety of different employers such as tour companies or tour agencies, where they are paid a daily rate or half-daily rate to escort a group of tourists. There is another source of income: working for corporate clients where guides are employed by companies to accompany employees – either from the UK or from abroad – on tours or visits. Tourist guiding can be seasonal with the busy period running from April through to October, so it is common for guides to juggle another job, such as teaching, in order to make a reasonable living. In the winter months tourist guides will often look for casual work with tourist boards or work in other parts of the industry. It is also usual to spend time in the winter updating your knowledge, because information is constantly changing. Days can be long, with some guides putting in up to 50 hours a week in the summer months, and evening and weekend work is common.

The culture

Most people who become tour guides choose it as a second career, so it is common to find guides in their 40s and older. They can come from a variety of backgrounds, but the profession appeals particularly to ex-teachers, because it is a job which requires a wealth of general knowledge, and actors, because most guides have to be 'performers' capable of engaging and entertaining their clients. It is the natural destination for former tour managers who crave a UK base, but it also appeals to former policemen, accountants and lawyers. Tourist guide training is quick – the gold standard of the profession, the Blue Badge, can be obtained in about 18 months – and the costs are not prohibitive, with training course fees of around £3,400. Training courses often run in the evenings and weekends so it is easy to fit in around an existing job. It is also a job that may appeal to career changers because it involves no overheads – once you have completed the training your only expense is going to be, as one guide puts it, a mobile phone and a good pair of walking shoes.

Do I need a degree?

You do not need a degree to become a qualified tourist guide, although a degree in tourism, history or arts may be useful. Modern language graduates will also have an advantage, because if you are fluent in other languages you are entitled to charge higher fees. You do need a broad general knowledge and must be able to absorb information easily.

What professional qualifications do I need?

The Institute of Tourist Guiding is the organisation responsible for accrediting training courses for tourist guides. It does not run training itself. This is run by course providers, which can be private providers or further or higher education institutions. There are three levels of entry into tourist guiding, from level 2 to 4.

A **level 2 qualification** will entitle you to be a tourist guide for a specific individual site such as St Paul's Cathedral in London, or working to a fixed route such as a tour guide on an open-top bus or riverboat trip.

A **level 3 qualification** is known as the **Green Badge**. This is the qualification you need if you want to be a guide for a particular city or town or area of the countryside. It will give you skills such as heritage interpretation and how to deliver a commentary, and will cover general presentation skills as well.

Level 4, the **Blue Badge in Tourist Guiding**, is the gold standard of the profession. Blue Badge training courses are run annually in London but in other regions they are only run according to demand, which is usually once every five years.

There are Blue Badges for 11 regions: the Heart of England, East of England, South-east England, Southern England, the South West, Wales, North-west England, Yorkshire, Northumbria, Cumbria, and Northern Ireland. London has its own Blue Badge and people who hold this qualification will be trained to guide in the capital but also at other venues outside London which can be visited within a day. This includes places such as Oxford, Stratford-upon-Avon, Bath and Canterbury. All Blue Badge guides will have core guide knowledge, which includes general knowledge about the UK, but they will also be trained to have an in-depth knowledge of their own area. They will be taught all aspects of guiding techniques for different environments such as churches and cathedrals, stately homes, museums and art galleries. The Blue Badge course takes 17 months part time and costs around £3,400.

What personal skills do I need?

Personal stamina and good health are crucial. This is a job where you will be on your feet for most of the day so it can be physically demanding. You must be interested in people and enjoy working with them. You must be sympathetic, be good at solving problems and be unflappable – you have to think on your feet. It is important to have a sense of humour and to be a bit of a performer – you have to engage your audience, often for hours, if not days at a time. A thirst for knowledge is important but also the ability to absorb that knowledge and to be prepared constantly to update what you know. You also have to like sharing your knowledge with other people. Excellent communication skills are a must and you should have a clear voice that people can easily understand.

Starting salary

The recommended minimum fees are set down by the two professional organisations, the Guild of Registered Tourist Guides and the Association of Professional Tourist Guides, which represents qualified guides in the capital. Fees are set according to half a day or a day's work. In London for 2006/7 the minimum rate was £105 for half a day or £159 for a full day. There is a structured fee scale with higher rates payable if you are able to offer a foreign language. The more foreign languages you can offer the higher the fee. Overtime, the size of the group and public holiday working all influence how much you will be paid.

Jobs on qualification

A qualified tourist guide.

Current employment prospects ★ ★ ★
Good, but this is a competitive job market as most guides are self-employed. Domestic tourism is a volatile market which can be influenced by the strength of the pound, and more recently by the threat of terrorism.

Is a career change a reality? ★ ★ ★ ★ ★

Welcomes older entrants? ★ ★ ★ ★ ★

Potential high earner? £ £ £

Useful contacts:

Institute of Tourist Guiding
Lloyd's Court, 1 Goodman's Yard
London E1 8AT
020 7953 1257
www.itg.org.uk

The Guild of Registered Tourist Guides
52D Borough High Street
London SE1 1XN
020 7403 1115
www.blue-badge.org.uk

Association of Professional Tourist Guides
33–37 Moreland Street
London EC1V 8HA
020 7939 7690
www.aptg.org.uk

Scottish Tourist Guides Association
St John Street
Stirling
FK8 1EA
01786 447784
www.stga.co.uk

The sector skills council for the hospitality, leisure, travel and tourism industries
Armstrong House
38 Market Square
Uxbridge
UB8 1LH
0870 060 2550
www.people1st.co.uk

Springboard UK
3 Denmark Street
London WC2H 8LP
020 7497 8654
www.springboarduk.org.uk

University lecturer

'I would say it's best to start off working part time to get to know what it's all about, that's what I did and then I ended up working full time.' Elaine Payne, career changer from marketing professional to university business lecturer.

The job

University lecturers share their time between lecturing students and working on academic research that contributes to the department's academic profile. Since it is essential to keep on top of the subject, continuing professional development is expected. As career changer Elaine Payne comments: 'Universities are sponsored for learning, and there is an expectation that lecturers will go on learning too.' Contact with students comes through lectures, seminars and tutorials, and it is likely that there will be some pastoral responsibility as well. It is not a nine-to-five job. The hours expected to be spent on lecturing and research will depend on the individual contract, but according to the University and College Union (UCU), whose members include lecturers, the average working week can reach 55 hours and beyond. Busy times of the year could find you working in the daytime as well as evenings and weekends to meet deadlines for student assessments. Annual holiday entitlement is usually seven weeks a year, but it does not match student holidays. Lecturers are still expected to work when the students are on vacation. Lecturing offers a variety of different types of employment contracts, such as permanent, fixed term or fractional. Different contracts will offer different benefits, but it does mean lecturing has flexible working opportunities. Being a lecturer is not a soft option, but according to Steve Wharton, joint president of the UCU and a French and communications lecturer, 'It is the most exciting, stimulating job that can be done. It's hard work but it's fantastic.'

The culture

Higher education can be a highly competitive environment where you are judged on your academic record and your own personal qualifications. Some universities, usually the older pre-1992 institutions, will expect their lecturers to show evidence of recent research and be working towards, or have, a PhD. Somebody hoping to change career may have more luck with one of the newer universities, which offer more vocational degrees and where experience in the workplace might carry more weight. But even at these universities, which are traditionally the former polytechnics, a first degree and probably a Masters will be required. In the past 10 years, there has been increasing demand for would-be lecturers, at both the old and new institutions, to have evidence of research because of the contribution it makes to statutory academic assessment, which in turn influences funding. Professional qualifications will, however, be given some recognition and if you have a professional qualification with a decade of work experience behind you, it could get you in.

Do I need a degree?

It is unlikely that you could become a university lecturer without a degree. However, a professional qualification with career experience may open doors, especially in departments where there are skills shortages (see current employment prospects below). Each institution, and each department within that institution, will have its own minimum qualifications. Contact the department directly to check what their requirements are.

Older universities are likely to ask for evidence of recent research and expect lecturers to have, or be working towards, a PhD. The newer universities are likely to require at least a first degree, with some demanding a Masters as well as evidence of research, but it will depend on individual departments and the current recruitment market.

What professional qualifications do I need?

There is no mandatory obligation on a university lecturer to have a teaching qualification, but in practice anybody working in this competitive academic environment would be expected to have, or be prepared to study for, a postgraduate certificate in learning and teaching in higher education, or equivalent. The university would be likely to pay for you to study for the teaching qualification, which would be worked around your other teaching and research commitments.

What personal skills do I need?

An up-to-date knowledge in your subject as well as a continuing enthusiasm for it are crucial. But it is equally important to be able to pass on that information to students in an informative and clear fashion, so excellent communication skills are needed. It is important to have the confidence to be able to speak in public. Good written skills are essential. Excellent analytical ability, original thought and maintaining an interest in research are essential. Good IT skills are important as well as the ability to work alone and as part of a team. A sense of humour is needed and patience is key.

Starting salary

The University and Colleges Employers' Association, the body that represents university employers, admits that anybody taking up a lecturer post after 10 to 15 years in private industry would be likely to face a pay cut. But it argues that there are compensations when working in higher education, such as the flexible working opportunities it offers compared to private industry. The starting salary for a lecturer in an older pre-1992 university, according to 2005 pay rates, is £24,435, reaching £43,850 after 15 years. Extra discretionary payments can push this up to £47,262. In the new universities lecturers' pay starts at £24,352, according to 2005 figures, reaching £44,328 after 20 years.

Jobs on qualification
University lecturer.

Current employment prospects ★ ★ ★ ★ ★
The latest recruitment and retention survey by the University and Colleges Employers' Association (UCEA), published in 2005, revealed lecturer shortages in subjects where there is competition from other prospective employers. The report highlighted law, business and management, finance and accountancy, IT and computing, education and health-related subjects as areas where there were problems in recruiting. As the government remains committed to increasing higher education student numbers, job opportunities in higher education should also rise. A recruitment 'bulge' is also predicted in the next five to ten years as a significant number of lecturers now in their 50s are due to retire.

Is a career change a reality? ★ ★ ★ ★ ★

Welcomes older entrants? ★ ★ ★ ★ ★

Potential high earner? £ £ £

Useful contacts:

The Higher Education Academy
Innovation Way
York Science Park
Heslington
York
YO10 5BR
01904 717500
www.heacademy.ac.uk

University and Colleges Employers' Association
Woburn House
20 Tavistock Square
London WC1H 9HU
020 7383 2444
www.ucea.ac.uk

Association of University Teachers (AUT)
Egmont House
25–31 Tavistock Place
London WC1H 9UT
020 7670 9700
www.aut.org.uk

National Association of Teachers in Further and Higher Education (NATFHE)
27 Britannia Street
London WC1X 9JP
020 7837 3636
www.natfhe.org.uk

Higher Education and Research Opportunities in the UK (HERO)
www.hero.ac.uk

Web designer

'If you want to change career and get a job in web design for an IT company, it won't be easy because of age and also because you lack experience. But if you have a leaning towards web design and have some formal training you could succeed as a freelance.' Howard Gerlis, chairman of the British Computer Society's internet specialist group.

The job
A website designer is somebody who designs the pages that make up a website. It is a job that requires technical knowledge about how the computer systems that create the pages work (known as the 'back end') but also a flair for design (known as the 'front end') so that you can create a website that looks good. Designers create the website working to a brief from a client. Alternatively they may work within IT departments of large organisations with responsibility for their internet websites or intranet. Web designers have to decide on design features including the size of the text, style and colour, as well as the general layout of the pages. Designers may also be expected to bring video, sound, graphics or animation to the site. They will come up with a draft design and following further discussions with the client, or with their employer, approve a final version. It is then up to the web designer to make sure that the site functions properly before it is uploaded and goes live on the internet. Designers may also have to maintain the site to make sure it continues to work properly, and if necessary, upgrade elements of it. Other responsibilities could include registering the site on search engines and establishing other internet links so that it is widely marketed.

The culture
During the dot com explosion of the 1990s, web design in particular experienced significant growth, and was seen as the dynamic part of the information technology (IT) industry. Web design still attracts the enthusiastic amateur looking for a career change, and researchers at e-skills UK, the sector skills council for the IT industry, estimate it gets a handful of enquiries every week from people wishing to go down this route. The IT industry has a reputation, according to the British Computer Society, of being ageist. Even though the law changed last October (2006) to make it illegal to discriminate in employment on the grounds of age, it probably means that an age-positive culture in IT may be slow in coming.

There is another route you can take if you really are keen to break into web design: freelance web design. However, this is not an option if you want to become involved in the more high-tech roles in the industry such as software development. Working as a freelance web designer and creating sites for local businesses and organisations is possible if you have the technical training (see professional qualifications below). Your fees could range from around £200 for creating a simple static web page to more than £1,000 for one which is more complex, if, for example, it contains interactive features. As it is a freelance career, it requires little investment in overheads. All you need is somewhere to work from and a computer.

Do I need a degree?

The percentage of graduates working in information technology is 60 per cent – double the graduate rate in the general workforce. But it is not essential to have an IT degree to work in the IT industry.

What professional qualifications do I need?

The IT industry is not regulated and there is no recognised gold standard professional qualification. However, you must be able to demonstrate that you have technical skills, experience and understanding of HTML, web editors such as Dreamweaver, FrontPage and Go Live, and graphic design programs including Photoshop, Illustrator and Paint Shop Pro. Knowledge of programs that create interactivity such as Shockwave and Flash are also useful. Understanding of Java and Javascript is an advantage.

The British Computer Society does offer members the opportunity to achieve **chartered status** through a combination of experience and academic achievement. Many people working in the industry as web designers are self-taught, although training is traditionally offered in-house by employers.

Training courses available include the **certified internet webmaster (CIW)** courses, which have global recognition and show that you have reached a certain competency in computer skills. They are aimed both at newcomers to the industry and at those who are already established but want to improve their IT skills. The professional organisation, the British Computer Society, accredits training courses while the British Web Design and Marketing Association has its own recommendations. The UK Web Design Association, which also has a membership of web designers, has links to training options on its website. Learndirect is also a useful internet resource for courses at further education colleges (see useful contacts below).

What personal skills do I need?

This is a job that crosses different sectors so you could come from a design background or an IT background. Whichever group you fall into, you are going to have to have a knowledge of internet programming and scripting language. You must be good at solving problems, be methodical and logical and be able to explain IT issues simply and in a language that is clear to audiences who are not technically minded. The job can be high pressure and you must be able to work as part of a team. Technologies are constantly changing so you must be prepared to keep your knowledge and skills up to date.

Starting salary

As a freelance web designer you could earn £200 for creating a simple static website but around £1,000 or considerably more if the site is more interactive and more complex. A web designer working as an employee for a large company could expect to start on around £24,000 increasing to a maximum of £50,000 with experience.

Jobs on qualification

Website designer, sometimes called web master, web author or web architect.

Current career prospects ★

According to e-skills, the sector skills council for the IT industry, the demand for web designers is currently high and is expected to stay high for the foreseeable future. According to its statistics, just over a quarter of a million people are computer software professionals – which includes web designers – making up around 25 per cent of the IT workforce in the UK. The IT industry is a growth industry; the workforce is currently growing at the rate of 2.5 per cent, faster than any other sector of the UK economy. However the boom days of the late 1990s when the job market was expanding at the rate of 11 per cent are over. It is a competitive job market that, according to the British Computer Society, favours younger entrants, so although the prospects for employment may be good it may be difficult to break through if you are over 40.

Is a career change a reality? ★ ★ ★

If you can bring business skills and experience to the IT workplace it will be an advantage, but you are also going to need IT experience, although being an enthusiastic amateur might be useful. Lack of a gold standard professional qualification means an employer may be prepared to take a risk, take you on and then train you. If you can build up a portfolio of web design work you have already done, maybe in a voluntary capacity, and you have some transferable business skills which would benefit the organisation, it may be enough to get you in.

Welcomes older entrants? ★

This is not an industry that has historically welcomed older entrants, according to the British Computer Society. The industry will however have to change with the times as from October 2006 it became illegal to discriminate in the workplace on the basis of a person's age.

Potential high earner? £ £ £ £

Useful contacts:

e-skills UK
1 Castle Lane
London SW1E 6DR
020 7963 8920
www.e-skills.com

The British Computer Society
1 Sanford Street
Swindon
Wiltshire
SN1 1HJ
01793 417417
www.bcs.org.uk

UK Web Design Association
www.ukwda.org

British Web Design and Marketing Association
PO Box 3227
London NW9 9LX
020 8204 2474
www.bwdma.com

Certified Internet Webmaster
www.ciwcertified.com

Yoga teacher

'I would say the majority of students on our teacher diploma are mature, in their 30s and 40s, and are people on their second or third careers.' Pierre Bibby, chief executive officer of the British Wheel of Yoga.

The job

A qualified yoga teacher is able to instruct people in yoga techniques which can be used to improve fitness, health and wellbeing. They are trained in relaxation, breathing and meditation skills and visualisation. Qualified teachers also have an understanding of the philosophy and theory of yoga. Most professionally qualified yoga teachers are self-employed and are paid per session or per hour. They can work in health clubs, sports studios and leisure centres. The most common yoga styles taught in the UK are hatha, ashtanga, viniyoga and iyengar.

The culture

Yoga classes are becoming increasingly popular and training to become a yoga teacher is a common destination for career changers. The profession attracts people from a variety of different backgrounds, such as former business managers and nurses, and is also a popular choice for occupational therapists or physiotherapists looking to diversify. People who have benefited from practising yoga are especially drawn to train as teachers; some go on to take additional qualifications to become a yoga therapist (see jobs on qualification entry below). There is a part-time route to qualification, so it can be a practical career change, and fees are not prohibitive. Both the British Wheel of Yoga, the national governing body of yoga in the UK, and the Yoga Biomedical Trust, the organisation devoted to promoting yoga therapy and its training in the UK, predict yoga in health and fitness is a growth area, so career opportunities are good.

Do I need a degree?

You do not need a degree to train as a yoga teacher.

What professional qualifications do I need?

SkillsActive is the sector skills council for active leisure and learning. In May 2005, it launched the first national occupational standards for yoga teachers. The move opens the door for more training providers to seek approval for their courses, provided they match the standards. This should bring an increase in both the number of teacher training courses available and the number of qualified yoga teachers who will be able to become level three members of the Register of Exercise Professionals (REP).

Entry to training to be a yoga teacher is not dependent on any statutory qualifications, but you will need to have at least two years' experience of practising yoga before you are eligible to start a teacher training course with the British Wheel of Yoga (BWY), which is the national governing body for yoga in the UK.

The BWY offers a **teacher training diploma** that entitles you to be registered with the REP – the organisation that sets national minimum standards for professionals working in the fitness industry. The yoga teacher qualification offered by the Scottish Yoga Teachers Association in Aberdeen is also endorsed by the REP and entitles graduates to REP registration. Both qualifications bring registration at level three – the top level of entry on the REP register.

The BWY recommends that you complete its **foundation course** first. This can be completed part time over one year and requires 60 hours of study. The course lays the foundation for the teacher diploma and covers practical and theoretical work on asana, pranayama, concentration and meditation as well as looking at the history of yoga and its different paths and schools. The teacher diploma can be completed over three years part time and is made up of 500 hours of teaching and study. It requires one day per month tuition. The tuition is available all over the UK and the BWY puts students in touch with a tutor close to their home. The tuition often takes place in hired halls or studios and course dates are decided by each individual tutor. The BWY diploma teacher training course is made up of four units – anatomy and physiology; stress and relaxation; yoga philosophy; and health and safety in teaching and practical aspects of teaching yoga postures. The qualification is based on continuous assessment and assignments, both written and practical.

Graduates of the diploma can join the BWY's register of qualified teachers. Registration has to be renewed annually and is linked to continuing professional development. The diploma course fees are decided by individual tutors and are in the region of £2,500.

What personal skills do I need?

You need to be supple and flexible to train as a yoga teacher. A personal experience of at least two years with a qualified teacher is also recommended. Communication skills are crucial, as you need to be able to speak to a group of individuals and enthuse them. It is also important to be well organised and it is an advantage to have good marketing and business skills as you are more than likely to be self-employed.

Starting salary

As yoga teachers are traditionally self-employed, income is determined by individual reputation and employment opportunity. A qualified yoga teacher can charge between £20 and £60 an hour or session. A professionally qualified yoga teacher can earn a reasonable income from teaching the BWY teacher diploma and working as a yoga teacher.

Jobs on qualification

A qualified yoga teacher. There are additional post-diploma modules run by the BWY, which are available to qualified teachers to improve their skills. They are: teaching yoga to children, yoga in pregnancy and post-pregnancy, teaching yoga meditation and yoga in prisons. An advanced diploma in special needs, which covers areas including autism and other disabilities, is also planned.

With additional study, a qualified yoga teacher can go on to become a yoga therapist who is trained to use yoga techniques as a therapy in the management of medical conditions, including chronic complaints such as asthma, irritable bowel syndrome or hypertension. The Yoga Biomedical Trust (YBT) and the Life Centre (LC) in London have developed a **foundation course in yoga therapy**. The course, which spans four weekends, is open to qualified yoga teachers and is the entry qualification for the YBT and LC modular **yoga therapy diploma**. The diploma takes two years to complete part time and is based on weekends of tuition and a summer retreat. The diploma is recognised by the NHS and the Institute for Complementary Medicine. Diploma graduates are entitled to register with the NHS Registered Complementary and Alternative Medical Practitioners. The cost of completing the diploma is around £4,500. The YBT, which promotes yoga as a complementary therapy, says the use of yoga therapists is becoming increasingly popular in the UK. They are already being employed by some GP surgeries while others can be found working in alternative therapy health centres. Most are self-employed private practitioners. Yoga therapy is well established in India and is increasingly popular in the US. The trend is expected to follow in the UK, says the YBT. There are currently 130 registered yoga therapists in the UK.

Current employment prospects ★ ★ ★ ★ ★

Good. Yoga is becoming increasingly popular and demand for qualified teachers to work in a range of different health and fitness environments is expected to grow. Demand for qualified yoga therapists is also expected to increase as the therapy becomes more established in the UK.

Is a career change a reality? ★ ★ ★ ★ ★

Training to become a yoga teacher is relatively cheap and practical. The overhead costs for setting yourself up in practice are also low – all you need is the cost of a yoga mat and the fee for hiring a studio or hall. So long as you have at least two years' experience of practising yoga with a qualified teacher it could prove a successful and rewarding career change with the opportunity for professional development.

Welcomes older entrants? ★ ★ ★ ★ ★

Potential high earner? £ £

Useful contacts:

British Wheel of Yoga
25 Jermyn Street
Sleaford
Lincolnshire
NG34 7RU
01529 306851
www.bwy.org.uk

Scottish Yoga Teachers Association
36 Woodhill Road
Aberdeen
AB15 5JU

Register of Exercise Professionals
3rd Floor
8–10 Crown Hill
Croydon
Surrey
CR0 1RZ
020 8686 6464
www.exerciseregister.org

Yoga Biomedical Trust (YBT)
90–92 Pentonville Street
Islington
London N1 9HS
020 7689 3040
www.yogatherapy.org

The Life Centre
15 Edge Street
London W8 7PN
020 7221 2626
www.thelifecentre.org

SkillsActive
Castlewood House
77-91 New Oxford Street
London WC1A 1PX
020 7632 2000
www.skillsactive.com

FUNDING FOR MATURE STUDENTS

Bank funding available to mature students

All banks advise that in all cases you should talk to them before making any decisions. It is also important to obtain accurate information from your local education authority and mortgage provider. The options you have will depend on your financial track record, the course you want to do, how much you've saved or what financial stake of your own you are putting towards your course costs or expenses.

What can you offer a mature student on a full-time three-year degree course who has to pay annual tuition fees of £3,000?

Barclays

The person would be eligible for a career development loan for the last two years of study and one year practical or industrial placement. The amount available is between £300 and £8,000. Repayments would commence two months after completion of the study. Students can apply for a loan to cover 100 per cent of course fees if they have been unemployed for three months prior to the course commencing. All other applicants may apply for up to 80 per cent of the course fees, funding the remaining 20 per cent themselves. The loan is repayable over 12 to 60 months after completed study. All courses and learning providers need to be approved by the LSC (Learning Skills Council).

Co-operative Bank

A student account with a free overdraft is available to any mature student providing they are in full-time education. The overdraft amount available works as follows: year one £1,400, year two £1,700 and year three £2,000. The customer could use the student account to fund part of their course and consider using a low-rate credit card.

NatWest

This case study would qualify for our student account as long as they were a UK resident on a full-time higher education course lasting two years or more and would therefore be entitled to an interest-free overdraft as follows: year one £1,250; year two £1,400; year three £1,600; year four £1,800 and year five £2,000.

HSBC

Our student service is available to people who are 18 years or older, have been resident in the UK for the past three years or have a bank account with the HSBC Group in their home country, and agree that their only student account is with HSBC. To be eligible, students must be studying for an undergraduate degree, postgraduate degree, diploma of higher education, BTEC higher national certificate, BTEC higher national diploma, national vocational qualifications levels 4 and 5, or a nursing and midwifery diploma. The student service offers: a current account with an interest-free overdraft up to certain limits; price promise insurance to ensure our customers never pay over the odds on high-street purchases; student credit card (subject to status); low-cost insurance; a discount card; and commission-free travel money.

Lloyds TSB

A student account is available where we offer an interest-free overdraft of up to £1,000 in the first year at college, £1,250 in the second year, £1,500 in year three and up to £2,000 in years four and five. The account is on condition that you are a permanent UK resident and are either studying on a course of at least three years' duration leading to an honours degree or have an unconditional offer letter or a UCAS acceptance letter for a full-time honours degree course.

Nationwide

Nationwide does not offer a specific career development loan. Nationwide does offer personal loans of £1,000–£25,000. Generally speaking, to be eligible you would need to be in full-time employment. In some circumstances those in part-time employment may be eligible, depending on the amount they wish to borrow, their income and their credit history. Personal loans may also be worth considering as an option for paying tuition fees; however, as explained above, the applicant would need some form of income to be eligible.

What can you offer a student on a one-year full-time or two-year part-time postgraduate course for a Masters degree or a professional diploma who is looking for help with meeting tuition fees for one or two years?

Barclays

A career development loan would be a product available for this scenario.

Co-operative Bank

A career development loan is available to fund vocational courses of up to two years, maximum amount £8,000. The loan only becomes payable one month after the course is finished. The course provider must be registered with the Department for Education and Skills (DfES) in order for the course to be eligible. Loans can cover 80 per cent of course fees, and the full cost of books and related materials. Repayment can be deferred by up to a maximum of 18 months if the customer is unable to find employment. If the student was studying full time then the student account overdraft is an alternative.

NatWest

Depending on the type of course, they may qualify for a graduate loan (within five years of graduation from an undergraduate course) or could look at a career development loan with RBS.

HSBC

Students studying for a postgraduate degree could be eligible to extend their student account and could apply for a professional studies loan. The professional studies loan offers borrowing up to £25,000 (subject to status) with repayments spread over one to five years for loans up to £15,000, or one to eight years for loans over £15,000. Students must be studying an eligible course – detailed at:
*www.hsbc.co.uk/1/2/personal/current-accounts/graduate-service/
post-graduate/loan*

Lloyds TSB

Our graduate account offers an interest-free overdraft of up to £2,000 in the first year after graduation, £1,500 in the second and £1,000 in the third year. A low-cost loan of between £1,000 and £10,000 with up to five years to repay your loan and option to make no repayments for the first four months is also available. But you must be a permanent UK resident and have confirmation of graduation, have graduated within the last three years with a degree from a UK-based university and be prepared to transfer your current account from your existing bank if you're not already a Lloyds TSB customer. You must also commit to pay at least £500 into your account per month (if you are moving your account to us).

Nationwide

Nationwide does not offer a specific career development loan. Nationwide does offer personal loans of £1,000–£25,000. Generally speaking, to be eligible you would need to be in full-time employment. In some circumstances those in part-time employment may be eligible, depending on the amount they wish to borrow, their income and their credit history. Personal loans may also be worth considering as an option for paying tuition fees; however, as explained above, the applicant would need some form of income to be eligible.

What can you offer somebody who is studying on a five-year part-time degree course at a private college with fees of £15,000 in total?

Barclays
From the information provided, the above person would be eligible for a career development loan for the last two years of study.

Co-operative Bank
No specific product available.

NatWest
Depending on the type of course, they may qualify for a graduate loan (within five years of graduation from an undergraduate course) or could look at career development loans with RBS.

Lloyds TSB
A student account is available where we offer an interest-free overdraft of up to £1,000 in the first year at college, £1,250 in the second year, £1,500 in year three and up to £2,000 in years four and five. The account is on condition that you are a permanent UK resident and are either studying on a course of at least three years' duration leading to an honours degree or have an unconditional offer letter or a UCAS acceptance letter for a full-time honours degree course.

Nationwide
Nationwide does not offer a specific career development loan. Nationwide does offer personal loans of £1,000–£25,000. Generally speaking, to be eligible you would need to be in full-time employment. In some circumstances those in part-time employment may be eligible, depending on the amount they wish to borrow, their income and their credit history. Personal loans may also be worth considering as an option for paying tuition fees; however, as explained above, the applicant would need some form of income to be eligible.

HSBC

Our student service is available to people who are 18 years or older, have been resident in the UK for the past three years or have a bank account with the HSBC Group in their home country, and agree that their only student account is with HSBC. To be eligible, students must be studying for: an undergraduate degree, postgraduate degree, diploma of higher education, BTEC higher national certificate, BTEC higher national diploma, national vocational qualifications levels 4 and 5, or a nursing and midwifery diploma. The student service offers: a current account with an interest-free overdraft up to certain limits; price promise insurance to ensure our customers never pay over the odds on high-street purchases; student credit card (subject to status); low-cost insurance; a discount card; and commission-free travel money.

What can you offer a mature medical student (aged in their 30s or 40s) with little statutory funding support?

Barclays

A professional studies loan is the most appropriate for this scenario. It is available to full-time students in at least their second year, with £25,000 being the maximum amount we would lend. The scenario listed is acceptable but as with any case the personal circumstances of any applicants would be considered and each application would be subject to risk assessment.

Co-operative Bank

A career development loan is possible.

NatWest

Depending on the type of course, students could apply for a professional trainee loan scheme. Students must be in full-time study to become one of the following professionals: barrister; solicitor (postgraduate diploma in law, legal practice course and bar vocational courses only); doctor; vet; optician; dentist; pharmacist; osteopath; chiropractor; podiatrist; physiotherapist. The money is available to cover course fees and living expenses.

Our professional trainee loan is market-leading, with the following options:
- You can borrow up to £20,000, or £25,000 if you're studying full time for the graduate diploma in law (GDL), legal practice course (LPC) or bar vocational course (BVC).
- You can draw the loan in one lump sum or instalments.
- There are no repayments for at least six months after you finish your course.
- You have up to ten years to repay your loan from date of initial drawdown.
- You can choose a fixed or variable interest rate.

- No arrangement or administration fees.
- You can borrow up to the cost of course fees if studying part time for a GDL, LPC or BVC.

HSBC
Students studying for a postgraduate degree could be eligible to extend their student account and could apply for a professional studies loan. The professional studies loan offers borrowing up to £25,000 (subject to status) with repayments spread over one to five years for loans up to £15,000, or one to eight years for loans over £15,000. Students must be studying an eligible course – detailed at:
www.hsbc.co.uk/1/2/personal/current-accounts/graduate-service/post-graduate/loan

Lloyds TSB
The further education loan is available to all eligible Lloyds TSB-franchised customers who are taking a course through a recognised institution, e.g. those studying to be a doctor, dentist, veterinary surgeon, optometrist, architect, surveyor or accountant. It is sole borrowing only; individuals must be aged between 18 and 35, although we will consider applications from people 36 and over. The minimum available is £1,000, the maximum £10,000. The money must be taken in a single drawdown within 30 calendar days of taking out the loan. The repayment term is five years, once the loan repayments commence. The first repayment is deferred for 47 months from drawdown, with the first payment being collected during the 48th month.

Nationwide
Nationwide does not offer a specific career development loan. Nationwide does offer personal loans of £1,000–£25,000. Generally speaking, to be eligible you would need to be in full-time employment. In some circumstances those in part-time employment may be eligible, depending on the amount they wish to borrow, their income and their credit history. Personal loans may also be worth considering as an option for paying tuition fees; however, as explained above, the applicant would need some form of income to be eligible.

What options are there to defer payment on a mortgage while you are studying or retraining until you have a full-time income again?

Barclays
Someone with a mortgage can take a payment holiday whilst studying but this is linked to the equity in their home. For example, if they have a mortgage of £50,000 and the house is worth £200,000, they could have £130,000 in their reserve account (the flexible mortgage pot to use for things like payment holidays, DIY, etc.). Any money used from this pot will be charged interest at the mortgage rate. If people are

thinking about studying they should contact the Woolwich, which runs our mortgage arm, whilst they are in full-time employment to establish what we can lend them.

Co-operative Bank

Our mortgages do allow for payment holidays of up to six months (with the bank's agreement). Interest continues to accrue throughout this period and for this reason any customer planning to use this should really seek professional financial advice beforehand to ensure it is cost-effective.

NatWest

An offset mortgage will allow you to take a payment holiday of 6 months in any rolling 12-month period, however a standard mortgage will have to be paid even if you are studying or retraining.

Lloyds TSB

The mortgage options we can offer are repayment holidays – i.e. not making repayments of either interest or capital – but this is generally an option for four payments in any year. You could switch from repayment to an interest-only mortgage during your period of study to keep outgoings as low as possible. You should talk to your mortgage provider to ask what they suggest, as there may be an option to overpay your mortgage in the lead-up to quitting work and starting study, and to make use of those overpayments to stop mortgage payments. Alternatively you could save this money in a separate savings account and use that to make the minimum interest repayments during your study time. You should also look into offset mortgages, as pooling your current account and savings with your mortgage may be an option that gives more flexibility.

If you have equity in your property you could have a further advance on your mortgage, but you would need to think seriously about this and consider your ability to meet increased repayments in the future. Potentially, for example, you could withdraw the amount you need for tuition, plus the amount needed to meet the monthly repayments during the time you're studying. If you consider this option, think carefully about the total interest cost to you to appreciate the true cost of the loan, and offset that against your potential for future earnings/repayment potential. Obviously your home is at stake, so think carefully about this – and ensure that the value of the loan isn't too high when compared to the equity.

Nationwide

We do accept the deferment of mortgage payments. However, the period of time very much depends on the borrower's circumstances and how much equity they have in their property. It is unlikely, however, that we would be able to defer payments for five years. Usually it is for a period of months. Again, depending on the borrower's circumstances, there could be an option to refinance, increasing the mortgage term and lowering the monthly payments.

Information correct at the time of researching May 2006.

Government bursaries and help with course tuition fees

Government bursaries are financial grants towards study that do not have to be repaid. These bursaries are different from any other bursaries that may be available from individual universities or charities. They are available to students studying for degrees or professional qualifications in three career categories: **teaching**, **NHS careers** and **social work**. Some are means-tested, so are linked to income, while others are non-means-tested and paid regardless of income. The government has introduced them to help boost recruitment in health, social care and education, and prevent further skills shortages. Bursaries are an attractive option for career changers because they are payable even if you have received funding for higher education in the past, or if you have had an NHS bursary in the past and now want to train for another NHS career.

If you enrol on an NHS degree or diploma course your tuition fees will also be paid. Students on the professional social work degree course have to pay their own tuition fees, although the non-means-tested bursary they are given has been increased to help offset some of the cost.

NHS bursaries

The NHS offers two types of bursary (figures are for 2005/6):

- A **non-means-tested bursary** is paid every year to students studying for a nursing, midwifery or operating department practitioner diploma course. The bursary is paid for every year of study and is not linked to family income. In 2006, the annual non-means-tested bursary was £6,859 in London, £5,837 outside the capital, and £5,837 if you are still living with parents. Students on part-time courses can receive a proportion of the annual bursary. If you are on a diploma course and receiving a non-means-tested bursary you are not entitled to apply for a student loan.

Other financial help for students on these diploma courses: students on these diploma courses who are aged over 26 when they enrol are eligible for an older students' allowance of £682 per year. They are also entitled to the single parent allowance of £1,001, but are not entitled to claim both. Other discretionary awards, which are means-tested, are: a dependants' allowance worth between £429 and £2,029 per year if you have children or adults who are dependent on you; practice placements expenses to cover essential travel and accommodation; and a contribution towards childcare costs in the form of a childcare allowance to a maximum of £114.75 per week for one child or £170 per week for two children.

• A **means-tested bursary** is available to students on degree-level NHS courses and those on postgraduate courses. This is available if you are on an NHS degree course to train as an audiologist; chiropodist; podiatrist; dental hygienist; dental nurse; dental therapist; midwife; nurse; occupational therapist; physiotherapist; radiographer; speech and language therapist; prosthetist; orthotist or dietician. The amount of bursary you receive is dependent on income, so it will vary from student to student. Students on part-time degree courses will be eligible for 75 per cent of the full bursary.

The bursary available for 2006 was £2,837 per year in London or £2,309 per year outside London, and £1,889 if you are still living with your parents. If you are on an NHS degree course you will also be able to apply for a reduced student loan to help towards your maintenance costs.

Other financial help for students on NHS degree courses: students on NHS degree and postgraduate courses are also eligible for an older students' allowance if aged over 26 before the first academic year of starting the course. This allowance is from £406 for 26-year-olds, up to a maximum £1,381 for the over-29s. If you are a single parent you are eligible for an allowance called a single parent addition which is £1,181 for a year. If you are over 26 and claim this benefit you forfeit the older students' allowance.

If you have family dependants who are entirely dependent on you, such as children or a partner, you are also eligible for additional financial support in the form of a dependants' allowance. This can range from £500 to £2,393 per year. A contribution towards childcare costs in the form of a childcare allowance to a maximum of £114.75 per week for one child or £170 per week for two children is also available.

If you are having to pay for the cost of two homes (i.e. a home for dependants and one for yourself during term-time) you are entitled to a two homes grant of £833 for an academic year. Costs towards practice placements are also available and include travel and accommodation costs.

The NHS hardship grant is available to students who are in serious financial difficulty if you have also received a means-tested bursary.

Medical Students

The means-tested bursaries on offer to medical students studying to become a doctor or a dentist vary according to the kind of degree course you are studying.

Graduate students are entitled to apply for a means-tested bursary in the second, third and fourth year of the course if they are on a four-year graduate-entry degree course. Tuition fees will also be paid for the same period. They are also entitled to claim for a student loan in their first year.

Graduate students who are studying medicine on a five-year undergraduate degree course, who have completed two years of higher education previously, are eligible for an annual means-tested bursary from year five of their study as well as a reduced maintenance loan. The Department of Health will also pay tuition fees from year five.

Undergraduate students on five-year medical degree courses will have their tuition fees paid from year five by the Department of Health, and will also be eligible to apply for a means-tested NHS bursary. A reduced maintenance loan is also available. Medical students on six-year courses are entitled to the NHS bursary in their fifth and sixth years.

Useful contacts:

In England, the NHS Bursary Scheme is administered by:
NHS Student Grants Unit
NHS Pensions Agency
200-220 Broadway
Fleetwood
Lancashire
FY7 8SS
0845 358 6655
www.nhsstudentgrants.co.uk

For Wales:
NHS Wales Students Awards Unit
2nd Floor Golate House
101 St Mary Street
Cardiff
CF10 1DX
029 2026 1495

For Scotland:
The Students Awards Agency for Scotland
3 Redheughs Rigg
South Gyle
Edinburgh
EH12 9HH
0131 476 8212

For Northern Ireland:
The Department of Higher and Further Education Training and Employment
Student Support Branch
4th Floor Adelaide House
39–49 Adelaide Street
Belfast
BT2 8FD
028 9025 7777

Social work bursaries

Students who study for the undergraduate social work degree are eligible for a non-means-tested annual bursary. In 2006/7 this was £4,000 for full-time students outside London, £4,400 for those studying full time in the Capital. Unlike some NHS bursaries, this bursary is not linked to income. Undergraduates studying part time are entitled to 50 per cent of the bursary. All students are however expected to pay their own tuition fees.

Students on full-time postgraduate courses which include the professional qualification are also entitled to a non-means-tested bursary. For 2006/7 this was £2,500 outside London or £2,900 in London. They are also able to claim a maximum £3,162 towards their tuition fees, wherever they study. A means-tested maintenance grant of £3,745 if they study in London or £2,450 if they study outside London is also available.

Students on part-time postgraduate courses are entitled to £1,200 towards their tuition fees and a non-means-tested bursary of £1,250 outside London or £1,450 in London. But these students are not entitled to apply for a maintenance grant.

You will not be eligible for the social work bursary if your employer sponsors your study.

For details of bursaries available to students in other UK countries, contact their care councils (see useful contacts).

Useful contacts:

General Social Care Council (GSCC)
Goldings House
2 Hay's Lane
London SE1 2HB
020 7397 5100
Bursaries helpline: 020 7397 5835
www.gscc.org.uk

Scottish Social Services Council (SSSC)
Compass House
11 Riverside Drive
Dundee
DD1 4NY
01382 207101
www.sssc.uk.com

Care Council for Wales (CCW)
South Gate House
Wood Street
Cardiff
CF10 1EW
029 2022 6257
www.ccwales.org.uk

Northern Ireland Social Care Council (NISCC)
7th Floor Millennium House
Great Victoria Street
Belfast
BT2 7AQ
028 9041 7600
www.socialworkcareers.co.uk

Teacher training bursaries

The type and amount of extra financial help you will be given if you decide to retrain as a teacher will depend on the type of training course you are doing, the subject you plan to teach and whether you are following an employment or university-based training path.

Students studying a postgraduate course in initial teacher training that includes the qualified teacher status award will receive a £9,000 non-means-tested bursary if they are training to teach in a subject where there are skills shortages. These include: maths, science, modern foreign languages, design and technology, information and communications technology, music, religious education and geography. This is usually paid in monthly instalments over nine months. This is non-taxable income. Postgraduate students on other initial teacher training courses including QTS will receive a £6,000 non-means-tested untaxed bursary.

You are also entitled to apply for student loans to help fund your course. But if your tuition fees are already covered through another source you will only be able to apply for the maintenance loan, and not a second loan to cover the cost of your tuition fees.

'Golden hellos' of £4,000 are available for postgraduate trainee teachers teaching secondary school mathematics, English and drama, science, modern foreign languages, design and technology or information technology.

Financial support for student teachers in employment-based training

Students who have decided to take the school-centred initial teacher training (SCITT) programme to qualify as a teacher are eligible for a tax-free non-means-tested bursary of between £6,000 and £9,000. The SCITT initiative is aimed at graduates and is provided by a consortium of schools and colleges working together. Training is delivered exclusively in schools, with teachers acting as mentors and trainers. While training you are likely to be based in a 'lead school' with practice placements at other schools in the consortium. SCITT training runs for one academic year.

If you are working as an unqualified teacher in a school and are seeking your qualified teacher status through the graduate or registered teacher programmes, you will be entitled to a salary during training, normally on the unqualified teachers' scale in the region of £14,000.

Students training to be teachers who are having difficulty meeting their living costs may apply for the Access to Learning fund.

FUNDING FOR SETTING UP YOUR OWN BUSINESS

Raising the money

The Department for Trade and Industry (DTI) recommends two financial initiatives with government backing which will help anybody looking for financial help to launch their new business.

The Small Firms Loan Guarantee and Enterprise Capital Funds are aimed at new businesses which are unable to secure start-up funding from traditional sources because they do not have any assets to act as security. Under the scheme more than £4 billion has been made available to businesses since it was launched in 1981. These are joint initiatives between the DTI and venture capitalists where financial support of between £250,000 and £2 million is available to newly established businesses seeking investment to develop their business.

Small Firms Loan Guarantee (SFLG)

This initiative is managed by the Small Business Services organisation, which is a DTI agency. The scheme is aimed at small and medium-sized businesses or enterprises which are unable to secure conventional loans because they do not have any assets to offer as security. It is a joint venture between the DTI and a number of lenders (see list of current lenders below).

The lenders administer the eligibility criteria and make all the commercial decisions about borrowing. The DTI's role is to stand as guarantor for the loan. The cost to the borrower for the government guarantee is 2 per cent per year on the outstanding amount of the loan.

The main features of the scheme are:
- The DTI stands guarantor for 75 per cent of any outstanding loan in the event of the company going under. In return the borrower pays a 2 per cent premium on the outstanding balance of the loan per year.
- Loans will be guaranteed up to a maximum £250,000, repayable over up to 10 years.
- Businesses are eligible if they are under five years old and have an annual turnover of less than £5.6 million.

• The scheme is open to most businesses in most areas but there are some restrictions.

• Financial lenders participating in the SFLG are:

Airdrie Savings Bank

Bank of Baroda

Bank of Ireland (NI only)

Bank of Scotland plc

Barclays Bank plc

Bibby Financial Services

Doncaster Business Advice Centre (Donbac)

Clydesdale Bank plc

Euro Sales Finance PLC

First Trust Bank (NI only)

General Asset Management

HSBC Bank plc

Lloyds TSB Group plc

National Westminster Bank plc

Northern Bank (NI only)

Northern Enterprise Ltd

One London Ltd

State Securities plc

Triodos Bank

The Co-operative Bank plc

The Enterprise Fund

The Royal Bank of Scotland

UK Steel Enterprise Ltd

Ulster Bank Ltd (NI only)

Venture Finance plc

YFM Group Ltd

Yorkshire Bank plc

Enterprise Capital Funds

The Enterprise Capital Funds (ECF) scheme is a partnership between the government, the DTI and private sector finance to help bridge the need for equity faced by established small or medium-sized businesses that have been running for only a few years. It is aimed at those businesses that are looking for a cash injection so they can expand, but need more money than friends or family can supply. The cash boost required is also likely to be too small to attract funding from traditional commercial capital venturists, who usually look to larger investments. The amount available under this scheme is a minimum £250,000, up to a maximum £2 million. The financial arrangements for the investment will differ according to the sector the business is in and the individual lender.

The first two ECFs were announced in March 2006. They are:

• The IQ Capital Fund, which has funds of £25 million. It operates across Cambridge, Oxford and Bristol but can invest anywhere in the UK. It focuses on technology-based businesses. The fund is being managed by NW Brown Group in Cambridge but other key partners in the fund are: Cambridge-based Great Eastern Investment Forum; Oxford-based Oxford Opportunities Investment Network and South West Angel Investor Network (SWAIN) in Bristol.

• The 21st Century Sustainable Technology Growth Fund, which has funds of £30 million and operates across the UK. Its focus is high-growth companies that embrace cutting edge sustainable technology. E-Synergy Ltd in London is managing the fund.

The DTI is expected to announce more ECFs. Further information will be made available on its website (see useful contacts below).

Community Development Venture Fund

This is an equity fund financed by the government and private investors, which was launched in May 2002. It is aimed at supporting small and medium businesses that are capable of substantial growth but are located in the top 25 per cent of deprived wards in England. The fund is being managed by Bridges Community Ventures Ltd (see details below for contact information).

Regional Venture Capital Funds

Regional Venture Capital Funds (RVCFs) are available to small or medium-sized businesses in England. There is a fund for each of the nine regional development agencies. An RVCF can invest up to £250,000 in equity or debt into any qualifying business. The money can be for start-up costs, or for capital to meet development, growth or acquisition costs. There are restrictions on the types of businesses that are eligible. Those sectors that do not qualify for RVCFs include accountancy and legal services; land and property development; hotels; nursing and residential care homes; agriculture; forestry and timber production and horticulture. Eligibility is also linked to the size of the company and its annual turnover. Anybody interested in the RVCF should contact their regional development agency for more details.

Community Development Finance Institutions (CDFI)

This is another source of funding which includes either a loan or equity. CDFI is a sustainable and independent financial institution whose aim is to create wealth in disadvantaged communities or within under-served markets. The CDFI is an option for funding if you have had your loan application turned down by other more traditional sources of funding such as the high-street banks.

A CDFI can provide money for working capital; bridging loans; property and equipment funding; start-up capital and money for business purchases. They are also able to provide personal finance.

The loans can range from £50 to £1,000,000. The average loan a CDFI makes to a 'micro enterprise' is £7,250, with £30,000 to a small business and £43,500 to a social enterprise. But the amount can vary depending on the business plan. The financial arrangements for each loan or equity deal will depend on the kind of business you plan to set up, the amount of money you want to borrow and for what purpose – the issues that would traditionally affect any financial package. But the CDFI's umbrella organisation, the Community Development Finance Association (CDFA), says none of its members will charge an Annualised Percentage Rate (APR) of more than 20 per cent.

The CDFA says its members differ from the traditional high-street banks in the way that they assess whether to provide funding. It says a CDFI is likely to be more flexible than a high-street bank and does not rely on an automatic credit score rating when reaching a decision.

The CDFA has 67 members working across the UK. Some institutions specialise in investments in particular kinds of businesses while others have a national brief. To find a CDFI in your area you should go to the CDFA website (see useful contacts below) to access its directory of institutions.

The CDFA revealed in its 2005 annual report that its members are now providing £181,000,000 in loans or investments – a 23 per cent increase on 2004.

Mortgage equity

Business advisers suggest releasing equity in your home as a potential source of money to fund the start-up costs of a new business. You would need to discuss this with your mortgage lender, but advisers say this is a better option than appealing to friends or family to lend money.

Bank loans available from private banks

Question: I want to start up my own business and am looking to borrow around £30,000. What can the different high-street banks offer me?

Barclays

As a general rule, personal circumstances would not affect how much we can lend to small businesses. For people setting up in business for the very first time, the maximum we would lend would be 50 per cent of the total cost of the proposition. The applicant would have to put in the other 50 per cent and should be able to show that their stake is not borrowed money. Ideally this would work as follows:

- Amount required: £30,000
- Client's stake: £15,000
- Bank loan: £15,000

If the £30,000 is needed for more than one thing (shop fitting, equipment, car/van, etc.) we would ask to see a shopping list to understand what they need the money for. If the client has no stake, there have been occasions where the applicant has been referred to a charity such as the Prince's Youth Trust.

Co-operative Bank

No specific product available.

NatWest

Each business idea is looked at on its own merits in terms of lending. Applications for borrowing are assessed on the specific business proposition and will take into consideration your experience, knowledge and ability to demonstrate that you can successfully manage the business. The best way to start is to produce a detailed business plan, cash flow and sales forecasts and then make an appointment with a business manager to discuss your proposition and funding options. You may be asked to provide security so it is worth spending some time considering what this will be. Regardless of whether or not they will be able to lend you the funds you require, your business manager will certainly be able to provide sound advice regarding other sources of funding including business angels, government schemes such as the small firms loan guarantee scheme, or investors that can help. When you do find funding opportunities, evaluate all the options open to you. With loan finance you will keep total ownership and control. Lenders will look at gearing (the ratio of loan finance to total finance) and will not lend if the gearing is too high. They will also look at interest cover – the number of times that the forecast profit exceeds the interest – and will not lend if it is too low. If you decide to take a loan, consider whether a variable or fixed rate product would meet your requirements. If you would like the peace of mind of regular repayments then a fixed option may be right for you. If you only require funding temporarily it may also be worth considering an overdraft or business card to cover initial costs.

HSBC

Our decision to lend and the amount offered is based upon the business plan presented to us and a credit assessment of the individual/business. The solutions proposed will be most appropriate for the customer and their needs. These could include: an overdraft facility – suitable if a short-term 'in and out' trading facility is required, e.g. purchase stock for resale; a small business loan (up to £25k) – more appropriate to fund asset purchases which are used over a longer period, e.g. buying a taxi, franchise or leasehold on premises, etc.; a business card – beneficial for very short-term, informal borrowing (this type of card is extremely useful as it enables the small business to separate business expenditure from personal expenditure, which would make keeping tax records much simpler).

Lloyds TSB

We could offer a business loan, where we can offer borrowing up to £100,000. For loans over £25,000 there will be an additional cost if you close your loan early. You can choose a loan term between one and ten years. There are fixed monthly payments for the whole term of your loan. You tell us about your plans and needs, we will let you know if we require any security and we will agree the interest rate with you. An arrangement fee will apply and is dependent on the amount you choose to borrow. These terms will be discussed with you before you are committed.

Nationwide

Nationwide does not offer business start-up loans or loans for commercial purposes. The only business loans we do are for property, via our commercial lending division – the minimum we lend on such properties is £250,000.

* Information collected May 2006.

USEFUL CONTACTS

AGE DISCRIMINATION

The Employers Forum on Age
Floor 3 Downstream
1 London Bridge
London SE1 9BG
0845 456 2495
www.efa.org.uk

Age Positive (government campaign to promote age diversity in the workplace)
Age Positive Team
Department for Work and Pensions
Room W8D
Moorfoot
Sheffield
S1 4PQ
www.agepositive.gov.uk

TRAINING

Learndirect
0800 100 900
www.learndirect.co.uk

nextstep
www.nextstepstakeholder.co.uk

TUC Learning Services
The Cotton Exchange
Suite 506–510
Old Hall Street
Liverpool
L3 9LQ
0151 236 7678
www.unionlearningfund.org.uk

Train to Gain
Learning and Skills Council
0870 900 6800
www.traintogain.gov.uk

Open University
Enquiries about OU study and help with registering for your course:
Student Registration & Enquiry Service
The Open University
PO Box 197
Milton Keynes
MK7 6BJ
general-enquiries@open.ac.uk
0870 333 4340 (Monday to Friday 08.30 to 21.00 and Saturday 09.00 to 17.00)

OU headquarters:
The Open University
Walton Hall
Milton Keynes
MK7 6AA
01908 274066
www.open.ac.uk

Training and Development Agency for Schools
Portland House
Bressenden Place
London SW1E 5TT
www.tda.gov.uk

The College of Law
Braboeuf Manor
St Catherine's
Portsmouth Road
Guildford
Surrey
GU3 1HA
General enquiries:
01483 460200
0800 317 249
admissions:
01483 460382
0800 328 0153
www.college-of-law.co.uk

Aimhigher
www.aimhigher.ac.uk

SETTING UP YOUR OWN BUSINESS

Business Link
www.businesslink.gov.uk

Small Business Service
www.sbs.gov.uk

Department of Trade and Industry
1 Victoria Street
London SW1H 0ET
020 7215 5000
www.dti.gov.uk

Regional Development Agencies (national secretariat)
Broadway House
Tothill Street
London SW1H 9NQ
020 7222 8180
www.englandsrdas.com

National Federation of Enterprise Agencies
12 Stephenson Court
Fraser Road
Priory Business Park
Bedford
MK44 3WH
01234 831623
www.nfea.com

Community Development Finance Association (CDFA)
Room 101
Hatton Square Business Centre
16-16A Baldwins Gardens
London EC1N 7RJ
020 7430 0222
www.cdfa.org.uk

IQ Capital Fund contacts:
NW Brown Group Ltd
Richmond House
16-20 Regent Street
Cambridge
CB2 1DB
01223 357131
www.nwbrown.co.uk

Oxfordshire Investment Opportunity Network (OION)
Oxford Centre For Innovation
Mill Street
Oxford
OX2 0JX
01865 811143
www.oion.co.uk

Great Eastern Investment Forum (GEIF)
Richmond House
16–20 Regent Street
Cambridge
CB2 1DB
01223 720312
www.geif.co.uk

The South West Angel and Investor Network (SWAIN)
Argentum
510 Bristol Business House
Coldharbour Lane
Bristol
BS16 1EJ
08700 606560
www.swain.org.uk

21st Century Sustainable Technology Growth Fund contact:
E-Synergy Ltd
Bride House
18–20 Bride Lane
London EC4Y 8JT
020 7583 3503
www.e-synergy.com

Bridges Community Ventures Ltd
1 Craven Hill
London W2 3EN
020 7262 5566
www.bridgesventures.com

PRIME
Astral House
1268 London Road
London SW16 4ER
020 8765 7833
Helpline 0800 783 1904
www.primeinitiative.org.uk

ShellLiveWire
Design Works Unit 15
William Street
Felling
Gateshead
Tyne and Wear
NE10 0JP
0191 423 6229
www.shell-livewire.org

Business Volunteer Mentor programme
www.bvm.org.uk

FUNDING

Learndirect
0800 100 900
www.learndirect.co.uk

nextstep
www.nextstepstakeholder.co.uk

Educational Grants Advisory Service (EGAS)
501–505 Kingsland Road
London E8 4AU
Helpline open Tuesday, Wednesday, Thursday 14.00 to 16.00
020 7254 6251
www.egas-online.org.uk

General Social Care Council (GSCC)
Goldings House
2 Hay's Lane
London SE1 2HB
020 7397 5100
Bursaries helpline: 020 7397 5835
www.gscc.org.uk

Scottish Social Services Council (SSSC)
Compass House
11 Riverside Drive
Dundee
DD1 4NY
01382 207101
www.sssc.uk.com

Care Council for Wales (CCW)
South Gate House
Wood Street
Cardiff
CF10 1EW
029 2022 6257
www.ccwales.org.uk

Northern Ireland Social Care Council (NISCC)
7th Floor Millennium House
Great Victoria Street
Belfast
BT2 7AQ
028 9041 7600
www.socialworkcareers.co.uk

The Training and Development Agency for Schools
Portland House
Bressenden Place
London SW1E 5TT
www.tda.gov.uk

Department for Education and Skills (DfES)
There are offices in London, Sheffield, Darlington and Runcorn.
www.dfes.gov.uk

NHS Student Grants Unit
NHS Pensions Agency
200–220 Broadway
Fleetwood
Lancashire
FY7 8SS
www.nhsstudentgrants.co.uk

NHS Bursaries helpline 0845 358 6655

For Wales:
NHS Wales Students Awards Unit
2nd Floor Golate House
101 St Mary Street
Cardiff
CF10 1DX
029 2026 1495

For Scotland:
The Students Awards Agency for Scotland
3 Redheughs Rigg
South Gyle
Edinburgh
EH12 9HH
0131 4768212

For Northern Ireland:
The Department of Higher and Further Education Training and Employment
Student Support Branch
4th Floor Adelaide House
39–49 Adelaide Street
Belfast
BT2 8FD
028 9025 7777

FINDING A JOB

General

Website for brad directory entries:
www.intellagencia.com

Job boards:
www.jobcentreplus.co.uk
www.jobsite.co.uk
www.jobserve.com
www.jobs.guardian.co.uk
www.monster.co.uk

Workthing
Beaumont House
Kensington Village
Avonmore Road
London W14 8TS
0870 898 0022
www.workthing.co.uk

fish4jobs
3rd floor
Broadway Chambers
14–26 Hammersmith Broadway
London W6 7AF
www.fish4jobs.co.uk

Specialist job boards

For public sector jobs:
www.jobsgopublic.com
www.guardian.co.uk

For NHS jobs:
www.nhsjobs.gov.uk

Specialist agencies and organisations

Forties People Ltd
11–13 Dowgate Hill
London EC4R 2ST
020 7329 4044
01923 212444
www.fortiespeople.co.uk

Aged2Excel Ltd
PO Box 13060
Redditch
B97 9DB
01527 457843
www.aged2excel.co.uk

The Employers Forum on Age
Floor 3 Downstream
1 London Bridge
London SE1 9BG
0845 456 2495
www.efa.org.uk

Age Positive (government campaign to promote age diversity in the workplace)
Age Positive Team
Department for Work and Pensions
Room W8D
Moorfoot
Sheffield
S1 4PQ
www.agepositive.gov.uk
General enquiries
agepositive@dwp.gsi.gov.uk

PRIME
Astral House
1268 London Road
London SW16 4ER
020 8765 7833
Help line 0800 783 1904
www.primeinitiative.org.uk

Learndirect
0800 100 900
www.learndirect.co.uk

Recruitment and Employment Confederation (REC)
36-38 Mortimer Street
London W1W 7RG
020 7462 3260
www.rec.uk.com

Chartered Institute of Personnel and Development (CIPD)
151 The Broadway
London SW19 1JQ
020 8612 6200
www.cipd.co.uk

MAKING YOUR CV WORK FOR YOU

Learndirect
0800 100 900
www.learndirect.co.uk

Recruitment and Employment Confederation (REC)
36-38 Mortimer Street
London W1W 7RG
020 7462 3260
www.rec.uk.com

Chartered Institute of Personnel and Development (CIPD)
151 The Broadway
London SW19 1JQ
020 8612 6200
www.cipd.co.uk

NOTES

1 *Nursing Standard,* 24 August 2005
2 Botanic and Historic Gardens Skills Research Project, 27 April 2005
3 'Challenging times: flexibility and flexible working in the UK', December 2005
4 Experian, May 2006. 2,233 men aged 18+ surveyed
5 Security in Retirement: Towards a New Pension System, May 2006
6 Extract from 'Practical Tips for Effective Career Discussions at Work', a National Institute for Careers Education and Counselling (NICEC) guide by NICEC Fellows Wendy Hirsh and Charles Jackson, and Jenny Kidd, senior lecturer in the Department of Organisational Psychology, Birkbeck, University of London and NICEC Associate
7 Morgan Hunt Recruitment
8 Morgan Hunt Recruitment